Bret Harte

The Poetical Works

Bret Harte

The Poetical Works

ISBN/EAN: 9783337336868

Printed in Europe, USA, Canada, Australia, Japan

Cover: Foto ©Thomas Meinert / pixelio.de

More available books at **www.hansebooks.com**

THE POETICAL WORKS

INCLUDING THE DRAMA OF "THE TWO MEN OF SANDY BAR"

OF

BRET HARTE

BOSTON
HOUGHTON, MIFFLIN AND COMPANY
NEW YORK: 11 EAST SEVENTEENTH STREET
The Riverside Press, Cambridge
1882

CONTENTS.

	PAGE
INTRODUCTION	1

NATIONAL POEMS.

JOHN BURNS OF GETTYSBURG	13
"HOW ARE YOU, SANITARY?"	17
BATTLE BUNNY	19
THE REVEILLE	22
OUR PRIVILEGE	24
RELIEVING GUARD	25
THE GODDESS	26
ON A PEN OF THOMAS STARR KING	28
A SECOND REVIEW OF THE GRAND ARMY	29
THE COPPERHEAD	32
A SANITARY MESSAGE	33
THE OLD MAJOR EXPLAINS	35
CALIFORNIA'S GREETING TO SEWARD	37
THE AGED STRANGER	39
THE IDYL OF BATTLE HOLLOW	41
CALDWELL OF SPRINGFIELD	43
POEM, DELIVERED ON THE FOURTEENTH ANNIVERSARY OF CALIFORNIA'S ADMISSION INTO THE UNION	45
MISS BLANCHE SAYS	48
AN ARCTIC VISION	52
ST. THOMAS	55
OFF SCARBOROUGH	58

SPANISH IDYLS AND LEGENDS.

THE MIRACLE OF PADRE JUNIPERO	65
THE WONDERFUL SPRING OF SAN JOAQUIN	68

Contents.

	PAGE
THE ANGELUS	72
CONCEPCION DE ARGUELLO	74
"FOR THE KING"	81
RAMON	88
DON DIEGO OF THE SOUTH	91
AT THE HACIENDA	95
FRIAR PEDRO'S RIDE	96
IN THE MISSION GARDEN	102
THE LOST GALLEON	104

POEMS IN DIALECT.

"JIM"	113
CHIQUITA	116
DOW'S FLAT	119
IN THE TUNNEL	123
"CICELY"	125
PENELOPE	129
PLAIN LANGUAGE FROM TRUTHFUL JAMES	131
THE SOCIETY UPON THE STANISLAUS	134
LUKE	136
"THE BABES IN THE WOODS"	141
THE LATEST CHINESE OUTRAGE	144
TRUTHFUL JAMES TO THE EDITOR	148
AN IDYL OF THE ROAD	151
THOMPSON OF ANGELS	155
THE HAWK'S NEST	158
HER LETTER	160
HIS ANSWER TO "HER LETTER"	163
"THE RETURN OF BELISARIUS"	166
FURTHER LANGUAGE FROM TRUTHFUL JAMES	168
AFTER THE ACCIDENT	171
THE GHOST THAT JIM SAW	173
"SEVENTY-NINE"	176
THE STAGE-DRIVER'S STORY	179

MISCELLANEOUS POEMS.

A GREYPORT LEGEND	185
A NEWPORT ROMANCE	187

	PAGE
SAN FRANCISCO	190
THE MOUNTAIN HEART'S EASE	192
GRIZZLY	194
MADRONO	196
COYOTE	198
TO A SEA-BIRD	199
WHAT THE CHIMNEY SANG	200
DICKENS IN CAMP	202
TWENTY YEARS	204
FATE	206
GRANDMOTHER TENTERDEN	207
GUILD'S SIGNAL	210
ASPIRING MISS DE LAINE	212
A LEGEND OF COLOGNE	219
THE TALE OF A PONY	228
ON A CONE OF THE BIG TREES	232
LONE MOUNTAIN	235
ALNASCHAR	237
THE TWO SHIPS	239
ADDRESS DELIVERED AT THE OPENING OF THE CALIFORNIA THEATRE, SAN FRANCISCO, JANUARY 19, 1870	240
DOLLY VARDEN	242
TELEMACHUS VERSUS MENTOR	244
WHAT THE WOLF REALLY SAID TO LITTLE RED RIDING-HOOD	248
HALF-AN-HOUR BEFORE SUPPER	249
WHAT THE BULLET SANG	252

PARODIES, ETC.

BEFORE THE CURTAIN	255
TO THE PLIOCENE SKULL	256
THE BALLAD OF MR. COOKE	258
THE BALLAD OF THE EMEU	263
MRS. JUDGE JENKINS	265
A GEOLOGICAL MADRIGAL	268
AVITOR	270
THE WILLOWS	272
NORTH BEACH	275
THE LOST TAILS OF MILETUS	276
THE RITUALIST	278
A MORAL VINDICATOR	279

CALIFORNIA MADRIGAL	281
WHAT THE ENGINES SAID	283
THE LEGENDS OF THE RHINE	286
SONGS WITHOUT SENSE	288

LITTLE POSTERITY.

MASTER JOHNNY'S NEXT-DOOR NEIGHBOR	293
MISS EDITH'S MODEST REQUEST	296
MISS EDITH MAKES IT PLEASANT FOR BROTHER JACK	300
MISS EDITH MAKES ANOTHER FRIEND	302
ON THE LANDING	304

DRAMA.

TWO MEN OF SANDY BAR	307
CADET GREY	431

INTRODUCTION.

IN rearranging and editing the following pages, the author is impelled by a desire to present under his own supervision a complete edition of his writings which shall show as nearly as possible the order in which his several tales and sketches have appeared in America; shall contain those writings and sketches which have appeared in England at various times and under various shapes and editions; and shall, more particularly, take the place of a volume known as his "Complete Works." This volume, published in 1872, before the author's presence in Europe made his personal cognisance and supervision of such a work possible, was desultory and incomplete, even for the time of its publication. The present edition aims to contain the substance of that volume, duly corrected, with all that was then omitted by the editor or has since been published by the author.

The opportunity here offered to give some account of the genesis of these Californian sketches, and the conditions under which they were conceived, is peculiarly tempting to an author who has been obliged to retain a decent professional reticence under a cloud of ingenious surmise, theory, and misinterpretation. It might seem hardly necessary to assure an intelligent English audience that the idea and invention of these stories was not due to the success of a satirical poem known as the "Heathen Chinee," or that the author obtained a hearing for his prose writings through this happy local parable; yet it is within the past year that he has had the satisfaction of reading this ingenious theory in a literary review of no mean eminence. He very gladly seizes this opportunity to establish the chronology of the sketches, and incidentally to show that what are considered the "happy accidents" of literature are very apt to be the results of quite logical and often prosaic processes.

The author's *first* volume was published in 1865 in a thin book of verse, containing, besides the titular poem, "The Lost Galleon," various patriotic contributions to the lyrics of the civil war, then raging, and certain better known humorous pieces, which have been hitherto interspersed with his later poems in separate volumes, but are now restored to their former companionship. This was followed in 1867 by "The Condensed Novels," originally contributed to the *San Francisco Californian*, a journal then edited by the author, and a number of local sketches entitled "Bohemian Papers," making a single not very plethoric volume, the author's first book of prose. But he deems it worthy of consideration that during this period, *i.e.*, from 1862 to 1866, he produced "The Society upon the Stanislaus" and "The Story of Mliss,"—the first a dialectical poem, the second a Californian romance,—his first efforts toward indicating a peculiarly characteristic Western American literature. He would like to offer these facts as evidence of his very early, half-boyish, but very enthusiastic, belief in such a possibility—a belief which never deserted him, and which, a few years later, from the better-known pages of the *Overland Monthly*, he was able to demonstrate to a larger and more cosmopolitan audience in the story of "The Luck of Roaring Camp" and the poem of the "Heathen Chinee." But it was one of the anomalies of the very condition of life that he worked amidst, and endeavoured to portray, that these first efforts were rewarded by very little success; and, as he will presently show, even "The Luck of Roaring Camp" depended for its recognition in California upon its success elsewhere. Hence the critical reader will observe that the bulk of these earlier efforts, as shown in the first two volumes, were marked by very little flavour of the soil, but were addressed to an audience half foreign in their sympathies, and still imbued with Eastern or New England habits and literary traditions. "Home" was still potent with these voluntary exiles in their moments of relaxation. Eastern magazines and current Eastern literature formed their literary recreation, and the sale of the better class of periodicals was singularly great. Nor was the taste confined to American literature. The illustrated and satirical English journals were as frequently seen in California as in Massachusetts; and the author records that he has experienced more difficulty in procuring a copy of *Punch* in an English provincial town than was his fortune at "Red Dog" or "One-Horse Gulch." An audience thus liberally equipped and familiar with the best modern writers was naturally critical and exacting, and no one appreciates more than he does the salutary effects of this severe discipline upon his earlier efforts.

When the first number of the *Overland Monthly* appeared, the author, then its editor, called the publisher's attention to the lack of any distinctive Californian romance in its pages, and averred that, should no other contribution come in, he himself would supply the omission in the next number. No other contribution was offered, and the author, having the plot and general idea already in his mind, in a few days sent the manuscript of "The Luck of Roaring Camp" to the printer. He had not yet received the proof-sheets when he was suddenly summoned to the office of the publisher, whom he found standing the picture of dismay and anxiety with the proof before him. The indignation and stupefaction of the author can be well understood when he was told that the printer, instead of returning the proofs to him, submitted them to the publisher, with the emphatic declaration that the matter thereof was so indecent, irreligious, and improper, that his proof-reader—a young lady—had with difficulty been induced to continue its perusal, and that he, as a friend of the publisher and a well-wisher of the magazine, was impelled to present to him personally this shameless evidence of the manner in which the editor was imperilling the future of that enterprise. It should be premised that the critic was a man of character and standing, the head of a large printing establishment, a church member, and, the author thinks, a deacon. In which circumstances the publisher frankly admitted to the author that, while he could not agree with all of the printer's criticisms, he thought the story open to grave objection, and its publication of doubtful expediency.

Believing only that he was the victim of some extraordinary typographical blunder, the author at once sat down and read the proof. In its new dress, with the metamorphosis of type—that metamorphosis which every writer so well knows changes his relations to it and makes it no longer seem a part of himself—he was able to read it with something of the freshness of an untold tale. As he read on he found himself affected, even as he had been affected in the conception and writing of it—a feeling so incompatible with the charges against it, that he could only lay it down and declare emphatically, albeit hopelessly, that he could really see nothing objectionable in it. Other opinions were sought and given. To the author's surprise, he found himself in the minority. Finally, the story was submitted to three gentlemen of culture and experience, friends of publisher and author,—who were unable, however, to come to any clear decision. It was, however, suggested to the author that, assuming the natural hypothesis that his editorial reasoning might be warped by his literary predilections in a consideration of one of his own productions, a personal sacrifice would at this juncture be in the last degree heroic. This last suggestion had the effect of ending all further discussion; for he at once informed the publisher that the question of the propriety of the story was no longer at issue; the only question was of his capacity to exercise the proper editorial judgment; and that unless he was permitted to test that capacity by the publication of the story, and abide squarely by the result, he must resign his editorial position. The publisher, possibly struck with the author's confidence, possibly from kindliness of disposition to a younger man, yielded, and "The Luck of Roaring Camp" was published in the current number of the magazine for which it was written, as it was written, without emendation, omission, alteration, or apology. A no inconsiderable part of the grotesqueness of the situation was the feeling, which the author retained throughout the whole affair, of the perfect sincerity, good faith, and seriousness of his friend's—the printer's—objection, and for many days thereafter he was haunted by a consideration of the sufferings of this conscientious man, obliged to assist materially in disseminating the dangerous and subversive doctrines contained in this baleful fiction. What solemn protests must have been laid with the ink on the rollers and impressed upon those wicked sheets! what pious warnings must have been secretly folded and stitched in that number of the *Overland Monthly!* Across the chasm of years and distance the author stretches forth the hand of sympathy and forgiveness, not forgetting the gentle proof-reader, that chaste and unknown nymph, whose mantling cheeks and downcast eyes gave the first indications of warning.

But the troubles of the "Luck" were far from ended. It had secured an entrance into the world, but, like its own hero, it was born with an evil reputation and to a community that had yet to learn to love it. The secular press, with one or two exceptions, received it coolly, and referred to its "singularity;" the religious press frantically excommunicated it, and anathematised it as the offspring of evil; the high promise of the *Overland Monthly* was said to have been ruined by its birth; Christians were cautioned against pollution by its contact; practical business men were gravely urged to condemn and frown upon this picture of Californian society that was not conducive to Eastern immigration; its hapless author was held up to obloquy as a man who had abused a sacred trust. If its life and reputation had depended on its reception in California, this edition and explanation would alike have been needless. But, fortunately, the young *Overland Monthly* had in its first number secured a hearing and position throughout the American Union, and the author waited the larger verdict. The publisher, albeit his worst fears were confirmed, was not a man to weakly regret a position he had once taken, and waited also. The return mail from the East brought a letter addressed to the "Editor of the Overland Monthly," enclosing a letter from Fields, Osgood & Co., the publishers of the *Atlantic Monthly*, addressed to the—to them—unknown "Author of 'The Luck of Roaring Camp.'" This the author opened, and found to be a request, upon the most flattering terms, for a story for the *Atlantic* similar to the "Luck." The same mail brought newspapers and reviews welcoming the little foundling of Californian literature with an enthusiasm that half frightened its author; but with the placing of that letter in the hands of the publisher, who chanced to be standing by his side, and who during those dark days had, without the author's faith, sustained the author's position, he felt that his compensation was full and complete.

Thus encouraged, "The Luck of Roaring Camp" was followed by "The Outcasts of Poker Flat," "Miggles," "Tennessee's Partner," and those various other characters who had impressed the author when, a mere truant schoolboy, he had lived among them. It is hardly necessary to say to any observer of human nature that at this time he was advised by kind and well-meaning friends to content himself with the success of the "Luck," and not tempt criticism again; or that from that moment ever after he was in receipt of that equally sincere contemporaneous criticism which assured him gravely that each successive story was a falling off from the last. Howbeit, by reinvigorated confidence in himself and some conscientious industry, he managed to get together in a year six or eight of these sketches, which, in a volume called "The Luck of Roaring Camp and Other Sketches," gave him that encouragement in America and England that has since seemed to justify him in swelling these records of a picturesque passing civilisation into the compass of the present edition.

A few words regarding the peculiar conditions of life and society that are here rudely sketched, and often but barely outlined. The author is aware that, partly from a habit of thought and expression, partly from the exigencies of brevity in his narratives, and partly from the habit of addressing an audience familiar with the local scenery, he often assumes, as premises already granted by the reader, the existence of a peculiar and romantic state of civilisation, the like of which few English readers are inclined to accept without corroborative facts and figures. These he could only give by referring to the ephemeral records of Californian journals of that date, and the testimony of far-scattered witnesses, survivors of the exodus of 1849. He must beg the reader to bear in mind that this emigration was either across a continent almost unexplored, or by the way of a long and dangerous voyage around Cape Horn, and that the promised land itself presented the singular spectacle of a patriarchal Latin race who had been left to themselves, forgotten by the world, for nearly three hundred years. The faith, courage, vigour, youth, and capacity for adventure necessary to this emigration produced a body of men as strongly distinctive as the companions of Jason. Unlike most pioneers, the majority were men of profession and education; all were young, and all had staked their future in the enterprise. Critics who have taken large and exhaustive views of mankind and society from club windows in Pall Mall or the Fifth Avenue can only accept for granted the turbulent chivalry that thronged the streets of San Francisco in the gala days of her youth, and must read the blazon of their deeds like the doubtful quarterings of the shield of Amadis de Gaul. The author has been frequently asked if such and such incidents were real; if he had ever met such and such characters? To this he must return the one answer, that in only a single instance was he conscious of drawing purely from his imagination and fancy for a character and a logical succession of incidents drawn therefrom. A few weeks after his story was published, he received a letter, authentically signed, *correcting some of the minor details of his facts* (!), and enclosing as corroborative evidence a slip from an old newspaper, wherein the main incident of his supposed fanciful creation was recorded with a largeness of statement that far transcended his powers of imagination.

He has been repeatedly cautioned, kindly and unkindly, intelligently and unintelligently, against his alleged tendency to confuse recognised standards of morality by extenuating lives of recklessness, and often criminality, with a single solitary virtue. He might easily show that he has never written a sermon, that he has never moralised or commented upon the actions of his heroes, that he has never voiced a creed or obtrusively demonstrated an ethical opinion. He might easily allege that this merciful effect of his art arose from the reader's weak human sympathies, and hold himself irresponsible. But he would be conscious of a more miserable weakness in thus divorcing himself from his fellow-men who in the domain of art must ever walk hand in hand with him. So he prefers to say, that of all the various forms in which Cant presents itself to suffering humanity, he knows of none so outrageous, so illogical, so undemonstrable, so marvellously absurd as the Cant of "Too Much Mercy." When it shall be proven to him that communities are degraded and brought to guilt and crime, suffering or destitution, from a predominance of this quality; when he shall see pardoned ticket-of-leave men elbowing men of austere lives out of situation and position, and the repentant Magdalen supplanting the blameless virgin in society, then he will lay aside his pen and extend his hand to the new Draconian discipline in fiction. But until then he will, without claiming to be a religious man or a moralist, but simply as an artist, reverently and humbly conform to the rules laid down by a Great Poet who created the parable of the "Prodigal Son" and the "Good Samaritan," whose works have lasted eighteen hundred years, and will remain when the present writer and his generation are forgotten. And he is conscious of uttering no original doctrine in this, but of only voicing the beliefs of a few of his literary brethren happily living, and one gloriously dead, who never made proclamation of this "from the housetops."

POEMS.

National.

John Burns of Gettysburg.

Have you heard the story that gossips tell
Of Burns of Gettysburg?—No? Ah, well:
Brief is the glory that hero earns,
Briefer the story of poor John Burns:
He was the fellow who won renown,—
The only man who didn't back down
When the rebels rode through his native town:
But held his own in the fight next day,
When all his townsfolk ran away.
That was in July sixty-three,
The very day that General Lee,
Flower of Southern chivalry,
Baffled and beaten, backward reeled
From a stubborn Meade and a barren field.
I might tell how but the day before
John Burns stood at his cottage door,
Looking down the village street,
Where, in the shade of his peaceful vine,
He heard the low of his gathered kine,
And felt their breath with incense sweet;
Or I might say, when the sunset burned
The old farm gable, he thought it turned
The milk that fell like a babbling flood
Into the milk-pail red as blood!
Or how he fancied the hum of bees

Were bullets buzzing among the trees.
But all such fanciful thoughts as these
Were strange to a practical man like Burns,
Who minded only his own concerns,
Troubled no more by fancies fine
Than one of his calm-eyed, long-tailed, kine,—
Quite old-fashioned and matter-of-fact,
Slow to argue, but quick to act.
That was the reason, as some folk say,
He fought so well on that terrible day.

And it was terrible. On the right
Raged for hours the heady fight,
Thundered the battery's double bass,—
Difficult music for men to face;
While on the left—where now the graves
Undulate like the living waves
That all that day unceasing swept
Up to the pits the rebels kept—
Round shot ploughed the upland glades,
Sown with bullets, reaped with blades;
Shattered fences here and there
Tossed their splinters in the air;
The very trees were stripped and bare;
The barns that once held yellow grain
Were heaped with harvests of the slain;
The cattle bellowed on the plain,
The turkeys screamed with might and main,
And brooding barn-fowl left their rest
With strange shells bursting in each nest.

Just where the tide of battle turns,
Erect and lonely stood old John Burns.

John Burns of Gettysburg.

How do you think the man was dressed?
He wore an ancient long buff vest,
Yellow as saffron,—but his best;
And, buttoned over his manly breast,
Was a bright blue coat, with a rolling collar,
And large gilt buttons,—size of a dollar,—
With tails that the country-folk called "swaller."
He wore a broad-brimmed, bell-crowned hat,
White as the locks on which it sat.
Never had such a sight been seen
For forty years on the village green,
Since old John Burns was a country beau,
And went to the "quiltings" long ago.

Close at his elbows all that day,
Veterans of the Peninsula,
Sunburnt and bearded, charged away;
And striplings, downy of lip and chin,—
Clerks that the Home Guard mustered in,—
Glanced, as they passed, at the hat he wore,
Then at the rifle his right hand bore;
And hailed him, from out their youthful lore,
With scraps of a slangy *répertoire:*
"How are you, White Hat!" "Put her through!"
"Your head's level!" and "Bully for you!"
Called him "Daddy,"—begged he'd disclose
The name of the tailor who made his clothes,
And what was the value he set on those;
While Burns, unmindful of jeer and scoff,
Stood there picking the rebels off,—
With his long brown rifle and bell-crown hat,
And the swallow-tails they were laughing at.

'Twas but a moment, for that respect
Which clothes all courage their voices checked;

And something the wildest could understand
Spake in the old man's strong right hand,
And his corded throat, and the lurking frown
Of his eyebrows under his old bell-crown;
Until, as they gazed, there crept an awe
Through the ranks in whispers, and some men saw,
In the antique vestments and long white hair,
The Past of the Nation in battle there;
And some of the soldiers since declare
That the gleam of his old white hat afar,
Like the crested plume of the brave Navarre,
That day was their oriflamme of war.

So raged the battle. You know the rest:
How the rebels, beaten and backward pressed,
Broke at the final charge and ran.
At which John Burns—a practical man—
Shouldered his rifle, unbent his brows,
And then went back to his bees and cows.

That is the story of old John Burns;
This is the moral the reader learns:
In fighting the battle, the question's whether
You'll show a hat that's white, or a feather!

"How are you, Sanitary?"

Down the picket-guarded lane
    Rolled the comfort-laden wain,
Cheered by shouts that shook the plain,
    Soldier-like and merry:
Phrases such as camps may teach,
Sabre-cuts of Saxon speech,
Such as "Bully!" "Them's the peach!"
    "Wade in, Sanitary!"

Right and left the caissons drew
As the car went lumbering through,
Quick succeeding in review
    Squadrons military;
Sunburnt men with beards like frieze,
Smooth-faced boys, and cries like these,—
"U. S. San. Com." "That's the cheese!"
    "Pass in, Sanitary!"

In such cheer it struggled on
Till the battle front was won,
Then the car, its journey done,
    Lo! was stationary;
And where bullets whistling fly,
Came the sadder, fainter cry,
"Help us, brothers, ere we die,—
    Save us, Sanitary!"

Such the work. The phantom flies,
Wrapped in battle clouds that rise;
But the brave—whose dying eyes,
　　Veiled and visionary,
See the jasper gates swung wide,
See the parted throng outside—
Hears the voice to those who ride:
　　" Pass in, Sanitary!"

Battle Bunny.

(MALVERN HILL, 1864.)

["After the men were ordered to lie down, a white rabbit, which had been hopping hither and thither over the field swept by grape and musketry, took refuge among the skirmishers, in the breast of a corporal."—*Report of the Battle of Malvern Hill.*]

  Bunny, lying in the grass,
  Saw the shining column pass;
  Saw the starry banner fly,
  Saw the chargers fret and fume,
  Saw the flapping hat and plume—
  Saw them with his moist and shy
  Most unspeculative eye,
  Thinking only, in the dew,
  That it was a fine review—
  Till a flash, not all of steel,
  Where the rolling caissons wheel,
  Brought a rumble and a roar
  Rolling down that velvet floor,
  And like blows of autumn flail
  Sharply threshed the iron hail.

  Bunny, thrilled by unknown fears,
  Raised his soft and pointed ears,
  Mumbled his prehensile lip,
  Quivered his pulsating hip,

As the sharp vindictive yell
Rose above the screaming shell;
Thought the world and all its men—
All the charging squadrons meant—
All were rabbit-hunters then,
All to capture him intent.
Bunny was not much to blame:
Wiser folk have thought the same—
Wiser folk who think they spy
Every ill begins with "I."

Wildly panting here and there,
Bunny sought the freer air,
Till he hopped below the hill,
And saw, lying close and still,
Men with muskets in their hands.
(Never Bunny understands
That hypocrisy of sleep,
In the vigils grim they keep,
As recumbent on that spot
They elude the level shot.)

One—a grave and quiet man,
Thinking of his wife and child
Far beyond the Rapidan,
Where the Androsaggin smiled—
Felt the little rabbit creep,
Nestling by his arm and side,
Wakened from strategic sleep,
To that soft appeal replied,
Drew him to his blackened breast,
And—

But you have guessed the rest.
Softly o'er that chosen pair
Omnipresent Love and Care

Drew a mightier Hand and Arm,
Shielding them from every harm;
Right and left the bullets waved,
Saved the saviour for the saved.

———

Who believes that equal grace
God extends in every place,
Little difference he scans
'Twixt a rabbit's God and man's.

The Reveille.

    Hark! I hear the tramp of thousands,
      And of armèd men the hum;
    Lo! a nation's hosts have gathered
      Round the quick alarming drum,—
        Saying, "Come,
        Freemen, come!
Ere your heritage be wasted," said the quick alarming drum.

    "Let me of my heart take counsel:
      War is not of life the sum;
    Who shall stay and reap the harvest
      When the autumn days shall come?"
        But the drum
        Echoed, "Come!
Death shall reap the braver harvest," said the solemn-sounding drum.

    "But when won the coming battle,
      What of profit springs therefrom?
    What if conquest, subjugation,
      Even greater ills become?"
        But the drum
        Answered, "Come!
You must do the sum to prove it," said the Yankee-answering drum.

"What if, 'mid the cannons' thunder,
   Whistling shot and bursting bomb,
When my brothers fall around me,
   Should my heart grow cold and numb?"
      But the drum
      Answered, "Come!
Better there in death united, than in life a recreant,—
   Come!"

   Thus they answered,—hoping, fearing,
     Some in faith, and doubting some,
   Till a trumpet-voice proclaiming,
     Said, "My chosen people, come!"
      Then the drum,
      Lo! was dumb,
For the great heart of the nation, throbbing, answered
   "Lord, we come!"

Our Privilege.

Not ours, where battle smoke upcurls,
    And battle dews lie wet,
To meet the charge that treason hurls
    By sword and bayonet.

Not ours to guide the fatal scythe
    The fleshless Reaper wields;
The harvest moon looks calmly down
    Upon our peaceful fields.

The long grass dimples on the hill,
    The pines sing by the sea,
And Plenty, from her golden horn,
    Is pouring far and free.

O brothers by the farther sea!
    Think still our faith is warm;
The same bright flag above us waves
    That swathed our baby form.

The same red blood that dyes your fields
    Here throbs in patriot pride—
The blood that flowed when Lander fell,
    And Baker's crimson tide.

And thus apart our hearts keep time
    With every pulse ye feel,
And Mercy's ringing gold shall chime
    With Valour's clashing steel.

Relieving Guard.

T. S. K. OBIIT MARCH 4, 1864.

CAME the relief. "What, sentry, ho!
How passed the night through thy long waking?"
"Cold, cheerless, dark,—as may befit
The hour before the dawn is breaking."

"No sight? no sound?" "No; nothing save
The plover from the marches calling,
And in yon western sky, about
An hour ago, a star was falling."

"A star? There's nothing strange in that."
"No, nothing; but, above the thicket,
Somehow it seemed to me that God
Somewhere had just relieved a picket."

The Goddess.

FOR THE SANITARY FAIR.

"Who comes?" The sentry's warning cry
   Rings sharply on the evening air:
Who comes? The challenge: no reply,
   Yet something motions there.

A woman, by those graceful folds;
   A soldier, by that martial tread:
"Advance three paces. Halt! until
   Thy name and rank be said."

"My name? Her name, in ancient song
   Who fearless from Olympus came:
Look on me! Mortals know me best
   In battle and in flame."

"Enough! I know that clarion voice;
   I know that gleaming eye and helm;
Those crimson lips,—and in their dew
   The best blood of the realm.

"The young, the brave, the good and wise,
   Have fallen in thy curst embrace:
The juices of the grapes of wrath
   Still stain thy guilty face.

The Goddess.

" My brother lies in yonder field,
    Face downward to the quiet grass :
Go back ! he cannot see thee now ;
    But here thou shalt not pass."

A crack upon the evening air,
    A wakened echo from the hill :
The watchdog on the distant shore
    Gives mouth, and all is still.

The sentry with his brother lies
    Face downward on the quiet grass ;
And by him, in the pale moonshine,
    A shadow seems to pass.

No lance or warlike shield it bears :
    A helmet in its pitying hands
Brings water from the nearest brook,
    To meet his last demands.

Can this be she of haughty mien,
    The goddess of the sword and shield ?
Ah, yes ! The Grecian poet's myth
    Sways still each battlefield.

For not alone that rugged War
    Some grace or charm from Beauty gains ;
But, when the goddess' work is done,
    The woman's still remains.

On a Pen of Thomas Starr King.

This is the reed the dead musician dropped,
    With tuneful magic in its sheath still hidden;
The prompt allegro of its music stopped,
    Its melodies unbidden.

But who shall finish the unfinished strain,
    Or wake the instrument to awe and wonder,
And bid the slender barrel breathe again,
    An organ-pipe of thunder!

His pen! what humbler memories cling about
    Its golden curves! what shapes and laughing graces
Slipped from its point, when his full heart went out
    In smiles and courtly phrases?

The truth, half jesting, half in earnest flung;
    The word of cheer, with recognition in it;
The note of alms, whose golden speech outrung
    The golden gift within it.

But all in vain the enchanter's wand we wave:
    No stroke of ours recalls his magic vision:
The incantation that its power gave
    Sleeps with the dead magician.

A Second Review of the Grand Army.

I READ last night of the grand review
In Washington's chiefest avenue,—
Two hundred thousand men in blue,
    I think they said was the number,—
Till I seemed to hear their trampling feet,
The bugle blast and the drum's quick beat,
The clatter of hoofs in the stony street,
The cheers of people who came to greet,
And the thousand details that to repeat
    Would only my verse encumber,—
Till I fell in a reverie, sad and sweet,
    And then to a fitful slumber.

When, lo! in a vision I seemed to stand
In the lonely Capitol. On each hand
Far stretched the portico, dim and grand
Its columns ranged like a martial band
Of sheeted spectres, whom some command
    Had called to a last reviewing.
And the streets of the city were white and bare;
No footfall echoed across the square;
But out of the misty midnight air
I heard in the distance a trumpet blare,
And the wandering night-winds seemed to bear
    The sound of a far tattooing.

Then I held my breath with fear and dread;
For into the square, with a brazen tread,
There rode a figure whose stately head
    O'erlooked the review that morning,
That never bowed from its firm-set seat
When the living column passed its feet,
Yet now rode steadily up the street
    To the phantom bugle's warning.

Till it reached the Capitol square, and wheeled,
And there in the moonlight stood revealed
A well-known form that in State and field
    Had led our patriot sires:
Whose face was turned to the sleeping camp,
Afar through the river's fog and damp,
That showed no flicker, nor waning lamp,
    Nor wasted bivouac fires.

And I saw a phantom army come,
With never a sound of fife or drum,
But keeping time to a throbbing hum
    Of wailing and lamentation:
The martyred heroes of Malvern Hill,
Of Gettysburg and Chancellorsville,
The men whose wasted figures fill
    The patriot graves of the nation.

And there came the nameless dead,—the men
Who perished in fever swamp and fen,
The slowly-starved of the prison pen;
    And, marching beside the others,
Came the dusky martyrs of Pillow's fight,
With limbs enfranchised and bearing bright;
I thought—perhaps 'twas the pale moonlight—
    They looked as white as their brothers!

And so all night marched the nation's dead,
With never a banner above them spread,
Nor a badge, nor a motto brandished;
No mark—save the bare uncovered head
    Of the silent bronze Reviewer;
With never an arch save the vaulted sky;
With never a flower save those that lie
On the distant graves—for love could buy
    No gift that was purer or truer.

So all night long swept the strange array,
So all night long till the morning gray
I watched for one who had passed away,
    With a reverent awe and wonder,—
Till a blue cap waved in the length'ning line,
And I knew that one who was kin of mine
Had come; and I spake—and lo! that sign
    Awakened me from my slumber.

The Copperhead.
(1864.)

THERE is peace in the swamp where the Copperhead sleeps,
Where the waters are stagnant, the white vapour creeps,
Where the musk of Magnolia hangs thick in the air,
And the lilies' phylacteries broaden in prayer.
There is peace in the swamp, though the quiet is death,
Though the mist is miasma, the upas tree's breath,
Though no echo awakes to the cooing of doves,—
There is peace: yes, the peace that the Copperhead loves!

Go seek him: he coils in the ooze and the drip,
Like a thong idly flung from the slave-driver's whip;
But beware the false footstep,—the stumble that brings
A deadlier lash than the overseer swings.
Never arrow so true, never bullet so dread,
As the straight steady stroke of that hammer-shaped head;
Whether slave or proud panther, who braves that dull crest,
Woe to him who shall trouble the Copperhead's rest!

Then why waste your labours, brave hearts and strong men,
In tracking a trail to the Copperhead's den?
Lay your axe to the cypress, hew open the shade
To the free sky and sunshine Jehovah has made;
Let the breeze of the North sweep the vapours away,
Till the stagnant lake ripples, the freed waters play;
And then to your heel can you righteously doom
The Copperhead born of its shadow and gloom!

A Sanitary Message.

LAST night, above the whistling wind,
    I heard the welcome rain,—
A fusillade upon the roof,
    A tattoo on the pane:
The keyhole piped; the chimney-top
    A warlike trumpet blew;
Yet, mingling with these sounds of strife,
    A softer voice stole through.

"Give thanks, O brothers!" said the voice,
    "That He who sent the rains
Hath spared your fields the scarlet dew
    That drips from patriot veins:
I've seen the grass on Eastern graves
    In brighter verdure rise;
But, oh! the rain that gave it life
    Sprang first from human eyes.

"I come to wash away no stain
    Upon your wasted lea;
I raise no banners, save the ones
    The forest waves to me:
Upon the mountain side, where Spring
    Her farthest picket sets,
My réveille awakes a host
    Of grassy bayonets.

A Sanitary Message.

"I visit every humble roof;
  I mingle with the low:
Only upon the highest peaks
  My blessings fall in snow;
Until, in tricklings of the stream
  And drainings of the lea,
My unspent bounty comes at last
  To mingle with the sea."

And thus all night, above the wind,
  I heard the welcome rain,—
A fusillade upon the roof,
  A tattoo on the pane:
The keyhole piped; the chimney-top
  A warlike trumpet blew;
But, mingling with these sounds of strife,
  This hymn of peace stole through.

The Old Major Explains.

(RE-UNION, ARMY OF THE POTOMAC, 12TH MAY 1871.)

WELL, you see, the fact is, Colonel, I don't know as I can come :
For the farm is not half planted, and there's work to do at home ;
And my leg is getting troublesome,—it laid me up last Fall,
And the doctors, they have cut and hacked, and never found the ball.

And then, for an old man like me, it's not exactly right,
This kind o' playing soldier with no enemy in sight.
"The Union,"—that was well enough way up to '66 ;
But this "Re-Union," maybe now it's mixed with politics ?

No ? Well, you understand it best ; but then, you see, my lad,
I'm deacon now, and some might think that the example's bad.
And week from next is Conference. . . . You said the twelfth of May ?
Why, that's the day we broke their line at Spottsyl-van-i-a !

Hot work; eh, Colonel, wasn't it? Ye mind that narrow
    front:
They called it the "Death-Angle!" Well, well, my lad, we
    won't
Fight that old battle over now: I only meant to say
I really can't engage to come upon the twelfth of May.

How's Thompson? What! will he be there? Well, now
    I wan't to know!
The first man in the rebel works! they called him "Swearing
    Joe."
A wild young fellow, sir, I fear the rascal was; but then—
Well, short of heaven, there wa'n't a place he dursn't lead
    his men.

And Dick, you say, is coming too. And Billy? ah! it's
    true
We buried him at Gettysburg: I mind the spot; do you?
A little field below the hill,—it must be green this May;
Perhaps that's why the fields about bring him to me to-
    day.

Well, well, excuse me, Colonel! but there are some things
    that drop
The tail-board out one's feelings; and the only way's to
    stop.
So they want to see the old man; ah, the rascals! do they,
    eh?
Well, I've business down in Boston about the twelfth of
    May.

California's Greeting to Seward.

(1869.)

We know him well: no need of praise
   Or bonfire from the windy hill
To light to softer paths and ways
   The world-worn man we honour still.

No need to quote those truths he spoke
   That burned through years of war and shame,
While History carves with surer stroke
   Across our map his noonday fame.

No need to bid him show the scars
   Or blows dealt by the Scæan gate,
Who lived to pass its shattered bars,
   And see the foe capitulate:

Who lived to turn his slower feet
   Toward the western setting sun,
To see his harvest all complete,
   His dream fulfilled, his duty done,

The one flag streaming from the pole,
   The one faith borne from sea to sea:
For such a triumph, and such goal,
   Poor must our human greeting be.

Ah! rather that the conscious land
  In simpler ways salute the Man,—
The tall pines bowing where they stand,
  The bared head of El Capitan,

The tumult of the waterfalls,
  Pohono's kerchief in the breeze,
The waving from the rocky walls,
  The stir and rustle of the trees;

Till, lapped in sunset skies of hope,
  In sunset lands by sunset seas,
The Young World's Premier treads the slope
  Of sunset years in calm and peace.

The Aged Stranger.

AN INCIDENT OF THE WAR.

"I was with Grant—" the stranger said;
   Said the farmer, "Say no more,
But rest thee here at my cottage porch,
   For thy feet are weary and sore."

"I was with Grant—" the stranger said;
   Said the farmer, "Nay, no more,—
I prithee sit at my frugal board,
   And eat of my humble store.

"How fares my boy,—my soldier boy,
   Of the old Ninth Army Corps?
I warrant he bore him gallantly
   In the smoke and the battle's roar!"

"I know him not," said the aged man,
   "And, as I remarked before,
I was with Grant—" "Nay, nay, I know,"
   Said the farmer, "say no more:

"He fell in battle,—I see, alas!
   Thou'dst smooth these tidings o'er,—
Nay, speak the truth, whatever it be,
   Though it rend my bosom's core.

"How fell he?—with his face to the foe,
  Upholding the flag he bore?
Oh, say not that my boy disgraced
  The uniform that he wore!"

"I cannot tell," said the aged man,
  "And should have remarked before,
That I was with Grant,—in Illinois,—
  Some three years before the war."

Then the farmer spake him never a word,
  But beat with his fist full sore
That aged man, who had worked for Grant
  Some three years before the war.

The Idyl of Battle Hollow.

(WAR OF THE REBELLION, 1864.)

No, I won't—thar, now, so! And it ain't nothin',—no!
And thar's nary to tell that you folks yer don't know;
And it's "Belle, tell us, do!" and it's "Belle, is it true?"
And "Wot's this yer yarn of the Major and you?"
Till I'm sick of it all,—so I am, but I s'pose
Thet is nothin' to you. . . . . Well, then, listen! yer goes!

It was after the fight, and around us all night
Thar was poppin' and shootin' a powerful sight;
And the niggers had fled, and Aunt Chlo was abed,
And Pinky and Milly were hid in the shed:
And I ran out at daybreak and nothin' was nigh
But the growlin' of cannon low down in the sky.

And I saw not a thing as I ran to the spring,
But a splintered fence rail and a broken-down swing,
And a bird said "Kerchee!" as it sat on a tree,
As if it was lonesome and glad to see me;
And I filled up my pail and was risin' to go,
When up comes the Major a canterin' slow.

When he saw me, he drew in his reins, and then threw
On the gate-post his bridle, and—what does he do

But come down where I sat; and he lifted his hat,
And he says—well, thar ain't any need to tell *that*—
'Twas some foolishness, sure, but it 'mounted to this,
Thet he asked for a drink, and he wanted—a kiss.

Then I said (I was mad), "For the water, my lad,
You're too big and must stoop; for a kiss, it's as bad—
You ain't near big enough." And I turned in a huff,
When that Major he laid his white hand on my cuff,
And he says, "You're a trump! Take my pistol, don't fear!
But shoot the next man that insults you, my dear."

Then he stooped to the pool, very quiet and cool,
Leavin' me with that pistol stuck there like a fool,
When thar flashed on my sight a quick glimmer of light
From the top of the little stone-fence on the right,
And I knew 'twas a rifle, and back of it all
Rose the face of that bushwhacker, Cherokee Hall!

Then I felt in my dread that the moment the head
Of the Major was lifted, the Major was dead;
And I stood still and white, but Lord! gals, in spite
Of my care, that derned pistol went off in my fright!
Went off—true as gospil!—and, strangest of all,
It actooally injured that Cherokee Hall.

Thet's all—now, go long. Yes, some folks thinks it's wrong.
And thar's some wants to know to what side I belong;
But I says, "Served him right!" and I go, all my might,
In love or in war, for a fair stand-up fight;
And as for the Major—Sho! gals, don't you know
Thet—Lord!—thar's his step in the garden below.

Caldwell of Springfield.

(NEW JERSEY, 1780.)

Here's the spot. Look around you. Above on the height
Lay the Hessians encamped. By that church on the right
Stood the gaunt Jersey farmers. And here ran a wall—
You may dig anywhere and you'll turn up a ball.
Nothing more. Grasses spring, waters run, flowers blow,
Pretty much as they did ninety-three years ago.

Nothing more, did I say? Stay one moment; you've heard
Of Caldwell, the parson, who once preached the word
Down at Springfield? What, No? Come—that's bad. Why
    he had
All the Jerseys aflame! And they gave him the name
Of the "rebel high priest." He stuck in their gorge,
For he loved the Lord God—and he hated King George!

He had cause, you might say! When the Hessians that
    day
Marched up with Knyphausen, they stopped on their way
At the "farms," where his wife, with a child in her arms,
Sat alone in the house. How it happened none knew
But God—and that one of the hireling crew
Who fired the shot! Enough!—there she lay,
And Caldwell, the chaplain, her husband, away!

Did he preach—did he pray? Think of him as you stand
By the old church to-day :—think of him and that band
Of militant ploughboys! See the smoke and the heat
Of that reckless advance—of that straggling retreat!
Keep the ghost of that wife, foully slain, in your view—
And what could you, what should you, what would *you* do?

Why, just what *he* did! They were left in the lurch
For the want of more wadding. He ran to the church,
Broke the door, stripped the pews, and dashed out in the road
With his arms full of hymn-books, and threw down his load
At their feet! Then above all the shouting and shots
Rang his voice—" Put Watts into 'em—Boys, give 'em Watts!"

And they did. That is all. Grasses spring, flowers blow,
Pretty much as they did ninety-three years ago.
You may dig anywhere and you'll turn up a ball—
But not always a hero like this—and that's all.

Poem

DELIVERED ON THE FOURTEENTH ANNIVERSARY OF CALI-
FORNIA'S ADMISSION INTO THE UNION.

September 9, 1864.

We meet in peace, though from our native East
The sun that sparkles on our birthday feast
Glanced as he rose in fields whose dews were red
With darker tints than those Aurora spread.
Though shorn his rays—his welcome disc concealed
In the dim smoke that veiled each battlefield,
Still striving upward, in meridian pride,
He climbed the walls that East and West divide—
Saw his bright face flashed back from golden sand,
And sapphire seas that lave the Western land.

Strange was the contrast that such scenes disclose
From his high vantage o'er eternal snows;
There War's alarm the brazen trumpet rings—
Here his love-song the mailed cicala sings;
There bayonets glitter through the forest glades—
Here yellow cornfields stack their peaceful blades;
There the deep trench where Valour finds a grave—
Here the long ditch that curbs the peaceful wave;
There the bold sapper with his lighted train—
Here the dark tunnel and its stores of gain;
Here the full harvest and the wain's advance—
There the Grim Reaper and the ambulance.

With scenes so adverse, what mysterious bond
Links our fair fortunes to the shores beyond?
Why come we here—last of a scattered fold—
To pour new metal in the broken mould?
To yield our tribute, stamped with Cæsar's face,
To Cæsar, stricken in the market-place?

Ah! love of country is the secret tie
That joins these contrasts 'neath one arching sky;
Though brighter paths our peaceful steps explore—
We meet together at the Nation's door.
War winds her horn, and giant cliffs go down
Like the high walls that girt the sacred town,
And bares the pathway to her throbbing heart,
From clustered village and from crowded mart.

Part of God's providence it was to found
A Nation's bulwark on this chosen ground—
Not Jesuit's zeal nor pioneer's unrest
Planted these pickets in the distant West;
But He who first the Nation's fate forecast
Placed here His fountains sealed for ages past,
Rock-ribbed and guarded till the coming time
Should fit the people for their work sublime;
When a new Moses with his rod of steel
Smote the tall cliffs with one wide-ringing peal,
And the old miracle in record told
To the new Nation was revealed in gold.

Judge not too idly that our toils are mean,
Though no new levies marshal on our green;
Nor deem too rashly that our gains are small,
Weighed with the prizes for which heroes fall.

See, where thick vapour wreathes the battle-line;
There Mercy follows with her oil and wine;
Or when brown Labour with its peaceful charm
Stiffens the sinews of the Nation's arm.

What nerves its hands to strike a deadlier blow
And hurl its legions on the rebel foe?
Lo! for each town new rising o'er our State
See the foe's hamlet waste and desolate,
While each new factory lifts its chimney tall,
Like a fresh mortar trained on Richmond's wall.

For this, oh! brothers, swings the fruitful vine,
Spread our broad pastures with their countless kine;
For this o'erhead the arching vault springs clear,
Sunlit and cloudless for one half the year;
For this no snowflake, e'er so lightly pressed,
Chills the warm impulse of our mother's breast.

Quick to reply, from meadows brown and sere,
She thrills responsive to Spring's earliest tear;
Breaks into blossom, flings her loveliest rose
Ere the white crocus mounts Atlantic snows;
And the example of her liberal creed
Teaches the lesson that to-day we need.

Thus ours the lot with peaceful, generous hand
To spread our bounty o'er the suffering land;
As the deep cleft in Mariposa's wall
Hurls a vast river splintering in its fall—
Though the rapt soul who stands in awe below
Sees but the arching of the promised bow—
Lo! the far streamlet drinks its dews unseen,
And the whole valley makes a brighter green.

Miss Blanche Says.

AND you are the poet, and so you want
    Something—what is it?—a theme, a fancy?
Something or other the Muse won't grant
    In your old poetical necromancy;
Why one half your poets—you can't deny—
    Don't know the Muse when you chance to meet her,
But sit in your attics and mope and sigh
For a faineant goddess to drop from the sky,
When flesh and blood may be standing by
    Quite at your service, should you but greet her.

What if I told you my own romance?
    Women are poets, if you so take them,
One-third poet—the rest what chance
    Of man and marriage may choose to make them.
Give me ten minutes before you go,—
    Here at the window we'll sit together,
Watching the currents that ebb and flow;
Watching the world as it drifts below
Up to the hot Avenue's dusty glow:
    Isn't it pleasant—this bright June weather?

Well, it was after the war broke out,
    And I was a school-girl fresh from Paris;
Papa had contracts, and roamed about,
    And I—did nothing—for I was an heiress.

Miss Blanche Says.

Picked some lint, now I think ; perhaps
   Knitted some stocking—a dozen nearly;
Havelocks made for the soldiers' caps ;
Stood at fair tables and peddled traps
Quite at a profit. The "shoulder-straps"
   Thought I was pretty. Ah, thank you ! really ?

Still it was stupid. Rata-tat-tat !
   Those were the sounds of that battle summer,
Till the earth seemed a parchment round and flat,
   And every footfall the tap of a drummer ;
And day by day down the Avenue went
   Cavalry, infantry, all together,
Till my pitying angel one day sent
My fate in the shape of a regiment,
That halted, just as the day was spent,
   Here at our door in the bright June weather.

None of your dandy warriors they,
   Men from the West, but where I know not ;
Haggard and travel-stained, worn and grey,
   With never a ribbon or lace or bow-knot :
And I opened the window, and leaning there,
   I felt in their presence the free winds blowing ;
My neck and shoulders and arms were bare—
I did not dream that they might think me fair,
But I had some flowers that night in my hair,
   And here, on my bosom, a red rose glowing.

And I looked from the window along the line,
   Dusty and dirty and grim and solemn,
Till an eye like a bayonet flash met mine,
   And a dark face grew from the darkening column,

And a quick flame leaped to my eyes and hair,
   Till cheeks and shoulders burned all together,
And the next I found myself standing there
With my eyelids wet and my cheeks less fair,
And the rose from my bosom tossed high in air,
   Like a blood-drop falling on plume and feather.

Then I drew back quickly : there came a cheer,
   A rush of figures, a noise and tussle,
And then it was over, and high and clear
   My red rose bloomed on his gun's black muzzle.
Then far in the darkness a sharp voice cried,
   And slowly and steadily, all together,
Shoulder to shoulder and side to side,
Rising and falling, and swaying wide,
But bearing above them the rose, my pride,
   They marched away in the twilight weather.

And I leaned from my window and watched my rose
   Tossed on the waves of the surging column,
Warmed from above in the sunset glows,
   Borne from below by an impulse solemn.
Then I shut the window. I heard no more
   Of my soldier friend, my flower neither,
But lived my life as I did before.
I did not go as a nurse to the war—
Sick folks to me are a dreadful bore—
   So I didn't go to the hospital either.

You smile, O poet, and what do you ?
   You lean from your window, and watch life's column
Trampling and struggling through dust and dew,
   Filled with its purposes grave and solemn ;

An act, a gesture, a face—who knows ?—
   Touches your fancy to thrill and haunt you,
And you pluck from your bosom the verse that grows,
And down it flies like my red, red rose,
And you sit and dream as away it goes,
   And think that your duty is done—now don't you ?

I know your answer.   I'm not yet through.
   Look at this photograph—"In the Trenches !"
That dead man in the coat of blue
   Holds a withered rose in his hand.   That clenches
Nothing !—except that the sun paints true,
   And a woman is sometimes prophetic-minded.
And that's my romance.   And, poet, you
Take it and mould it to suit your view ;
And who knows but you may find it too
   Come to your heart once more, as mine did.

An Arctic Vision.

WHERE the short-legged Esquimaux
Waddle in the ice and snow,
And the playful Polar bear
Nips the hunter unaware;
Where by day they track the ermine,
And by night another vermin,—
Segment of the frigid zone,
Where the temperature alone
Warms on St. Elias' cone;
Polar dock, where Nature slips
From the ways her icy ships;
Land of fox and deer and sable,
Shore end of our western cable,—
Let the news that flying goes
Thrill through all your arctic floes,
And reverberate the boast
From the cliffs off Beechey's coast,
Till the tidings, circling round
Every bay of Norton Sound,
Throw the vocal tide-wave back
To the isles of Kodiac.
Let the stately Polar bears
Waltz around the pole in pairs,
And the walrus, in his glee,
Bare his tusk of ivory;

An Arctic Vision.

While the bold sea-unicorn
Calmly takes an extra horn;
All ye Polar skies, reveal your
Very rarest of parhelia;
Trip it all ye merry dancers,
In the airiest of "Lancers;"
Slide, ye solemn glaciers, slide,
One inch farther to the tide,
Nor in rash precipitation
Upset Tyndall's calculation.
Know you not what fate awaits you,
Or to whom the future mates you?
All ye icebergs make salaam,—
You belong to Uncle Sam!

On the spot where Eugene Sue
Led his wretched Wandering Jew,
Stands a form whose features strike
Russ and Esquimaux alike.
He it is whom Skalds of old
In their Runic rhymes foretold;
Lean of flank and lank of jaw,
See the real Northern Thor!
See the awful Yankee leering
Just across the Straits of Behring;
On the drifted snow, too plain,
Sinks his fresh tobacco stain,
Just beside the deep inden-
Tation of his Number 10.

Leaning on his icy hammer
Stands the hero of this drama,
And above the wild-duck's clamour,
In his own peculiar grammar,

With its linguistic disguises,
Lo! the Arctic prologue rises:—
"Wa'll, I reckon 'tain't so bad,
Seein' ez 'twas all they had;
True, the Springs are rather late,
And early Falls predominate;
But the ice crop's pretty sure,
And the air is kind o' pure;
'Tain't so very mean a trade,
When the land is all surveyed.
There's a right smart chance for fur-chase
All along this recent purchase,
And, unless the stories fail,
Every fish from cod to whale;
Rocks, too; mebbe quartz; let's see,—
'Twould be strange if there should be,—
Seems I've heerd such stories told;
Eh!—why, bless us,—yes, it's gold!"

While the blows are falling thick
From his California pick,
You may recognise the Thor
Of the vision that I saw,—
Freed from legendary glamour,
See the real magician's hammer.

St. Thomas.

(A GEOGRAPHICAL SURVEY, 1868.)

VERY fair and full of promise
Lay the island of St. Thomas:
Ocean o'er its reefs and bars
Hid its elemental scars;
Groves of cocoanut and guava
Grew above its fields of lava.
So the gem of the Antilles,—
"Isles of Eden," where no ill is,—
Like a great green turtle slumbered
On the sea that it encumbered.
Then said William Henry Seward,
As he cast his eye to leeward,
"Quite important to our commerce
Is this island of St. Thomas."

Said the Mountain ranges, "Thank'ee,
But we cannot stand the Yankee
O'er our scars and fissures poring,
In our very vitals boring,
In our sacred caverns prying,
All our secret problems trying,—
Digging, blasting, with dynamit
Mocking all our thunders! Damn it!

St. Thomas.

Other lands may be more civil,
Bust our lava crust if we will!"

Said the Sea, its white teeth gnashing
Through its coral-reef lips flashing,
"Shall I let this scheming mortal
Shut with stone my shining portal,
Curb my tide and check my play,
Fence with wharves my shining bay?
Rather let me be drawn out
In one awful waterspout!"

Said the black-browed Hurricane,
Brooding down the Spanish Main,
"Shall I see my forces, zounds!
Measured by square inch and pounds,
With detectives at my back
When I double on my track,
And my secret paths made clear,
Published o'er the hemisphere
To each gaping, prying crew?
Shall I? Blow me if I do!"

So the Mountains shook and thundered,
And the Hurricane came sweeping,
And the people stared and wondered
As the Sea came on them leaping:
Each, according to his promise,
Made things lively at St. Thomas.

Till one morn, when Mr. Seward
Cast his weather eye to leeward,
There was not an inch of dry land
Left to mark his recent island.

St. Thomas.

Not a flagstaff or a sentry,
Not a wharf or port of entry,—
Only—to cut matters shorter—
Just a patch of muddy water
In the open ocean lying,
And a gull above it flying.

Off Scarborough.

(SEPTEMBER 1779.)

I.

"Have a care!" the bailiffs cried
    From their cockleshell that lay
Off the frigate's yellow side,
    Tossing on Scarborough Bay,
While the forty sail it convoyed on a bowline stretched away;
    "Take your chicks beneath your wings,
        And your claws and feathers spread,
    Ere the hawk upon them springs—
        Ere around Flamborough Head
Swoops Paul Jones, the Yankee falcon, with his beak and talons red."

II.

How we laughed!—my mate and I—
    On the "Bon Homme Richard's" deck,—
As we saw that convoy fly
    Like a snow squall, till each fleck
Melted in the twilight shadows of the coast-line, speck by speck;
    And scuffling back to shore
        The Scarborough bailiffs sped,

As the " Richard," with a roar
    Of her cannon round the Head,
Crossed her royal yards and signalled to her consort:
    "Chase ahead!"

III.

But the devil seize Landais
    In that consort ship of France!
For the shabby, lubber way
    That he worked the "Alliance"
In the offing,—nor a broadside fired save to our mischance!—
    When tumbling to the van,
        With his battle-lanterns set,
    Rose the burly Englishman
        'Gainst our hull as black as jet—
Rode the yellow-sided "Serapis," and all alone we met!

IV.

All alone—though far at sea
    Hung his consort, rounding to;
All alone—though on our lee
    Fought our "Pallas," stanch and true!
For the first broadside around us both a smoky circle drew:
    And, like champions in a ring,
        There was cleared a little space—
    Scarce a cable's length to swing—
        Ere we grappled in embrace,
All the world shut out around us, and we only face to face!

V.

Then awoke all hell below
    From that broadside, doubly curst,
For our long eighteens in row
    Leaped the first discharge and burst!
And on deck our men came pouring, fearing their own
    guns the worst.
    And as dumb we lay, till, through
        Smoke and flame and bitter cry,
    Hailed the " Serapis "—" Have you
        Struck your colours?" Our reply,
"We have not yet begun to fight!" went shouting to the
    sky!

VI.

Roux of Brest, old fisher, lay
    Like a herring gasping here;
Bunker of Nantucket Bay,
    Blown from out the port, dropped sheer
Half a cable's length to leeward; yet we faintly raised a cheer
    As with his own right hand,
        Our Commodore made fast
    The foeman's head-gear and
        The "Richard's" mizzen-mast,
And in that death-lock clinging held us there from first to
    last!

VII.

Yet the foeman, gun on gun,
    Through the " Richard " tore a road—

With his gunners' rammers run
 Through our ports at every load,
Till clear the blue beyond us through our yawning timbers
  showed.
 Yet with entrails torn we clung
  Like the Spartan to our fox,
 And on deck no coward tongue
  Wailed the enemy's hard knocks,
Nor that all below us trembled like a wreck upon the rocks.

VIII.

 Then a thought rose in my brain,
  As through Channel mists the sun.
 From our tops a fire like rain
  Drove below decks every one
Of the enemy's ship's company to hide or work a gun,
 And that thought took shape as I
  On the "Richard's" yard lay out,
 That a man might do and die,
  If the doing brought about
Freedom for his home and country, and his messmates'
  cheering shout!

IX.

 Then I crept out in the dark
  Till I hung above the hatch
 Of the "Serapis"—a mark
  For her marksmen!—with a match
And a hand-grenade, but lingered just a moment more to
  snatch
 One last look at sea and sky!
  At the lighthouse on the hill!

At the harvest-moon on high!
 And our pine flag fluttering still;
Then turned and down her yawning throat I launched that
    devil's pill!

X.

Then a blank was all between
 As the flames around me spun!
Had I fired the magazine?
 Was the victory lost or won?
Nor knew I till the fight was o'er but half my work was
    done:
 For I lay among the dead
  In the cockpit of our foe,
 With a roar above my head—
  Till a trampling to and fro,
And a lantern showed my mate's face, and I knew what
    now you know!

SPANISH IDYLS AND LEGENDS.

The Miracle of Padre Junipero.

This is the tale that the Chronicle
Tells of the wonderful miracle
Wrought by the pious Padre Serro,
The very reverend Junipero.

The heathen stood on his ancient mound,
Looking over the desert bound
Into the distant, hazy South,
Over the dusty and broad champaign,
Where, with many a gaping mouth
And fissure, cracked by the fervid drouth,
For seven months had the wasted plain
Known no moisture of dew or rain.
The wells were empty and choked with sand;
The rivers had perished from the land;
Only the sea-fogs to and fro
Slipped like ghosts of the streams below.
Deep in its bed lay the river's bones,
Bleaching in pebbles and milk-white stones,
And tracked o'er the desert faint and far,
Its ribs shone bright on each sandy bar.

Thus they stood as the sun went down
Over the foot-hills bare and brown;

Thus they looked to the South, wherefrom
The pale-face medicine-man should come,
Not in anger or in strife,
But to bring—so ran the tale—
The welcome springs of eternal life,
The living waters that should not fail.

Said one, "He will come like Manitou,
Unseen, unheard, in the falling dew."
Said another, "He will come full soon
Out of the round-faced watery moon."
And another said, "He is here!" and lo,—
Faltering, staggering, feeble and slow,—
Out from the desert's blinding heat
The Padre dropped at the heathen's feet.
They stood and gazed for a little space
Down on his pallid and careworn face,
And a smile of scorn went round the band
As they touched alternate with foot and hand
This mortal waif, that the outer space
Of dim mysterious sky and sand
Flung with so little of Christian grace
Down on their barren, sterile strand.

Said one to him: "It seems thy God
Is a very pitiful kind of God;
He could not shield thine aching eyes
From the blowing desert sands that rise,
Nor turn aside from thy old grey head
The glittering blade that is brandishèd
By the sun He set in the heavens high;
He could not moisten thy lips when dry;
The desert fire is in thy brain;
Thy limbs are racked with the fever-pain:

The Miracle of Padre Junipero.

If this be the grace He showeth thee
Who art His servant, what may we,
Strange to His ways and His commands,
Seek at His unforgiving hands?"
"Drink but this cup," said the Padre, straight,
"And thou shalt know whose mercy bore
These aching limbs to your heathen door,
And purged my soul of its gross estate.
Drink in His name, and thou shalt see
The hidden depths of this mystery.
Drink!" and he held the cup. One blow
From the heathen dashed to the ground below
The sacred cup that the Padre bore,
And the thirsty soil drank the precious store
Of sacramental and holy wine,
That emblem and consecrated sign
And blessed symbol of blood divine.

Then, says the legend (and they who doubt
The same as heretics be accurst),
From the dry and feverish soil leaped out
A living fountain; a well-spring burst
Over the dusty and broad champaign,
Over the sandy and sterile plain,
Till the granite ribs and the milk-white stones
That lay in the valley—the scattered bones—
Moved in the river and lived again!
Such was the wonderful miracle
Wrought by the cup of wine that fell
From the hands of the pious Padre Serro,
The very reverend Junipero.

The Wonderful Spring of San Joaquin.

Of all the fountains that poets sing,—
Crystal, thermal, or mineral spring;
Ponce de Leon's Fount of Youth;
Wells with bottoms of doubtful truth;
In short, of all the springs of Time
That ever were flowing in fact or rhyme,
That ever were tasted, felt, or seen,—
There were none like the Spring of San Joaquin.

Anno Domini Eighteen-seven,
Father Dominguez (now in heaven,—
Obiit, Eighteen twenty-seven)
Found the spring, and found it, too,
By his mule's miraculous cast of a shoe;
For his beast—a descendant of Balaam's ass—
Stopped on the instant, and would not pass.

The Padre thought the omen good,
And bent his lips to the trickling flood;
Then—as the Chronicles declare,
On the honest faith of a true believer—
His cheeks, though wasted, lank, and bare,
Filled like a withered russet-pear
In the vacuum of a glass receiver,

And the snows that seventy winters bring
Melted away in that magic spring.

Such, at least, was the wondrous news
The Padre brought into Santa Cruz.
The Church, of course, had its own views
Of who were worthiest to use
The magic spring; but the prior claim
Fell to the aged, sick, and lame.
Far and wide the people came:
Some from the healthful Aptos Creek
Hastened to bring their helpless sick;
Even the fishers of rude Soquel
Suddenly found they were far from well;
The brawny dwellers of San Lorenzo
Said, in fact, they had never been so:
And all were ailing,—strange to say,—
From Pescadero to Monterey.

Over the mountain they poured in,
With leathern bottles and bags of skin;
Through the cañons a motley throng
Trotted, hobbled, and limped along.
The Fathers gazed at the moving scene
With pious joy and with souls serene;
And then—a result perhaps foreseen—
They laid out the Mission of San Joaquin.

Not in the eyes of faith alone
The good effects of the water shone;
But skins grew rosy, eyes waxed clear,
Of rough vaquero and mulcteer;

Angular forms were rounded out,
Limbs grew supple and waists grew stout;
And as for the girls—for miles about
They had no equal! To this day,
From Pescadero to Monterey,
You'll still find eyes in which are seen
The liquid graces of San Joaquin.

There is a limit to human bliss,
And the Mission of San Joaquin had this;
None went abroad to roam or stay,
But they fell sick in the queerest way,—
A singular *maladie du pays*,
With gastric symptoms: so they spent
Their days in a sensuous content,
Caring little for things unseen
Beyond their bowers of living green,—
Beyond the mountains that lay between
The world and the Mission of San Joaquin.

Winter passed and the summer came;
The trunks of *madroño*, all aflame,
Here and there through the underwood
Like pillars of fire starkly stood.
All of the breezy solitude
   Was filled with the spicing of pine and bay
And resinous odours mixed and blended,
   And dim and ghost-like, far away,
The smoke of the burning woods ascended.
Then of a sudden the mountains swam,
The rivers piled their floods in a dam,
The ridge above Los Gatos Creek

Arched its spine in a feline fashion;
The forests waltzed till they grew sick,
And Nature shook in a speechless passion;
And, swallowed up in the earthquake's spleen,
The wonderful Spring of San Joaquin
Vanished, and never more was seen!

Two days passed: the Mission folk
Out of their rosy dream awoke;
Some of them looked a trifle white,
But that, no doubt, was from earthquake fright.
Three days: there was sore distress,
Headache, nausea, giddiness.
Four days: faintings, tenderness
Of the mouth and fauces; and in less
Than one week,—here the story closes;
We won't continue the prognosis,—
Enough that now no trace is seen
Of Spring or Mission of San Joaquin.

MORAL.

You see the point? Don't be too quick
To break bad habits: better stick,
Like the Mission folk, to your *arsenic.*

The Angelus.

(HEARD AT THE MISSION DOLORES, 1868.)

BELLS of the Past, whose long-forgotten music
    Still fills the wide expanse,
Tingeing the sober twilight of the Present
    With colour of romance !

I hear your call, and see the sun descending
    On rock and wave and sand,
As down the coast the Mission voices, blending,
    Girdle the heathen land.

Within the circle of your incantation
    No blight nor mildew falls ;
Nor fierce unrest, nor lust, nor low ambition
    Passes those airy walls.

Borne on the swell of your long waves receding,
    I touch the farther Past,—
I see the dying glow of Spanish glory,
    The sunset dream and last !

Before me rise the dome-shaped Mission towers,
    The white Presidio ;
The swart commander in his leathern jerkin,
    The priest in stole of snow.

The Angelus.

Once more I see Portala's cross uplifting
    Above the setting sun ;
And past the headland, northward, slowly drifting
    The freighted galleon.

O solemn bells ! whose consecrated masses
    Recall the faith of old,—
O tinkling bells ! that lulled with twilight music
    The spiritual fold !

Your voices break and falter in the darkness,—
    Break, falter, and are still ;
And veiled and mystic, like the Host descending,
    The sun sinks from the hill !

Concepcion de Arguello.

(PRESIDIO DE SAN FRANCISCO, 1800.)

I.

Looking seaward, o'er the sandhills stands the fortress, old and quaint,
By the San Francisco friars lifted to their patron saint,—

Sponsor to that wondrous city, now apostate to the creed,
On whose youthful walls the Padre saw the angel's golden reed;

All its trophies long since scattered, all its blazon brushed away;
And the flag that flies above it but a triumph of to-day.

Never scar of siege or battle challenges the wandering eye—
Never breach of warlike onset holds the curious passer-by;

Only one sweet human fancy interweaves its threads of gold
With the plain and home-spun present, and a love that ne'er grows old:

Only one thing holds its crumbling walls above the meaner dust,—
Listen to the simple story of a woman's love and trust.

II.

Count von Resanoff, the Russian, envoy of the mighty Czar,
Stood beside the deep embrasures where the brazen cannon are;

He with grave provincial magnates long had held serene debate
On the Treaty of Alliance and the high affairs of state;

He from grave provincial magnates oft had turned to talk apart
With the Commandante's daughter on the questions of the heart,

Until points of gravest import yielded slowly one by one,
And by Love was consummated what Diplomacy begun;

Till beside the deep embrasures, where the brazen cannon are,
He received the twofold contract for approval of the Czar;

Till beside the brazen cannon the betrothèd bade adieu,
And, from sallyport and gateway, north the Russian eagles flew.

III.

Long beside the deep embrasures, where the brazen cannon are,
Did they wait the promised bridegroom and the answer of the Czar;

Day by day on wall and bastion beat the hollow, empty breeze,—
Day by day the sunlight glittered on the vacant, smiling seas;

Week by week the near hills whitened in their dusty leather cloaks,—
Week by week the far hills darkened from the fringing plain of oaks,

Till the rains came, and far-breaking, on the fierce south-wester tost,
Dashed the whole long coast with colour, and then vanished and were lost.

So each year the seasons shifted,—wet and warm and drear and dry;
Half a year of clouds and flowers,—half a year of dust and sky.

Still it brought no ship nor message,—brought no tidings, ill or meet,
For the statesmanlike Commander, for the daughter fair and sweet.

Yet she heard the varying message, voiceless to all ears beside :
" He will come," the flowers whispered ; " Come no more," the dry hills sighed.

Still she found him with the waters lifted by the morning breeze,—
Still she lost him with the folding of the great white-tented seas ;

Until hollows chased the dimples from her cheeks of olive brown,
And at times a swift, shy moisture dragged the long sweet lashes down ;

Or the small mouth curved and quivered as for some denied caress,
And the fair young brow was knitted in an infantine distress.

Then the grim Commander, pacing where the brazen cannon are,
Comforted the maid with proverbs,—wisdom gathered from afar ;

Bits of ancient observation by his fathers garnered, each
As a pebble worn and polished in the current of his speech :

"'Those who wait the coming rider travel twice as far as he ;'
'Tired wench and coming butter never did in time agree ;'

"'He that getteth himself honey, though a clown, he shall
   have flies;'
'In the end God grinds the miller;' 'In the dark the mole
   has eyes;'

"'He whose father is Alcalde of his trial hath no fear,'—
And be sure the Count has reasons that will make his conduct clear."

Then the voice sententious faltered, and the wisdom it would
   teach
Lost itself in fondest trifles of his soft Castilian speech;

And on "Concha," "Conchitita," and "Conchita" he would
   dwell
With the fond reiteration which the Spaniard knows so well.

So with proverbs and caresses, half in faith and half in doubt,
Every day some hope was kindled, flickered, faded, and
   went out.

IV.

Yearly, down the hillside sweeping, came the stately caval-
   cade,
Bringing revel to vaquero, joy and comfort to each maid;

Bringing days of formal visit, social feast and rustic sport;
Of bull-baiting on the plaza, of love-making in the court.

Vainly then at Concha's lattice, vainly as the idle wind,
Rose the thin high Spanish tenor that bespoke the youth
   too kind;

Vainly, leaning from their saddles, caballeros, bold and fleet,
Plucked for her the buried chicken from beneath their mustang's feet;

So in vain the barren hillsides with their gay serapes blazed,
Blazed and vanished in the dust-cloud that their flying hoofs had raised.

Then the drum called from the rampart, and once more, with patient mien,
The Commander and his daughter each took up the dull routine,—

Each took up the petty duties of a life apart and lone,
Till the slow years wrought a music in its dreary monotone.

v.

Forty years on wall and bastion swept the hollow idle breeze,
Since the Russian eagle fluttered from the California seas;

Forty years on wall and bastion wrought its slow but sure decay,
And St. George's cross was lifted in the port of Monterey;

And the citadel was lighted, and the hall was gaily drest,
All to honour Sir George Simpson, famous traveller and guest.

Far and near the people gathered to the costly banquet set,
And exchanged congratulations with the English baronet;

Till, the formal speeches ended, and amidst the laugh and wine,
Some one spoke of Concha's lover,—heedless of the warning sign.

Quickly then cried Sir George Simpson: "Speak no ill of him, I pray—
He is dead. He died, poor fellow, forty years ago this day.

"Died while speeding home to Russia, falling from a fractious horse.
Left a sweetheart, too, they tell me. Married, I suppose, of course!

"Lives she yet?" A death-like silence fell on banquet, guests, and hall,
And a trembling figure rising fixed the awestruck gaze of all.

Two black eyes in darkened orbits gleamed beneath the nun's white hood;
Black serge hid the wasted figure, bowed and stricken where it stood.

"Lives she yet?" Sir George repeated. All were hushed as Concha drew
Closer yet her nun's attire. "Señor, pardon, she died too!"

"For the King."

(NORTHERN MEXICO, 1640.)

As you look from the plaza at Leon west
You can see her house, but the view is best
From the porch of the church where she lies at rest,

Where much of her past still lives, I think,
In the scowling brows and sidelong blink
Of the worshipping throng that rise or sink

To the waxen saints that, yellow and lank,
Lean out from their niches, rank on rank,
With a bloodless Saviour on either flank;

In the gouty pillars, whose cracks begin
To show the *adobe* core within,—
A soul of earth in a whitewashed skin.

And I think that the moral of all, you'll say,
Is the sculptured legend that molds away
On a tomb in the choir: "Por el Rey."

"Por el Rey!" Well, the king is gone
Ages ago, and the Hapsburg one
Shot—but the Rock of the Church lives on.

"Por el Rey!" What matters, indeed,
If king or president succeed
To a country haggard with sloth and greed,

As long as one granary is fat,
And yonder priest, in a shovel hat,
Peeps out from the bin like a sleek brown rat?

What matters? Nought, if it serves to bring
The legend nearer,—no other thing,—
We'll spare the moral, "Live the king!"

Two hundred years ago, they say,
The Viceroy, Marquis of Monte-Rey,
Rode with his retinue that way;

Grave, as befitted Spain's grandee,
Grave, as the substitute should be
Of His Most Catholic Majesty;

Yet, from his black plume's curving grace
To his slim black gauntlet's smaller space,
Exquisite as a piece of lace!

Two hundred years ago—e'en so—
The Marquis stopped where the lime-trees blow,
While Leon's seneschal bent him low,

And begged that the Marquis would that night take
His humble roof for the royal sake,
And then, as the custom demanded, spake

The usual wish, that his guest would hold
The house, and all that it might enfold,
As his—with the bride scarce three days old.

"For the King."

Be sure that the Marquis, in his place,
Replied to all with the measured grace
Of chosen speech and unmoved face;

Nor raised his head till his black plume swept
The hem of the lady's robe, who kept
Her place, as her husband backward stept.

And then (I know not how nor why)
A subtle flame in the lady's eye—
Unseen by the courtiers standing by—

Burned through his lace and titled wreath,
Burned through his body's jewelled sheath,
Till it touched the steel of the man beneath!

(And yet, mayhap, no more was meant
Than to point a well-worn compliment,
And the lady's beauty, her worst intent.)

Howbeit, the Marquis bowed again:
"Who rules with awe well serveth Spain,
But best whose law is love made plain."

Be sure that night no pillow pressed
The seneschal, but with the rest
Watched,—as was due a royal guest,—

Watched from the wall till he saw the square
Fill with the moonlight, white and bare,—
Watched till he saw two shadows fare

Out from his garden, where the shade
That the old church tower and belfry made
Like a benedictory hand was laid.

Few words spoke the seneschal as he turned
To his nearest sentry: "These monks have learned
That stolen fruit is sweetly earned.

"Myself shall punish yon acolyte
Who gathers my garden grapes by night;
Meanwhile, wait thou till the morning light."

Yet not till the sun was riding high
Did the sentry meet his commander's eye,
Nor then till the Viceroy stood by.

To the lovers of grave formalities
No greeting was ever so fine, I wis,
As this host's and guest's high courtesies!

The seneschal feared, as the wind was west,
A blast from Morena had chilled his rest;
The Viceroy languidly confessed

That cares of state, and—he dared to say—
Some fears that the King could not repay
The thoughtful zeal of his host, some way

Had marred his rest. Yet he trusted much
None shared his wakefulness; though such
Indeed might be! If he dared to touch

A theme so fine—the bride, perchance,
Still slept! At least, they missed her glance
To give this greeting countenance.

Be sure that the seneschal, in turn,
Was deeply bowed with the grave concern
Of the painful news his guest should learn:

"Last night, to her father's dying bed
By a priest was the lady summoned;
Nor know we yet how well she sped,

"But hope for the best." The grave Viceroy
(Though grieved his visit had such alloy)
Must still wish the seneschal great joy

Of a bride so true to her filial trust!
Yet now, as the day waxed on, they must
To horse, if they'd 'scape the noonday dust.

"Nay," said the seneschal, "at least,
To mend the news of this funeral priest,
Myself shall ride as your escort east."

The Viceroy bowed. Then turned aside
To his nearest follower: "With me ride—
You and Felipe—on either side.

"And list! Should anything me befall,
Mischance of ambush or musket-ball,
Cleave to his saddle yon seneschal!

"No more." Then gravely in accents clear
Took formal leave of his late good cheer;
Whiles the seneschal whispered a musketeer,

Carelessly stroking his pommel top:
"If from the saddle ye see me drop,
Riddle me quickly yon solemn fop!"

So these, with many a compliment,
Each on his own dark thought intent,
With grave politeness onward went,

Riding high, and in sight of all,
Viceroy, escort, and seneschal,
Under the shade of the Almandral;

Holding their secret hard and fast,
Silent and grave they ride at last
Into the dusty travelled Past.

Even like this they passed away
Two hundred years ago to-day.
What of the lady?   Who shall say?

Do the souls of the dying ever yearn
To some favoured spot for the dust's return—
For the homely peace of the family urn?

I know not.   Yet did the seneschal,
Chancing in after years to fall
Pierced by a Flemish musket-ball,

Call to his side a trusty friar,
And bid him swear, as his last desire,
To bear his corse to San Pedro's choir

At Leon, where 'neath a shield azure
Should his mortal frame find sepulture;
This much, for the pains Christ did endure.

Be sure that the friar loyally
Fulfilled his trust by land and sea,
Till the spires of Leon silently

Rose through the green of the Almandral,
As if to beckon the seneschal
To his kindred dust 'neath the choir wall.

"For the King."

I wot that the saints on either side
Leaned from their niches open-eyed
To see the doors of the church swing wide—

That the wounds of the Saviour on either flank
Bled fresh, as the mourners, rank by rank,
Went by with the coffin, clank on clank.

For why? When they raised the marble door
Of the tomb, untouched for years before,
The friar swooned on the choir floor;

For there, in her laces and festal dress,
Lay the dead man's wife, her loveliness
Scarcely changed by her long duress;

As on the night she had passed away—
Only that near her a dagger lay,
With the written legend, "Por el Rey."

What was their greeting—the groom and bride,
They whom that steel and the years divide?
I know not. Here they lie side by side.

Side by side! Though the king has his way,
Even the dead at last have their day.
Make you the moral. "Por el Rey!"

Ramon.

(REFUGIO MINE, NORTHERN MEXICO.)

    Drunk and senseless in his place,
    Prone and sprawling on his face,
More like brute than any man
        Alive or dead,—
    By his great pump out of gear,
    Lay the peon engineer,
    Waking only just to hear,
        Overhead,
    Angry tones that called his name,
    Oaths and cries of bitter blame—
Woke to hear all this, and, waking, turned and fled!

    "To the man who'll bring to me,"
    Cried Intendant Harry Lee,—
Harry Lee, the English foreman of the mine,—
    "Bring the sot alive or dead,
    I will give to him," he said,
    "Fifteen hundred *pesos* down,
    Just to set the rascal's crown
Underneath this heel of mine:
        Since but death
    Deserves the man whose deed,
    Be it vice or want of heed,

Stops the pumps that give us breath,—
Stops the pumps that suck the death
From the poisoned lower levels of the mine!"

No one answered; for a cry
From the shaft rose up on high,
And shuffling, scrambling, tumbling from below,
Came the miners each, the bolder
Mounting on the weaker's shoulder,
Grappling, clinging to their hold or
    Letting go,
As the weaker gasped and fell
From the ladder to the well,—
To the poisoned pit of hell
    Down below!

"To the man who sets them free,"
Cried the foreman, Harry Lee,—
Harry Lee, the English foreman of the mine,—
"Brings them out and sets them free,
I will give that man," said he,
"Twice that sum, who with a rope
Face to face with Death shall cope.
Let him come who dares to hope!"
"Hold your peace!" some one replied,
Standing by the foreman's side;
"There has one already gone, whoe'er he be!"

Then they held their breath with awe,
Pulling on the rope, and saw
Fainting figures reappear,
On the black rope swinging clear,
Fastened by some skilful hand from below;

Till a score the level gained,
And but one alone remained,—
He the hero and the last,
He whose skilful hand made fast
The long line that brought them back to hope and cheer!

Haggard, gasping, down dropped he
At the feet of Harry Lee,—
Harry Lee, the English foreman of the mine.
"I have come," he gasped, "to claim
Both rewards. Señor, my name
    Is Ramon!
I'm the drunken engineer,
I'm the coward, Señor—" Here
He fell over, by that sign,
    Dead as stone!

Don Diego of the South.

(REFECTORY, MISSION SAN GABRIEL, 1869.)

GOOD !—said the Padre,—believe me still,
" Don Giovanni," or what you will,
The type's eternal ! We knew him here
As Don Diego del Sud. I fear
The story's no new one ! Will you hear?

One of those spirits you can't tell why
God has permitted. Therein I
Have the advantage, for *I* hold
That wolves are sent to the purest fold,
And we'd save the wolf if we'd get the lamb.
You're no believer? Good ! I am.

Well, for some purpose, I grant you dim,
The Don loved women, and they loved him.
Each thought herself his *last* love ! Worst,
Many believed that they were his *first!*
And, such are these creatures since the Fall,
The very doubt had a charm for all !

You laugh ! You are young, but *I*—indeed
I have no patience . . . To proceed—
You saw, as you passed through the upper town,
The *Eucinal* where the road goes down

To San Felipe! There one morn
They found Diego,—his mouth torn,
And as many holes through his doublet's band
As there were wronged husbands—you understand!

"Dying," so said the gossips. . "Dead"
Was what the friars who found him said.
May be. *Quien sabe?* Who else should know—
It was a hundred years ago.
There was a funeral. Small indeed—
Private. What would you? To proceed :—

Scarcely the year had flown. One night
The Commandante awoke in fright,
Hearing below his casement's bar
The well-known twang of the Don's guitar;
And rushed to the window, just to see
His wife a-swoon on the balcony.

One week later, Don Juan Ramirez
Found his own daughter, the Doña Inez,
Pale as a ghost, leaning out to hear
The song of that phantom cavalier.
Even Alcalde Pedro Blas
Saw, it was said, through his niece's glass,
The shade of Diego twice repass.

What these gentlemen each confessed
Heaven and the Church only knows. At best
The case was a bad one. How to deal
With Sin as a Ghost, they couldn't but feel
Was an awful thing. Till a certain Fray
Humbly offered to show the way.

And the way was this. Did I say before
That the Fray was a stranger? No, Señor?
Strange! very strange! I should have said
That the very week that the Don lay dead
He came among us. Bread he broke
Silent, nor ever to one he spoke.
So he had vowed it! Below his brows
His face was hidden. There are such vows!

Strange! are they not? You do not use
Snuff? A bad habit!

      Well, the views
Of the Fray was this: That the penance done
By the caballeros was right; but one
Was due from the *cause*, and that, in brief,
Was Donna Dolores Gomez, chief,
And Inez, Sanchicha, Concepcion,
And Carmen—Well, half the girls in town
On his tablets the Friar had written down.

These were to come on a certain day
And ask at the hands of the pious Fray
For absolution. That done, small fear
But the shade of Diego would disappear.

They came; each knelt in her turn and place
To the pious Fray with his hidden face
And voiceless lips, and each again
Took back her soul freed from spot or stain,
Till the Doña Inez, with eyes downcast
And a tear on their fringes, knelt her last.

And then—perhaps that her voice was low
From fear or from shame—the monks said so—
But the Fray leaned forward, when, presto! all
Were thrilled by a scream, and saw her fall
Fainting beside the confessional.

And so was the ghost of Diego laid
As the Fray had said. Never more his shade
Was seen at San Gabriel's Mission. Ah!
The girl interests you? I dare say!
"Nothing," said she, when they brought her to—
"Only a faintness!" They spoke more true
Who said 'twas a stubborn soul. But then—
Women are women and men are men!

So, to return. As I said before,
Having got the wolf, by the same high law
We saved the lamb in the wolf's own jaw,
And that's my moral. The tale, I fear,
But poorly told. Yet it strikes me here
Is stuff for a moral. What's your view?
You smile, Don Pancho,—Ah! that's like you!

At the Hacienda.

Know I not whom thou mayst be
  Carved upon this olive tree—
    "Manuela of La Torre,"
For around on broken walls
Summer sun and Spring rain falls,
And in vain the low wind calls
    "Manuela of La Torre."

Of that song no words remain
  But the musical refrain :
    "Manuela of La Torre."
Yet at night, when winds are still,
Tinkles on the distant hill
A guitar, and words that thrill
  Tell to me the old, old story—
Old when first thy charms were sung,
Old when these old walls were young,
    "Manuela of La Torre."

Friar Pedro's Ride.

It was the morning season of the year;
    It was the morning era of the land;
The watercourses rang full loud and clear;
    Portala's cross stood where Portala's hand
Had planted it when Faith was taught by Fear,
    When monks and missions held the sole command
Of all that shore beside the peaceful sea,
Where spring-tides beat their long-drawn réveille.

Out of the Mission of San Luis Rey,
    All in that brisk, tumultuous spring weather,
Rode Friar Pedro, in a pious way,
    With six dragoons in cuirasses of leather,
Each armed alike for either prayer or fray,
    Handcuffs and missals they had slung together;
And as in aid the gospel truth to scatter
Each swung a lasso—*alias* a "riata."

In sooth, that year the harvest had been slack,
    The crop of converts scarce worth computation;
Some souls were lost, whose owners had turned back
    To save their bodies frequent flagellation;
And some preferred the songs of birds, alack!
    To Latin matins and their soul's salvation,
And thought their own wild whoopings were less dreary
Than Father Pedro's droning *miserere*.

To bring them back to matins and to prime,
  To pious works and secular submission,
To prove to them that liberty was crime,—
  This was, in fact, the Padre's present mission;
To get new souls perchance at the same time,
  And bring them to a "sense their condition"—
That easy phrase, which, in the past and present,
Means making that condition most unpleasant.

He saw the glebe land guiltless of a furrow;
  He saw the wild oats wrestle on the hill;
He saw the gopher working in his burrow;
  He saw the squirrel scampering at his will;—
He saw all this and felt no doubt a thorough
  And deep conviction of God's goodness; still
He failed to see that in His glory He
Yet left the humblest of His creatures free.

He saw the flapping crow, whose frequent note
  Voiced the monotony of land and sky,
Mocking with graceless wing and rusty coat
  His priestly presence as he trotted by.
He would have cursed the bird by bell and rote,
  But other game just then was in his eye—
A savage camp, whose occupants preferred
Their heathen darkness to the living Word.

He rang his bell, and at the martial sound
  Twelve silver spurs their jingling rowels clashed;
Six horses sprang across the level ground
  As six dragoons in open order dashed;
Above their heads the lassos circled round,
  In every eye a pious fervour flashed;

They charged the camp, and in one moment more
They lassoed six and reconverted four.

The Friar saw the conflict from a knoll,
   And sang *Laus Deo* and cheered on his men :
"Well thrown, Bautista—that's another soul ;
   After him, Gomez—try it once again ;
This way, Felipe—there the heathen stole ;
   Bones of St. Francis !—surely that makes *ten ;*
Te deum laudamus—but they're very wild ;
Non nobis dominus—all right, my child !"

When at that moment—as the story goes—
   A certain squaw, who had her foes eluded,
Ran past the Friar—just before his nose.
   He stared a moment, and in silence brooded,
Then in his breast a pious frenzy rose
   And every other prudent thought excluded ;
He caught a lasso, and dashed in a canter
After that Occidental Atalanta.

High o'er his head he swirled the dreadful noose,
   But, as the practice was quite unfamiliar,
His first cast tore Felipe's captive loose
   And almost choked Tiburcio Camilla,
And might have interfered with that brave youth's
   Ability to gorge the tough *tortilla ;*
But all things come by practice, and at last
His flying slip-knot caught the maiden fast.

Then rose above the plain a mingled yell
   Of rage and triumph—a demoniac whoop ;
The Padre heard it like a passing knell,
   And would have loosened his unchristian loop ;

Friar Pedro's Ride.

But the tough raw-hide held the captive well,
    And held, alas ! too well the captor-dupe ;
For with one bound the savage fled amain,
Dragging horse, Friar, down the lonely plain.

Down the *arroyo*, out across the mead,
    By heath and hollow, sped the flying maid,
Dragging behind her still the panting steed
    And helpless Friar, who in vain essayed
To cut the lasso or to check his speed.
    He felt himself beyond all human aid,
And trusted to the saints—and, for that matter,
To some weak spot in Felipe's *riata*.

Alas ! the lasso had been duly blessed,
    And, like baptism, held the flying wretch—
A doctrine that the priest had oft expressed—
    Which, like the lasso, might be made to stretch
But would not break ; so neither could divest
    Themselves of it, but, like some awful *fetch*,
The holy Friar had to recognise
The image of his fate in heathen guise.

He saw the glebe land guiltless of a furrow ;
    He saw the wild oats wrestle on the hill ;
He saw the gopher standing in his burrow ;
    He saw the squirrel scampering at his will ;—
He saw all this, and felt no doubt how thorough
    The contrast was to his condition ; still
The squaw kept onward to the sea, till night
And the cold sea-fog hid them both from sight.

The morning came above the serried coast,
    Lighting the snow-peaks with its beacon fires,

Driving before it all the fleet-winged host
    Of chattering birds above the Mission spires,
Filling the land with light and joy—but most
    The savage woods with all their leafy lyres;
In pearly tints and opal flame and fire
The morning came, but not the holy Friar.

Weeks passed away. In vain the Fathers sought
    Some trace or token that might tell his story;
Some thought him dead, or, like Elijah, caught
    Up to the heavens in a blaze of glory.
In this surmise some miracles were wrought
    On his account, and souls in purgatory
Were thought to profit from his intercession;
In brief, his absence made a "deep impression."

A twelvemonth passed; the welcome Spring once more
    Made green the hills beside the white-faced Mission,
Spread her bright dais by the western shore,
    And sat enthroned—a most resplendent vision.
The heathen converts thronged the chapel door
    At morning mass, when, says the old tradition,
A frightful whoop throughout the church resounded,
And to their feet the congregation bounded.

A tramp of hoofs upon the beaten course,
    Then came a sight that made the bravest quail:
A phantom Friar on a spectre horse,
    Dragged by a creature decked with horns and tail.
By the lone Mission, with the whirlwind's force,
    They madly swept, and left a sulphurous trail—
And that was all—enough to tell the story
And leave unblessed those souls in purgatory.

And ever after, on that fatal day
   That Friar Pedro rode abroad lassoing,
A ghostly couple came and went away
   With savage whoop and heathenish hallooing,
Which brought discredit on San Luis Rey,
   And proved the Mission's ruin and undoing;
For ere ten years had passed, the squaw and Friar
Performed to empty walls and fallen spire.

The Mission is no more; upon its walls
   The golden lizards slip, or breathless pause
Still as the sunshine brokenly that falls
   Through crannied roof and spider-webs of gauze;
No more the bell its solemn warning calls—
   A holier silence thrills and overawes;
And the sharp lights and shadows of to-day
Outline the Mission of San Luis Rey.

In the Mission Garden.

(1865.)

FATHER FELIPE.

I SPEAK not the English well, but Pachita
She speak for me; is it not so, my Pancha?
Eh, little rogue?   Come, salute me the stranger
      Americano.

Sir, in my country we say, "Where the heart is,
There live the speech."   Ah! you not understand?   So!
Pardon an old man,—what you call "ol fogy,"—
      Padre Felipe!

Old, Señor, old! just so old as the Mission.
You see that pear-tree?   How old you think, Señor?
Fifteen year?   Twenty?   Ah, Señor, just *fifty*
      Gone since I plant him!

You like the wine?   It is some at the Mission,
Made from the grape of the year Eighteen Hundred;
All the same time when the earthquake he come to
      San Juan Bautista.

But Pancha is twelve, and she is the rose-tree;
And I am the olive, and this is the garden:
And Pancha we say; but her name is Francisca,
      Same like her mother.

In the Mission Garden.

Eh, you knew *her?* No? Ah! it is a story;
But I speak not, like Pachita, the English:
So! if I try, you will sit here beside me,
     And shall not laugh, eh?

When the American come to the Mission,
Many arrive at the house of Francisca:
One,—he was fine man,—he buy the cattle
     Of José Castro.

So! he came much, and Francisca she saw him:
And it was love,—and a very dry season;
And the pears bake on the tree,—and the rain come,
     But not Francisca.

Not for one year; and one night I have walk much
Under the olive-tree, when comes Francisca,—
Comes to me here, with her child, this Francisca,—
     Under the olive-tree.

Sir, it was sad; . . . but I speak not the English;
So! . . . she stay here, and she wait for her husband:
He come no more, and she sleep on the hillside;
     There stands Pachita.

Ah! there's the Angelus. Will you not enter?
Or shall you walk in the garden with Pancha?
Go, little rogue—sit—attend to the stranger.
     Adios, Señor.

   PACHITA (*briskly*).
So, he's been telling that yarn about mother!
Bless you! he tells it to every stranger:
Folks about yer say the old man's my father;
     What's your opinion?

The Lost Galleon.

In sixteen hundred and forty-one,
The regular yearly galleon,
Laden with odorous gums and spice,
India cottons and India rice,
And the richest silks of far Cathay,
Was due at Acapulco Bay.
Due she was, and over-due,—
Galleon, merchandise, and crew,
Creeping along through rain and shine,
Through the tropics, under the line.
The trains were waiting outside the walls,
The wives of sailors thronged the town,
The traders sat by their empty stalls,
And the Viceroy himself came down;
The bells in the tower were all a-trip,
Te Deums were on each Father's lip,
The limes were ripening in the sun
For the sick of the coming galleon.

All in vain. Weeks passed away,
And yet no galleon saw the bay:
India goods advanced in price;
The Governor missed his favourite spice;
The Señoritas mourned for sandal
And the famous cottons of Coromandel;

And some for an absent lover lost,
And one for a husband,—Donna Julia,
Wife of the captain tempest-tossed,
In circumstances so peculiar:
Even the Fathers, unawares,
Grumbled a little at their prayers;
And all along the coast that year
Votive candles were scarce and dear.

Never a tear bedims the eye
That time and patience will not dry;
Never a lip is curved with pain
That can't be kissed into smiles again;
And these same truths, as far as I know,
Obtained on the coast of Mexico
More than two hundred years ago,
In sixteen hundred and fifty-one,—
Ten years after the deed was done,—
And folks had forgotten the galleon:
The divers plunged in the gulf for pearls,
White as the teeth of the Indian girls;
The traders sat by their full bazaars;
The mules with many a weary load,
And oxen, dragging their creaking cars,
Came and went on the mountain road.

Where was the galleon all this while?
Wrecked on some lonely coral isle,
Burnt by the roving sea-marauders,
Or sailing north under secret orders?
Had she found the Anian passage famed,
By lying Moldonado claimed,
And sailed through the sixty-fifth degree
Direct to the North Atlantic Sea?

Or had she found the "River of Kings,"
Of which De Fonte told such strange things?

In sixteen forty! Never a sign,
East or west or under the line,
They saw of the missing galleon;
Never a sail or plank or chip
They found of the long-lost treasure-ship,
Or enough to build a tale upon.
But when she was lost, and where and how,
Are the facts we're coming to just now.

Take, if you please, the chart of that day,
Published at Madrid,—*por el Rey;*
Look for a spot in the old South Sea,
The hundred and eightieth degree
Longitude west of Madrid : there,
Under the equatorial glare,
Just where the east and west are one,
You'll find the missing galleon,—
You'll find the "San Gregorio," yet
Riding the seas, with sails all set,
Fresh as upon the very day
She sailed from Acapulco Bay.

How did she get there? What strange spell
Kept her two hundred years so well,
Free from decay and mortal taint?
What but the prayers of a patron saint!
A hundred leagues from Manilla town,
The "San Gregorio's" helm came down;
Round she went on her heel, and not
A cable's length from a galliot
That rocked on the waters just abreast
Of the galleon's course, which was west-sou-west.

The Lost Galleon.

Then said the galleon's commandante,
General Pedro Sobriente
(That was his rank on land and main,
A regular custom of Old Spain),
"My pilot is dead of scurvy: may
I ask the longitude, time, and day?"
The first two given and compared;
The third,—the commandante stared!
"The *first* of June? I make it second."
Said the stranger, "Then you've wrongly-reckoned;
I make it *first:* as you came this way,
You should have lost, d'ye see, a day;
Lost a day, as plainly see,
On the hundred and eightieth degree."
"Lost a day?"   "Yes; if not rude,
When did you make east longitude?"
"On the ninth of May,—our patron's day."
"On the ninth?—*you had no ninth of May!*
Eighth and tenth was there; but stay"—
Too late; for the galleon bore away.

Lost was the day they should have kept,
Lost unheeded and lost unwept;
Lost in a way that made search vain,
Lost in a trackless and boundless main;
Lost like the day of Job's awful curse,
In his third chapter, third and fourth verse;
Wrecked was their patron's only day,—
What would the holy Fathers say?

Said the Fray Antonio Estavan,
The galleon's chaplain,—a learned man,—

"Nothing is lost that you can regain;
And the way to look for a thing is plain,
To go where you lost it, back again.
Back with your galleon till you see
The hundred and eightieth degree.
Wait till the rolling year goes round,
And there will the missing day be found;
For you'll find—if computation's true—
That sailing *east* will give to you
Not only one ninth of May, but two,—
One for the good saint's present cheer,
And one for the day we lost last year."

Back to the spot sailed the galleon;
Where, for a twelvemonth, off and on
The hundred and eightieth degree
She rose and fell on a tropic sea:
But lo! when it came to the ninth of May,
All of a sudden becalmed she lay
One degree from that fatal spot,
Without the power to move a knot;
And of course the moment she lost her way,
Gone was her chance to save that day.

To cut a lengthening story short,
She never saved it. Made the sport
Of evil spirits and baffling wind,
She was always before or just behind,
One day too soon, or one day too late,
And the sun, meanwhile, would never wait.
She had two eighths, as she idly lay,
Two tenths, but never a *ninth* of May;

And there she rides through two hundred years
Of dreary penance and anxious fears;
Yet, through the grace of the saint she served,
Captain and crew are still preserved.

By a computation that still holds good,
Made by the Holy Brotherhood,
The "San Gregorio" will cross that line
In nineteen hundred and thirty-nine:
Just three hundred years to a day
From the time she lost the ninth of May.
And the folk in Acapulco town,
Over the waters looking down,
Will see in the glow of the setting sun
The sails of the missing galleon,
And the royal standard of Philip Rey,
The gleaming mast and glistening spar,
As she nears the surf of the outer bar.
A *Te Deum* sung on her crowded deck,
An odour of spice along the shore,
A crash, a cry from a shattered wreck,—
And the yearly galleon sails no more
In or out of the olden bay;
For the blessed patron has found his day.

Such is the legend. Hear this truth:
  Over the trackless past, somewhere,
Lie the lost days of our tropic youth,
  Only regained by faith and prayer,
Only recalled by prayer and plaint:
Each lost day has its patron saint!

IN DIALECT.

"Jim."

Say there! P'r'aps
Some on you chaps
   Might know Jim Wild?
Well,—no offence:
Thar ain't no sense
   In gittin' riled!

Jim was my chum
   Up on the Bar:
That's why I come
   Down from up yar,
Lookin' for Jim.
Thank ye, sir! *You*
Ain't of that crew,—
   Blest if you are!

Money?—Not much:
   That ain't my kind:
I ain't no such.
   Rum?—I don't mind,
Seein' it's you.

Well, this yer Jim,
Did you know him?—

Jess 'bout your size;
Same kind of eyes;—
Well, that is strange:
  Why, it's two year
  Since he came here,
Sick, for a change.

Well, here's to us:
  Eh?
The h—— you say!
  Dead?
That little cuss?

What makes you star,—
You over thar?
Can't a man drop
's glass in yer shop
But you must rar'?
  It wouldn't take
  D—— much to break
You and your bar.

  Dead!
Poor—little—Jim!
Why, thar was me,
Jones, and Bob Lee,
Harry and Ben,—
No-account men:
Then to take *him!*

Well, thar—Good by,—
No more, sir,—I—
  Eh?
What's that you say?—

Why, dern it!—sho!—
No? Yes! By Joe!
   Sold!
Sold! Why, you limb,
You ornery,
   Derned old
Long-legged Jim!

Chiquita.

BEAUTIFUL! Sir, you may say so. Thar isn't her match
  in the county.
Is thar, old gal,—Chiquita, my darling, my beauty?
Feel of that neck, sir,—thar's velvet! Whoa! steady,—ah,
  will you, you vixen!
Whoa! I say. Jack, trot her out; let the gentleman look
  at her paces.

Morgan!—she ain't nothing else, and I've got the papers to
  prove it.
Sired by Chippewa Chief, and twelve hundred dollars won't
  buy her.
Briggs of Tuolumne owned her. Did you know Briggs of
  Tuolumne?—
Busted hisself in White Pine, and blew out his brains down
  in 'Frisco?

Hedn't no savey—hed Briggs. Thar, Jack! that'll do,—
  quit that foolin'!
Nothin' to what she kin do, when she's got her work cut out
  before her.
Hosses is hosses, you know, and likewise, too, jockeys is
  jockeys:
And 'tain't ev'ry man as can ride as knows what a hoss has
  got in him.

Chiquita.

Know the old ford on the Fork, that nearly got Flanigan's
    leaders?
Nasty in daylight, you bet, and a mighty rough ford in low
    water!
Well, it ain't six weeks ago that me and the Jedge and his
    nevey
Struck for that ford in the night, in the rain, and the water
    all round us;

Up to our flanks in the gulch, and Rattlesnake Creek just a
    bilin',
Not a plank left in the dam, and nary a bridge on the river.
I had the grey, and the Jedge had his roan, and his nevey,
    Chiquita;
And after us trundled the rocks jest loosed from the top of
    the cañon.

Lickity, lickity, switch, we came to the ford, and Chiquita
Buckled right down to her work, and afore I could yell to
    her rider,
Took water jest at the ford, and there was the Jedge and
    me standing,
And twelve hundred dollars of hoss-flesh afloat, and a
    driftin' to thunder!

Would ye b'lieve it? that night that hoss, that ar' filly,
    Chiquita,
Walked herself into her stall, and stood there, all quiet and
    dripping:
Clean as a beaver or rat, with nary a buckle of harness,
Just as she swam the Fork,—that hoss, that ar' filly,
    Chiquita.

That's what I call a hoss! and—What did you say?—Oh,
    the nevey?
Drownded, I reckon,—leastways, he never kem back to
    deny it.
Ye see the derned fool had no seat,—ye couldn't have made
    him a rider;
And then, ye know, boys will be boys, and hosses—well,
    hosses is hosses '

Dow's Flat.

(1856.)

Dow's FLAT. That's its name;
   And I reckon that you
Are a stranger? The same?
   Well, I thought it was true,—
For thar isn't a man on the river as can't spot the place at
   first view.

It was called after Dow,—
   Which the same was an ass,—
And as to the how
   Thet the thing kem to pass,—
Jest tie up your hoss to that buckeye, and sit ye down here
   in the grass.

You see this 'yer Dow
   Hed the worst kind of luck;
He slipped up somehow
   On each thing thet he struck.
Why, ef he'd a straddled thet fence-rail, the derned thing
   'ed get up and buck.

He mined on the bar
   Till he couldn't pay rates;

He was smashed by a car
    When he tunnelled with Bates;
And right on the top of his trouble kem his wife and five
    kids from the States.

It was rough,—mighty rough;
    But the boys they stood by,
And they brought him the stuff
    For a house, on the sly;
And the old woman,—well, she did washing, and took on
    when no one was nigh.

But this 'yer luck of Dow's
    Was so powerful mean
That the spring near his house
    Dried right up on the green;
And he sunk forty feet down for water, but nary a drop to
    be seen.

Then the bar petered out,
    And the boys wouldn't stay;
And the chills got about,
    And his wife fell away;
But Dow in his well kept a peggin' in his usual ridikilous
    way.

One day,—it was June,—
    And a year ago, jest—
This Dow kem at noon
    To his work like the rest,
With a shovel and pick on his shoulder, and a derringer hid
    in his breast.

Dow's Flat.

      He goes to the well,
         And he stands on the brink,
      And stops for a spell
         Jest to listen and think:
For the sun in his eyes (jest like this, sir!), you see, kinder
         made the cuss blink.

      His two ragged gals
         In the gulch were at play,
      And a gownd that was Sal's
         Kinder flapped on a bay:
Not much for a man to be leavin', but his all,—as I've heer'd
         the folks say.

      And—That's a peart hoss
         Thet you've got,—ain't it now?
      What might be her cost?
         Eh? Oh!—Well, then, Dow—
Let's see,—well, that forty-foot grave wasn't his, sir, that
         day, anyhow.

      For a blow of his pick
         Sorter caved in the side,
      And he looked and turned sick,
         Then he trembled and cried.
For you see the dern cuss had struck — "Water?" — Beg
         your parding, young man,—there you lied!

      It was *gold*,—in the quartz,
         And it ran all alike;
      And I reckon five oughts
         Was the worth of that strike;
And that house with the coopilow's his'n,—which the same
         isn't bad for a Pike.

Thet's why it's Dow's Flat;
  And the thing of it is
That he kinder got that
  Through sheer contrairiness:
For 'twas *water* the derned cuss was seekin', and his luck
    made him certain to miss

Thet's so! Thar's your way,
  To the left of yon tree;
But—a—look h'yur, say?
  Won't you come up to tea?
No? Well, then the next time you're passin'; and ask after
    Dow,—and thet's *me*.

In the Tunnel.

Didn't know Flynn,—
Flynn of Virginia,—
Long as he's been 'yar?
Look 'ee here, stranger,
Whar *hev* you been?

Here in this tunnel
  He was my pardner,
That same Tom Flynn,—
  Working together,
  In wind and weather,
Day out and in.

Didn't know Flynn!
  Well, that *is* queer;
Why, it's a sin
To think of Tom Flynn,—
  Tom with his cheer,
  Tom without fear,—
Stranger, look 'yar!

Thar in the drift,
  Back to the wall,
He held the timbers
  Ready to fall;

Then in the darkness
I heard him call:
  "Run for your life, Jake!
  Run for your wife's sake!
  Don't wait for me."

And that was all
  Heard in the din,
  Heard of Tom Flynn,—
    Flynn of Virginia.

That's all about
  Flynn of Virginia.
That lets me out.
  Here in the damp,—
Out of the sun,—
  That 'ar derned lamp
Makes my eyes run.
Well, there,—I'm done!

But, sir, when you'll
Hear the next fool
  Asking of Flynn,—
Flynn of Virginia,—
  Just you chip in,
  Say you knew Flynn;
Say that you've been 'yar.

"Cicely."

(ALKALI STATION.)

CICELY says you're a poet; maybe,—I ain't much on rhyme:
I reckon you'd give me a hundred, and beat me every time.
Poetry!—that's the way some chaps puts up an idee,
But I takes mine "straight without sugar," and that's what's
    the matter with me.

Poetry!—just look round you,—alkali, rock, and sage;
Sage-brush, rock, and alkali; ain't it a pretty page!
Sun in the east at mornin', sun in the west at night,
And the shadow of this yer station the on'y thing moves in
    sight.

Poetry!—Well now—Polly! Polly, run to your mam;
Run right away, my pooty! By-by! Ain't she a lamb?
Poetry!—that reminds me o' suthin' right in that suit:
Jest shet that door thar, will yer?—for Cicely's ears is cute.

Ye noticed Polly,—the baby? A month afore she was born,
Cicely—my old woman—was moody-like and forlorn;
Out of her head and crazy, and talked of flowers and trees;
Family man yourself, sir? Well, you know what a woman
    be's.

Narvous she was, and restless,—said that she "couldn't
　　stay."
Stay !—and the nearest woman seventeen miles away.
But I fixed it up with the doctor, and he said he would be
　　on hand,
And I kinder stuck by the shanty, and fenced in that bit o'
　　land.

One night,—the tenth of October,—I woke with a chill and
　　a fright,
For the door it was standing open, and Cicely warn't in
　　sight,
But a note was pinned on the blanket, which it said that she
　　"couldn't stay,"
But had gone to visit her neighbour,—seventeen miles away !

When and how she stampeded, I didn't wait for to see,
For out in the road, next minit, I started as wild as she ;
Running first this way and that way, like a hound that is off
　　the scent,
For there warn't no track in the darkness to tell me the way
　　she went.

I've had some mighty mean moments afore I kem to this
　　spot,—
Lost on the Plains in '50, drownded almost and shot ;
But out on this alkali desert, a hunting a crazy wife,
Was ra'ly as on-satis-factory as anything in my life.

"Cicely ! Cicely ! Cicely !" I called, and I held my breath,
And " Cicely !" came from the canyon,—and all was as still
　　as death.

And "Cicely! Cicely! Cicely!" came from the rocks below,
And jest but a whisper of "Cicely!" down from them peaks
   of snow.

I ain't what you call religious,—but I jest looked up to the
   sky,
And—this yer's to what I'm coming, and maybe ye think
   I lie:
But up away to the east'ard, yaller and big and far,
I saw of a suddent rising the singlerist kind of star.

Big and yaller and dancing, it seemed to beckon to me:
Yaller and big and dancing, such as you never see:
Big and yaller and dancing,—I never saw such a star,
And I thought of them sharps in the Bible, and I went for it
   then and thar.

Over the brush and bowlders I stumbled and pushed ahead;
Keeping the star afore me, I went wherever it led.
It might hev been for an hour, when suddent and peart and
   nigh,
Out of the yearth afore me thar riz up a baby's cry.

Listen! thar's the same music; but her lungs they are
   stronger now
Than the day I packed her and her mother,—I'm derned if
   I jest know how.
But the doctor kem the next minit, and the joke o' the
   whole thing is
That Cis never knew what happened from that very night
   to this!

But Cicely says you're a poet, and maybe you might, some day,
Jest sling her a rhyme 'bout a baby that was born in a curious way,
And see what she says; and, old fellow, when you speak of the star, don't tell
As how 'twas the doctor's lantern,—for maybe 'twon't sound so well.

Penelope.

(SIMPSON'S BAR, 1858.)

So you've kem 'yer agen,
    And one answer won't do?
Well, of all the derned men
    That I've struck, it is you.
O Sal! 'yer's that derned fool from Simpson's. cavortin'
    round 'yer in the dew.

Kem in, ef you *will*.
    Thar,—quit! Take a cheer.
Not that; you can't fill
    Them theer cushings this year,—
For that cheer was my old man's, Joe Simpson, and they
    don't make such men about 'yer.

He was tall, was my Jack,
    And as strong as a tree.
Thar's his gun on the rack,—
    Jest you heft it, and see.
And *you* come a courtin' his widder! Lord! where can
    that critter, Sal, be!

You'd fill my Jack's place?
And a man of your size,—
With no baird to his face,
Nor a snap to his eyes,
And nary—Sho! thar! I was foolin',—I was, Joe, for sartain,—don't rise.

Sit down. Law! why, sho!
I'm as weak as a gal.
Sal! Don't you go, Joe,
Or I'll faint,—sure, I shall.
Sit down,—*anywheer*, where you like, Joe,—in that cheer, if
you choose,—Lord! where's Sal?

Plain Language from Truthful James.

(TABLE MOUNTAIN, 1870.)

WHICH I wish to remark,
   And my language is plain,
That for ways that are dark
   And for tricks that are vain,
The heathen Chinee is peculiar,
   Which the same I would rise to explain.

Ah Sin was his name;
   And I shall not deny,
In regard to the same,
   What that name might imply;
But his smile it was pensive and childlike,
   As I frequent remarked to Bill Nye.

It was August the third,
   And quite soft was the skies;
Which it might be inferred
   That Ah Sin was likewise;
Yet he played it that day upon William
   And me in a way I despise.

Which we had a small game,
   And Ah Sin took a hand:
It was Euchre. The same
   He did not understand;
But he smiled as he sat by the table,
   With the smile that was childlike and bland.

Yet the cards they were stocked
   In a way that I grieve,
And my feelings were shocked
   At the state of Nye's sleeve,
Which was stuffed full of aces and bowers,
   And the same with intent to deceive.

But the hands that were played
   By that heathen Chinee,
And the points that he made,
   Were quite frightful to see,—
Till at last he put down a right bower,
   Which the same Nye had dealt unto me.

Then I looked up at Nye,
   And he gazed upon me;
And he rose with a sigh,
   And said, "Can this be?
We are ruined by Chinese cheap labour,"—
   And he went for that heathen Chinee.

In the scene that ensued
   I did not take a hand,
But the floor it was strewed
   Like the leaves on the strand
With the cards that Ah sin had been hiding,
   In the game "he did not understand."

Plain Language from Truthful James.

In his sleeves, which were long,
   He had twenty-four packs,—
Which was coming it strong,
   Yet I state but the facts;
And we found on his nails, which were taper,
   What is frequent in tapers,—that's wax.

Which is why I remark,
   And my language is plain,
That for ways that are dark
   And for tricks that are vain,
The heathen Chinee is peculiar,—
   Which the same I am free to maintain.

The Society upon the Stanislaus.

I reside at Table Mountain, and my name is Truthful James;
I am not up to small deceit or any sinful games;
And I'll tell in simple language what I know about the row
That broke up our Society upon the Stanislow.

But first I would remark, that it is not a proper plan
For any scientific gent to whale his fellow-man,
And, if a member don't agree with his peculiar whim,
To lay for that same member for to " put a head " on him.

Now nothing could be finer or more beautiful to see
Than the first six months' proceedings of that same Society,
Till Brown of Calaveras brought a lot of fossil bones
That he found within a tunnel near the tenement of Jones.

Then Brown he read a paper, and he reconstructed there,
From those same bones, an animal that was extremely rare;
And Jones then asked the Chair for a suspension of the rules,
Till he could prove that those same bones was one of his lost mules.

Then Brown he smiled a bitter smile, and said he was at
  fault,
It seemed he had been trespassing on Jones's family vault;
He was a most sarcastic man, this quiet Mr. Brown,
And on several occasions he had cleaned out the town.

Now I hold it is not decent for a scientific gent
To say another is an ass,—at least, to all intent;
Nor should the individual who happens to be meant
Reply by heaving rocks at him, to any great extent.

Then Abner Dean of Angel's raised a point of order, when
A chunk of old red sandstone took him in the abdomen,
And he smiled a kind of sickly smile, and curled up on the
  floor,
And the subsequent proceedings interested him no more.

For, in less time than I write it, every member did engage
In a warfare with the remnants of a palæozoic age;
And the way they heaved those fossils in their anger was
  a sin,
Till the skull of an old mammoth caved the head of
  Thompson in.

And this is all I have to say of these improper games,
For I live at Table Mountain, and my name is Truthful
  James;
And I've told in simple language what I knew about the
  row
That broke up our Society upon the Stanislow.

Luke.

(IN THE COLORADO PARK, 1873.)

Wot's that you're readin'?—a novel? A novel!—well darn my skin!
You a man grown and bearded and histin' such stuff ez that in—
Stuff about gals and their sweethearts! No wonder you're thin ez a knife.
Look at me!—clar two hundred—and never read one in my life!

That's my opinion o' novels. And ez to their lyin' round here,
They belong to the Jedge's daughter—the Jedge who came up last year
On account of his lungs and the mountains and the balsam o' pine and fir;
And his daughter—well, she read novels, and that's what's the matter with her.

Yet she was sweet on the Jedge, and stuck by him day and night,
Alone in the cabin up 'yer—till she grew like a ghost, all white.
She wus only a slip of a thing, ez light and ez up and away
Ez rifle smoke blown through the woods, but she wasn't my kind—no way!

Speakin' o' gals, d'ye mind that house ez you rise the hill,
A mile and a half from White's, and jist above Mattingly's mill?
You do? Well now *thar's* a gal! What! you saw her? Oh, come now, thar! quit!
She was only bedevlin' you boys, for to me she don't cotton one bit.

Now she's what I call a gal—ez pretty and plump ez a quail;
Teeth ez white ez a hound's, and they'd go through a tenpenny nail;
Eyes that kin snap like a cap. So she asked to know "whar I was hid?"
She did! Oh, it's jist like her sass, for she's peart ez a Katydid.

But what was I talking of?—Oh! the Jedge and his daughter—she read
Novels the whole day long, and I reckon she read them abed;
And sometimes she read them out loud to the Jedge on the porch where he sat,
And 'twas how "Lord Augustus" said this, and how "Lady Blanche" she said that.

But the sickest of all that I heerd was a yarn thet they read 'bout a chap,
"Leather-stocking" by name, and a hunter chock full o' the greenest o' sap;

And they asked me to hear, but I says, "Miss Mabel, not any for me;
When I likes I kin sling my own lies, and thet chap and I shouldn't agree."

Yet somehow or other she was always sayin' I brought her to mind
Of folks about whom she had read, or suthin belike of thet kind,
And thar warn't no end o' the names that she give me thet summer up here—
"Robin Hood," "Leather-stocking," "Rob Roy,"—Oh, I tell you, the critter was queer!

And yet, ef she hadn't been spiled, she was harmless enough in her way;
She could jabber in French to her dad, and they said that she knew how to play;
And she worked me that shot-pouch up thar, which the man doesn't live ez kin use;
And slippers—you see 'em down 'yer—ez would cradle an Injin's papoose.

Yet along o' them novels, you see, she was wastin' and mopin' away,
And then she got shy with her tongue, and at last had nothin' to say;
And whenever I happened around, her face it was hid by a book,
And it warn't until she left that she give me ez much ez a look.

And this was the way it was. It was night when I kem up
    here
To say to 'em all "good-bye," for I reckoned to go for
    deer
At "sun up" the day they left. So I shook 'em all round
    by the hand,
'Cept Mabel, and she was sick, ez they give me to under-
    stand.

But jist ez I passed the house next morning at dawn, some
    one,
Like a little waver o' mist got up on the hill with the sun;
Miss Mabel it was, alone—all wrapped in a mantle o'
    lace—
And she stood there straight in the road, with a touch o'
    the sun in her face.

And she looked me right in the eye—I'd seen suthin like
    it before
When I hunted a wounded doe to the edge o' the Clear
    Lake Shore,
And I had my knee on its neck, and jist was raisin' my
    knife,
When it give me a look like that, and—well, it got off with
    its life.

"We are going to-day," she said, "and I thought I would
    say good-bye
To you in your own house, Luke—these woods and the
    bright blue sky!
You've always been kind to us, Luke, and papa has found
    you still
As good as the air he breathes, and wholesome as Laurel
    Tree Hill.

"And we'll always think of you, Luke, as the thing we could not take away,—
The balsam that dwells in the woods, the rainbow that lives in the spray.
And you'll sometimes think of *me*, Luke, as you know you once used to say,
A rifle smoke blown through the woods, a moment, but never to stay."

And then we shook hands. She turned, but a-suddent she tottered and fell,
And I caught her sharp by the waist, and held her a minit. Well,
It was only a minit, you know, thet ez cold and ez white she lay
Ez a snowflake here on my breast, and then—well, she melted away—

And was gone . . . And thar are her books; but I says not any for me;
Good enough may be for some, but them and I mightn't agree.
They spiled a decent gal ez might hev made some chap a wife,
And look at me!—clar two hundred—and never read one in my life!

"The Babes in the Woods."

(BIG PINE FLAT, 1871.)

"SOMETHING characteristic," eh?
 Humph! I reckon you mean by that
Something that happened in our way,
 Here at the crossin' of Big Pine Flat.
Times aren't now as they used to be,
 When gold was flush and the boys were frisky,
And a man would pull out his battery
 For anything—maybe the price of whisky.

Nothing of that sort, eh? That's strange!
 Why, I thought you might be diverted
Hearing how Jones of Red Rock Range
 Drawed his "hint to the unconverted,"
And saying, "Whar will you have it?" shot
 Cherokee Bob at the last debating!
What was the question I forgot,
 But Jones didn't like Bob's way of stating.

Nothing of that kind, eh? You mean
 Something milder? Let's see!—O Joe!
Tell to the stranger that little scene
 Out of the "Babes in the Woods." You know,

"The Babes in the Woods."

"Babes" was the name that we gave 'em, sir,
   Two lean lads in their teens, and greener
Than even the belt of spruce and fir
   Where they built their nest, and each day grew
      leaner.

No one knew where they came from.   None
   Cared to ask if they had a mother.
Runaway scholboys, maybe.   One
   Tall and dark as a spruce; the other
Blue and gold in the eyes and hair,
   Soft and low in his speech, but rarely
Talking with us; and we didn't care
   To get at their secret at all unfairly.

For they were so quiet, so sad and shy,
   Content to trust each other solely,
That somehow we'd always shut one eye,
   And never seem to observe them wholly
As they passed to their work. 'Twas a worn-out
      claim,
   And it paid them grub. They could live with
      out it,
For the boys had a way of leaving game
   In their tent, and forgetting all about it.

Yet no one asked for their secret.   Dumb
   It lay in their big eyes' heavy hollows.
It was understood that no one should come
   To their tent unawares, save the bees and swallows.
So they lived alone. 'Until one warm night
   I was sitting here at the tent-door,—so, sir!
When out of the sunset's rosy light
   Up rose the Sheriff of Mariposa.

"The Babes in the Woods."

I knew at once there was something wrong,
    For his hand and his voice shook just a little,
And there isn't much you can fetch along
    To make the sinews of Jack Hill brittle.
"Go warn the Babes!" he whispered, hoarse;
    "Tell I'm coming—to get and scurry;
For I've got a story that's bad,—and worse,
    I've got a warrant: G—d d—n it, hurry!"

Too late! they had seen him cross the hill;
    I ran to their tent and found them lying
Dead in each other's arms, and still
    Clasping the drug they had taken flying.
And there lay their secret cold and bare,
    Their life, their trial—the old, old story!
For the sweet blue eyes and the golden hair
    Was a *woman's* shame and a *woman's* glory.

"Who were they?" Ask no more, or ask
    The sun that visits their grave so lightly;
Ask of the whispering reeds, or task
    The mourning crickets that chirrup nightly.
All of their life but its love forgot,
    Everything tender and soft and mystic,
These are our Babes in the Woods,—you've got,
    Well—human nature—that's characteristic.

The Latest Chinese Outrage.

It was noon by the sun; we had finished our game,
And was passin' remarks goin' back to our claim;
Jones was countin' his chips, Smith relievin' his mind
Of ideas that a "straight" should beat "three of a kind,"
When Johnson of Elko came gallopin' down,
With a look on his face 'twixt a grin and a frown,
And he calls, "Drop your shovels and face right about,
For them Chinees from Murphy's are cleanin' us out—
  With their ching-a-ring-chow
  And their chic-colorow
  They're bent upon making
  No slouch of a row."

Then Jones—my own pardner—looks up with a sigh
"It's your wash-bill," sez he, and I answers, "You lie!"
But afore he could draw or the others could arm,
Up tumbles the Bates' boys, who heard the alarm.
And a yell from the hill-top and roar of a gong,
Mixed up with remarks like "Hi! yi! Chang-a-wong,"
And bombs, shells, and crackers, that crashed through
 the trees,
Revealed in their war-togs four hundred Chinees!
  Four hundred Chinee;
  We are eight, don't ye see!
  That made a square fifty
  To just one o' we.

The Latest Chinese Outrage.

They were dressed in their best, but I grieve that that same
Was largely made up of our own, to their shame;
And my pardner's best shirt and his trousers were hung
On a spear, and above him were tauntingly swung;
While that beggar, Chey Lee, like a conjuror sat
Pullin' out eggs and chickens from Johnson's best hat;
And Bates' game rooster was part of their "loot,"
And all of Smith's pigs were skyugled to boot;
But the climax was reached and I like to have died
When my demijohn, empty, came down the hillside,—
      Down the hillside—
      What once held the pride
      Of Robertson County
      Pitched down the hillside!

Then we axed for a parley. When out of the din ;
To the front comes a-rockin' that heathen, Ah Sin!
"You owe flowty dollee—me washee you camp,
You catchee my washee—me catchee no stamp;
One dollar hap dozen, me no catchee yet,
Now that flowty dollee—no hab?—how can get?
Me catchee you piggee—me sellee for cash,
It catchee me licee—you catchee no 'hash;'
Me belly good Sheliff—me lebbee when can,
Me allee same halp pin as Melican man!
      But Melican man
      He washee him pan
      On *bottom* side hillee
      And catchee—how can?"

"Are we men?" says Joe Johnson, "and list to this jaw,
Without process of warrant or colour of law?

Are we men or—a-chew?"—here he gasped in his speech,
For a stink-pot had fallen just out of his reach.
"Shall we stand here as idle, and let Asia pour
Her barbaric hordes on this civilised shore?
Has the White Man no country? Are we left in the lurch?
And likewise what's gone of the Established Church?
One man to four hundred is great odds, I own,
But this 'yer's a White Man—I plays it alone!"
And he sprang up the hillside—to stop him none dare—
Till a yell from the top told a "White Man was there!"
   A White Man was there!
   We prayed he might spare
   Those misguided heathens
   The few clothes they wear.

They fled, and he followed, but no matter where;
They fled to escape him,—the "White Man was there,"—
Till we missed first his voice on the pine-wooded slope,
And we knew for the heathen henceforth was no hope;
And the yells they grew fainter, when Petersen said,
"It simply was human to bury his dead."
   And then, with slow tread,
   We crept up, in dread,
   But found nary mortal there,
   Living or dead.

But there was his trail, and the way that they came,
And yonder, no doubt, he was bagging his game.
When Jones drops his pickaxe, and Thompson says
  "Shoo!"
And both of 'em points to a cage of bamboo
Hanging down from a tree, with a label that swung

Conspicuous, with letters in some foreign tongue,
Which, when freely translated, the same did appear
Was the Chinese for saying, "A White Man is here!"
        And as we drew near,
        In anger and fear,
        Bound hand and foot, Johnson
        Looked down with a leer!

In his mouth was an opium pipe—which was why
He leered at us so with a drunken-like eye!
They had shaved off his eyebrows, and tacked on a cue,
They had painted his face of a coppery hue,
And rigged him all up in a heathenish suit,
Then softly departed, each man with his "loot."
        Yes, every galoot,
        And Ah Sin, to boot,
        Had left him there hanging
        Like ripening fruit.

At a mass meeting held up at Murphy's next day
There were seventeen speakers and each had his say;
There were twelve resolutions that instantly passed,
And each resolution was worse than the last;
There were fourteen petitions, which, granting the same,
Will determine what Governor Murphy's shall name;
And the man from our District that goes up next year
Goes up on one issue—that's patent and clear:
        " Can the work of a mean,
        Degraded, unclean
        Believer in Buddha
        Be held as a lien?"

Truthful James to the Editor.

(YREKA, 1873.)

WHICH it is not my style
    To produce needless pain
By statements that rile
    Or that go 'gin the grain,
But here's Captain Jack still a-livin', and Nye has no skelp on his brain!

On that Caucasian head
    There is no crown of hair;
It has gone, it has fled!
    And Echo sez "Where?"
And I asks, "Is this Nation a White Man's, and is generally things on the square?"

She was known in the camp
    As "Nye's other squaw,"
And folks of that stamp
    Hez no rights in the law,
But is treacherous, sinful, and slimly, as Nye might hev well known before.

But she said that she knew
    Where the Injins was hid,

And the statement was true
For it seemed that she did,
Since she led William where he was covered by seventeen
Modocs, and—slid!

Then they reached for his hair;
But Nye sez, "By the law
Of nations, forbear!
I surrenders—no more
And I looks to be treated,—you hear me?—as a pris'ner, a
pris'ner of war!"

But Captain Jack rose
And he sez, "It's too thin!
Such statements as those
It's too late to begin.
There's a *Modoc indictment* agin you, O Paleface, and you're
goin' in!

"You stole Schonchin's squaw
In the year sixty-two;
It was in sixty-four
That Long Jack you went through,
And you burned Nasty Jim's rancheria, and his wives and
his papooses too.

"This gun in my hand
Was sold me by you
'Gainst the law of the land,
And I grieves it is true!"
And he buried his face in his blanket and wept as he hid it
from view.

"But you're tried and condemned,
 And skelping's your doom,"
And he paused and he hemmed—
 But why this resume?
He was skelped 'gainst the custom of nations, and cut off
 like a rose in its bloom.

So I asks without guile,
 And I trusts not in vain,
If this is the style
 That is going to obtain—
If here's Captain Jack still a-livin', and Nye with no skelp
 on his brain?

An Idyl of the Road.

SIERRAS, 1876.

DRAMATIS PERSONÆ.

| *First Tourist.* | *"Yuba Bill," Driver.* |
| *Second Tourist.* | *A Stranger.* |

First Tourist.

Look how the upland plunges into cover,
   Green where the pines fade sullenly away.
Wonderful those olive depths! and wonderful, more-
     over——

Second Tourist.

The red dust that rises in a suffocating way.

First Tourist.

Small is the soul that cannot soar above it,
   Cannot but cling to its ever-kindred clay:
Better be yon bird, that seems to breathe and love
     it——

Second Tourist.

Doubtless a hawk or some other bird of prey.
Were we, like him, as sure of a dinner
   That on our stomachs would comfortably stay;

Or were the fried ham a shade or two just thinner,
    That must confront us at closing of the day:
Then might you sing like Theocritus or Virgil,
    Then might we each make a metrical essay;
But verse just now—I must protest and urge—ill
    Fits a digestion by travel led astray

Chorus of Passengers.

Speed, Yuba Bill! oh, speed us to our dinner!
Speed to the sunset that beckons far away.

Second Tourist.

William of Yuba, O Son of Nimshi, hearken!
    Check thy profanity, but not thy chariot's play.
Tell us, O William, before the shadows darken,
    Where, and, oh! how we shall dine? O William,
        say!

Yuba Bill.

It ain't my fault, nor the Kumpeney's, I reckon,
    Ye can't get ez square meal ez any on the Bay,
Up at yon place, whar the senset 'pears to beckon—
    Ez thet sharp allows in his airy sort o' way.
Thar woz a place wor yer hash ye might hev wrestled,
    Kept by a woman ez chipper ez a jay—
Warm in her breast all the morning sunshine nestled;
    Red on her cheeks all the evening's sunshine lay.

Second Tourist.

Praise is but breath, O chariot compeller!
Yet of that hash we would bid you farther say.

An Idyl of the Road.

Yuba Bill.

Thar woz a snipe—like you, a fancy tourist—
   Kem to that ranch ez if to make a stay,
Ran off the gal, and ruined jist the purist
   Critter that lived——

Stranger (quietly).
                  You're a liar, driver!

Yuba Bill (reaching for his revolver).
                                        Eh !
Here take my lines, somebody——

Chorus of Passengers.
                       Hush, boys! listen!
Inside there's a lady!   Remember!   No affray!

Yuba Bill.

Ef that man lives, the fault ain't mine or his'n.

Stranger.

Wait for the sunset that beckons far away,
   Then—as you will! But, meantime, friends, believe me,
Nowhere on earth lives a purer woman ; nay,
   If my perceptions do surely not deceive me,
She is the lady we have inside to-day.
   As for the man—you see that blackened pine tree,
Up which the green vine creeps heavenward away !
   He was that scarred trunk, and she the vine that sweetly
Clothed him with life again, and lifted——

Second Tourist.
                    Yes; but pray
How know you this?

                    Stranger.
                        She's my wife.

                    Yuba Bill.
The h—ll you say!

Thompson of Angels.

It is the story of Thompson—of Thompson, the hero of Angels.
Frequently drunk was Thompson, but always polite to the stranger;
Light and free was the touch of Thompson upon his revolver;
Great the mortality incident on that lightness and freedom.

Yet not happy or gay was Thompson, the hero of Angels;
Often spoke to himself in accents of anguish and sorrow,
"Why do I make the graves of the frivolous youth who in folly
Thoughtlessly pass my revolver, forgetting its lightness and freedom?

"Why in my daily walks does the surgeon drop his left eyelid,
The undertaker smile, and the sculptor of gravestone marbles
Lean on his chisel and gaze? I care not o'er much for attention;
Simple am I in my ways, save but for this lightness and freedom."

So spake that pensive man—this Thompson, the hero of
  Angels,
Bitterly smiled to himself, as he strode through the
  chapparal musing.
"Why, O why?" echoed the pines in the dark olive depth
  far resounding.
'Why, indeed?" whispered the sage brush that bent
  'neath his feet non-elastic.

Pleasant indeed was that morn that dawned o'er the bar-
  room at Angels,
Where in their manhood's prime was gathered the pride of
  the hamlet.
Six "took sugar in theirs," and nine to the barkeeper
  lightly
Smiled as they said, "Well, Jim, you can give us our
  regular fusil."

Suddenly as the grey hawk swoops down on the barnyard,
  alighting
Where, pensively picking their corn, the favourite pullets
  are gathered,
So in that festive bar-room dropped Thompson, the hero
  of Angels,
Grasping his weapon dread with his pristine lightness and
  freedom.

Never a word he spoke; divesting himself of his garments,
Danced the war-dance of the playful yet truculent Modoc,
Uttered a single whoop, and then, in the accents of chal-
  lenge,
Spake: "Oh, behold in me a Crested Jay Hawk of the
  mountain."

Then rose a pallid man—a man sick with fever and ague;
Small was he, and his step was tremulous, weak, and uncertain;
Slowly a Derringer drew, and covered the person of Thompson;
Said in his feeblest pipe, "I'm a Bald-headed Snipe of the Valley."

As on its native plains the kangaroo, startled by hunters,
Leaps with successive bounds, and hurries away to the thickets,
So leaped the Crested Hawk, and quietly hopping behind him
Ran, and occasionally shot, that Bald-headed Snipe of the Valley.

Vain at the festive bar still lingered the people of Angels,
Hearing afar in the woods the petulant pop of the pistol;
Never again returned the Crested Jay Hawk of the mountains,
Never again was seen the Bald-headed Snipe of the Valley.

Yet in the hamlet of Angels, when truculent speeches are uttered,
When bloodshed and life alone will atone for some trifling misstatement,
Maidens and men in their prime recall the last hero of Angels,
Think of and vainly regret the Bald-headed Snipe of the Valley!

The Hawk's Nest.

(SIERRAS.)

We checked our pace, the red road sharply rounding;
　　We heard the troubled flow
Of the dark olive depths of pines resounding
　　A thousand feet below.

Above the tumult of the cañon lifted,
　　The grey hawk breathless hung,
Or on the hill a wingèd shadow drifted
　　Where furze and thorn-bush clung;

Or where half-way the mountain side was furrowed
　　With many a seam and scar;
Or some abandoned tunnel dimly burrowed,—
　　A mole-hill seen so far.

We looked in silence down across the distant
　　Unfathomable reach:
A silence broken by the guide's consistent
　　And realistic speech.

"Walker of Murphy's blew a hole through Peters
　　For telling him he lied;
Then up and dusted out of South Hornitos
　　Across the Long Divide.

"We ran him out of Strong's, and up through Eden
 And 'cross the ford below,
And up this cañon (Peters' brother leadin'),
 And me and Clark and Joe.

"He fou't us game: somehow I disremember
 Jest how the thing kem round;
Some say 'twas wadding, some a scattered ember
 From fires on the ground.

"But in one minute all the hill below him
 Was just one sheet of flame;
Guardin' the crest, Sam Clark and I called to him,
 And,—well, the dog was game!

"He made no sign: the fires of hell were round him,
 The pit of hell below.
We sat and waited, but never found him;
 And then we turned to go.

"And then—you see that rock that's grown so bristly
 With chapparal and tan—
Suthin crep' out: it might hev been a grizzly,
 It might hev been a man;

"Suthin that howled, and gnashed its teeth, and shouted
 In smoke and dust and flame;
Suthin that sprang into the depths about it,
 Grizzly or man,—but game!

"That's all! Well, yes, it does look rather risky,
 And kinder makes one queer
And dizzy looking down. A drop of whisky
 Ain't a bad thing right here!"

Her Letter.

I'm sitting alone by the fire,
   Dressed just as I came from the dance,
In a robe even *you* would admire,—
   It cost a cool thousand in France;
I'm be-diamonded out of all reason,
   My hair is done up in a cue:
In short, sir, "the belle of the season"
   Is wasting an hour upon you.

A dozen engagements I've broken;
   I left in the midst of a set;
Likewise a proposal, half spoken,
   That waits—on the stairs—for me yet.
They say he'll be rich,—when he grows up,-
   And then he adores me indeed;
And you, sir, are turning your nose up,
   Three thousand miles off, as you read.

"And how do I like my position?"
   "And what do I think of New York?"
"And now, in my higher ambition,
   With whom do I waltz, flirt, or talk?"
"And isn't it nice to have riches,
   And diamonds and silks, and all that?"
"And aren't it a change to the ditches
   And tunnels of Poverty Flat?"

Her Letter.

Well, yes,—if you saw us out driving
    Each day in the Park, four-in-hand,—
If you saw poor dear mamma contriving
    To look supernaturally grand,—
If you saw papa's picture, as taken
    By Brady, and tinted at that,—
You'd never suspect he sold bacon
    And flour at Poverty Flat.

And yet, just this moment, when sitting
    In the glare of the grand chandelier,—
In the bustle and glitter befitting
    The " finest *soirée* of the year,"—
In the mists of a *gaze de Chambéry*,
    And the hum of the smallest of talk,—
Somehow, Joe, I thought of the " Ferry,"
    And the dance that we had on " The Fork;"

Of Harrison's barn, with its muster
    Of flags festooned over the wall;
Of the candles that shed their soft lustre
    And tallow on head-dress and shawl;
Of the steps that we took to one fiddle,
    Of the dress of my queer *vis-à-vis;*
And how I once went down the middle
    With the man that shot Sandy McGee;

Of the moon that was quietly sleeping
    On the hill, when the time came to go;
Of the few baby peaks that were peeping
    From under their bedclothes of snow;
Of that ride,—that to me was the rarest;
    Of—the something you said at the gate.

Ah! Joe, then I wasn't an heiress
   To "the best-paying lead in the State."

Well, well, it's all past; yet it's funny
   To think, as I stood in the glare
Of fashion and beauty and money,
   That I should be thinking, right there,
Of some one who breasted high water,
   And swam the North Fork, and all that,
Just to dance with old Folinsbee's daughter,
   The Lily of Poverty Flat.

But goodness! what nonsense I'm writing!
   (Mamma says my taste still is low),
Instead of my triumphs reciting,
   I'm spooning on Joseph,—heigh-ho!
And I'm to be "finished" by travel,—
   Whatever's the meaning of that.
Oh, why did papa strike pay gravel
   In drifting on Poverty Flat?

Good night!—here's the end of my paper;
   Good night!—if the longitude please,—
For maybe, while wasting my taper,
   Your sun's climbing over the trees.
But know, if you haven't got riches,
   And are poor, dearest Joe, and all that,
That my heart's somewhere there in the ditches,
   And you've struck it,—on Poverty Flat.

His Answer to "Her Letter."

(REPORTED BY TRUTHFUL JAMES.)

BEING asked by an intimate party,—
    Which the same I would term as a friend,—
Though his health it were vain to call hearty,
    Since the mind to deceit it might lend;
For his arm it was broken quite recent,
    And there's something gone wrong with his lung,—
Which is why it is proper and decent
    I should write what he runs off his tongue.

First, he says, Miss, he's read through your letter
    To the end,—and "the end came too soon;"
That a "slight illness kept him your debtor,"
    (Which for weeks he was wild as a loon);
That "his spirits are buoyant as yours is;"
    That with you, Miss, he "challenges Fate,"
(Which the language that invalid uses
    At times it were vain to relate).

And he says "that the mountains are fairer
    For once being held in your thought;"
That each rock "holds a wealth that is rarer
    Than ever by gold-seeker sought."

(Which are words he would put in these pages,
   By a party not given to guile ;
Though the claim not, at date, paying wages,
   Might produce in the sinful a smile.)

He remembers the ball at the Ferry,
   And the ride, and the gate, and the vow,
And the rose that you gave him,—that very
   Same rose he is "treasuring now."
(Which his blanket he's kicked on his trunk, Miss,
   And insists on his legs being free ;
And his language to me from his bunk, Miss,
   Is frequent and painful and free.)

He hopes you are wearing no willows,
   But are happy and gay all the while ;
That he knows—(which this dodging of pillows
   Imparts but small ease to the style,
And the same you will pardon)—he knows, Miss,
   That, though parted by many a mile,
"Yet, were *he* lying under the snows, Miss,
   They'd melt into tears at your smile."

And "you'll still think of him in your pleasures,
   In your brief twilight dreams of the past ;
In this green laurel spray that he treasures,—
   It was plucked where your parting was last ;
In this specimen,—but a small trifle,—
   It will do for a pin for your shawl."
(Which, the truth not to wickedly stifle,
   Was his last week's " clean up,"—and *his all.*)

He's asleep, which the same might seem strange, Miss,
   Were it not that I scorn to deny
That I raised his last dose, for a change, Miss,
   In view that his fever was high;
But he lies there quite peaceful and pensive.
   And now, my respects, Miss, to you;
Which my language, although comprehensive,
   Might seem to be freedom, it's true.

Which I have a small favour to ask you,
   As concerns a bull-pup, and the same,—
If the duty would not overtask you,—
   You would please to procure for me, *game;*
And send per express to the Flat, Miss,—
   For they say York is famed for the breed,
Which, though words of deceit may be that, Miss,
   I'll trust to your taste, Miss, indeed.

P.S.—Which this same interfering
   Into other folks' way I despise;
Yet if it so be I was hearing
   That it's just empty pockets as lies
Betwixt you and Joseph, it follers
   That, having no family claims,
Here's my pile, which it's six hundred dollars,
   As is *yours*, with respects,
                        TRUTHFUL JAMES.

"The Return of Belisarius."

(MUD FLAT, 1860.)

So you're back from your travels, old fellow,
    And you left but a twelvemonth ago;
You've hobnobbed with Louis Napoleon,
    Eugenie, and kissed the Pope's toe.
By Jove, it is perfectly stunning,
    Astounding,—and all that, you know;
Yes, things are about as you left them
    In Mud Flat a twelvemonth ago.

The boys!—they're all right,—Oh! Dick Ashley,
    He's buried somewhere in the snow;
He was lost on the Summit last winter,
    And Bob has a hard row to hoe.
You knew that he's got the consumption?
    You didn't! Well come, that's a go;
I certainly wrote you at Baden,—
    Dear me! that was six months ago.

I got all your outlandish letters,
    All stamped by some foreign P.O.
I handed myself to Miss Mary
    That sketch of a famous château.

"The Return of Belisarius."

Tom Saunders is living at 'Frisco,—
    They say that he cuts quite a show
You didn't meet Euchre-deck Billy
    Anywhere on your road to Cairo?

So you thought of the rusty old cabin,
    The pines, and the valley below,
And heard the North Fork of the Yuba
    As you stood on the banks of the Po?
'Twas just like your romance, old fellow;
    But now there is standing a row
Of stores on the site of the cabin
    That you lived in a twelvemonth ago.

But it's jolly to see you, old fellow,—
    To think it's a twelvemonth ago!
And you have seen Louis Napoleon,
    And look like a Johnny Crapaud.
Come in. You will surely see Mary,—
    You know we are married. What, no?—
Oh, ay! I forgot there was something
    Between you a twelvemonth ago.

Further Language from Truthful James.

(NYE'S FORD, STANISLAUS, 1870.)

Do I sleep? do I dream?
Do I wonder and doubt?
Are things what they seem?
Or is visions about?
Is our civilisation a failure?
Or is the Caucasian played out?

Which expressions are strong;
Yet would feebly imply
Some account of a wrong—
Not to call it a lie—
As was worked off on William, my pardner,
And the same being W. Nye.

He came down to the Ford
On the very same day
Of that lottery drawed
By those sharps at the Bay;
And he says to me, "Truthful, how goes it?"
I replied, "It is far, far from gay;

"For the camp has gone wild
On this lottery game,
And has even beguiled
'Injin Dick' by the same."
Then said Nye to me, "Injins is pizen:
But what is his number, eh? James?"

I replied, "7,2,
9,8,4, is his hand;"
When he started, and drew
Out a list, which he scanned;
Then he softly went for his revolver
With language I cannot command.

Then I said, "William Nye!"
But he turned upon me,
And the look in his eye
Was quite painful to see;
And he says, "You mistake; this poor Injin
I protects from such sharps as *you* be!"

I was shocked and withdrew;
But I grieve to relate,
When he next met my view
Injin Dick was his mate;
And the two around town was a-lying
In a frightfully dissolute state.

Which the war dance they had
Round a tree at the Bend
Was a sight that was sad;
And it seemed that the end

Would not justify the proceedings,
As I quiet remarked to a friend.

For that Injin he fled
The next day to his band;
And we found William spread
Very loose on the strand,
With a peaceful-like smile on his features,
And a dollar greenback in his hand;

Which the same, when rolled out,
We observed, with surprise,
Was what he, no doubt,
Thought the number and prize—
Them figures in red in the corner,
Which the number of notes specifies.

Was it guile, or a dream?
Is it Nye that I doubt?
Are things what they seem?
Or is visions about?
Is our civilisation a failure?
Or is the Caucasian played out?

After the Accident.

(MOUTH OF THE SHAFT.)

WHAT I want is my husband, sir,—
    And if you're a man, sir,
You'll give me an answer,—
    Where is my Joe?

Penrhyn, sir, Joe,—
    Caernarvonshire.
Six months ago
    Since we came here—
Eh?—Ah, you know!

Well, I am quiet
    And still,
But I must stand here,
    And will!
Please, I'll be strong,
    If you'll just let me wait
    Inside o' that gate
Till the news comes along.

    "Negligence!"—
That was the cause!—
    Butchery!

Are there no laws,—
　　Laws to protect such as we?

Well, then!
　　I won't raise my voice.
There, men!
　　I won't make no noise,
Only you just let me be.

Four, only four—did he say—
Saved! and the other ones?—Eh?
　　Why do they call?
　　Why are they all
Looking and coming this way?

What's that?—a message?
　　I'll take it.
I know his wife, sir,
　　I'll break it.
　　"Foreman!"
　　Ay, ay!
　　"Out by and by,—
　　Just saved his life.
　　Say to his wife
　　Soon he'll be free."
Will I?—God bless you!
　　It's me!

The Ghost that Jim Saw.

WHY, as to that, said the engineer,
Ghosts ain't things we are apt to fear;
Spirits don't fool with levers much,
And throttle-valves don't take to such.
    And as for Jim,
    What happened to him
Was one half fact and t'other half whim!

Running one night on the line, he saw
A house—as plain as the moral law—
Just by the moonlit bank, and thence
Came a drunken man with no more sense
    Than to drop on the rail
    Flat as a flail,
As Jim drove by with the midnight mail.

Down went the patents—steam reversed.
Too late! for there came a "thud." Jim cursed
As the fireman, there in the cab with him,
Kinder stared in the face of Jim,
    And says, "What now?"
    Says Jim, "What now!
I've just run over a man,—that's how!"

The Ghost that Jim Saw.

The fireman stared at Jim. They ran
Back, but they never found house nor man,—
Nary a shadow within a mile.
Jim turned pale, but he tried to smile,
    Then on he tore
    Ten mile or more,
In quicker time than he'd made afore.

Would you believe it! the very next night
Up rose that house in the moonlight white,
Out comes the chap and drops as before,
Down goes the brake and the rest encore;
    And so, in fact,
    Each night that act
Occurred, till folks swore Jim was cracked.

umph! let me see; it's a year now, 'most,
That I met Jim, East, and says, "How's your ghost?"
"Gone," says Jim; "and more, it's plain
That ghost don't trouble me again.
    I thought I shook
    That ghost when I took
A place on an Eastern line,—but look!

"What should I meet, the first trip out,
But the very house we talked about,
And the selfsame man! 'Well,' says I, 'I guess
It's time to stop this 'yer foolishness.'
    So I crammed on steam,
    When there came a scream
From my fireman, that jest broke my dream:

The Ghost that Jim Saw.

"'You've killed somebody!' Says I, 'Not much!
I've been thar often, and thar ain't no such,
And now I'll prove it!' Back we ran,
And,—darn my skin!—but thar *was* a man
    On the rail, dead,
      Smashed in the head!—
Now I call that meanness!" That's all Jim said.

"Seventy-Nine."

(MR. INTERVIEWER INTERVIEWED.)

KNOW me next time when you see me, won't you, old smarty?
Oh, I mean *you*, old figger-head,—just the same party!
Take out your pensivil, d—n you; sharpen it, do!
Any complaints to make? Lot's of 'em—one of 'em's *you*.

You! who are *you*, anyhow, goin' round in that sneakin' way?
Never in jail before, was you, old blatherskite, say?
Look at it; don't it look pooty? Oh, grin, and be d—d to you, do!
But if I had you this side o' that gratin', I'd just make it lively for you.

How did I get in here? Well what 'ud you give to know?
'Twasn't by sneakin' round where I hadn't no call to go:
'Twasn't by hangin' round a-spyin' unfortnet men.
Grin! but I'll stop your jaw if ever you do that agen.

Why don't you say suthin, blast you? Speak your mind if you dare.
Ain't I a bad lot, sonny? Say it, and call it square.

Hain't got no tongue, hey, hev ye? O guard! here's a little swell
A cussin' and swearin' and yellin', and bribin' me not to tell.

There! I thought that 'ud fetch ye! And you want to know my name?
"Seventy-nine" they call me, but that is their little game;
For I am werry highly connected, as a gent, sir, can understand,
And my family hold their heads up with the very furst in the land.

For 'twas all, sir, a put-up job on a pore young man like me;
And the jury was bribed a puppos, and at furst they couldn't agree;
And I sed to the judge, sez I,—Oh, grin! it's all right, my son!
But you're a werry lively young pup, and you ain't to be played upon!

Wot's that you got?—tobacco? I'm cussed but I thought 'twas a tract.
Thank ye! A chap t'other day—now, lookee, this is a fact—
Slings me a tract on the evils o' keepin' bad company,
As if all the saints was howlin' to stay here along o' we.

No, I hain't no complaints. Stop, yes; do you see that chap,—
Him standin' over there, a-hidin' his eyes in his cap?

Well, that man's stumick is weak, and he can't stand the
    pris'n fare ;
For the coffee is just half beans, and the sugar it ain't no-
    where.

Perhaps it's his bringin' up ; but he's sickenin' day by day,
And he doesn't take no food, and I'm seein' him waste
    away.
And it isn't the thing to see ; for, whatever he's been and
    done,
Starvation isn't the plan as he's to be saved upon.

For he cannot rough it like me ; and he hasn't the stamps,
    I guess,
To buy him his extry grub outside o' the pris'n mess.
And perhaps if a gent like you, with whom I've been sorter
    free,
Would—thank you ! But, say ! look here ! Oh, blast it!
    don't give it to ME !

Don't you give it to me ; now, don't ye, don't ye, *don't!*
You think it's a put-up job ; so I'll thank ye, sir, if you
    won't.
But hand him the stamps yourself : why, he isn't even my
    pal ;
And, if it's a comfort to you, why, I don't intend that he
    shall.

The Stage-Driver's Story.

It was the stage-driver's story, as he stood with his back to the wheelers,
Quietly flecking his whip, and turning his quid of tobacco;
While on the dusty road, and blent with the rays of the moonlight,
We saw the long curl of his lash and the juice of tobacco descending.

"Danger! Sir, I believe you,—indeed, I may say, on that subject,
You your existence might put to the hazard and turn of a wager.
I have seen danger? Oh, no! not me, sir, indeed, I assure you:
'Twas only the man with the dog that is sitting alone in yon waggon.

"It was the Geiger Grade, a mile and a half from the summit:
Black as your hat was the night, and never a star in the heavens.
Thundering down the grade, the gravel and stones we sent flying
Over the precipice side,—a thousand feet plumb to the bottom.

"Half-way down the grade I felt, sir, a thrilling and creaking,
Then a lurch to one side, as we hung on the bank of the cañon;
Then, looking up the road, I saw, in the distance behind me,
The off hind wheel of the coach, just loosed from its axle, and following.

"One glance alone I gave, then gathered together my ribbons,
Shouted, and flung them, outspread, on the straining necks of my cattle;
Screamed at the top of my voice, and lashed the air in my frenzy,
While down the Geiger Grade, on *three* wheels, the vehicle thundered.

"Speed was our only chance, when again came the ominous rattle:
Crack, and another wheel slipped away, and was lost in the darkness.
Two only now were left; yet such was our fearful momentum,
Upright, erect, and sustained on *two* wheels, the vehicle thundered.

"As some huge bowlder, unloosed from its rocky shelf on the mountain,
Drives before it the hare and the timorous squirrel, far leaping,

So down the Geiger Grade rushed the Pioneer coach, and before it
Leaped the wild horses, and shrieked in advance of the danger impending.

"But to be brief in my tale. Again, ere we came to the level,
Slipped from its axle a wheel; so that, to be plain in my statement,
A matter of twelve hundred yards or more, as the distance may be,
We travelled upon *one* wheel, until we drove up to the station.

"Then, sir, we sank in a heap; but, picking myself from the ruins,
I heard a noise up the grade; and looking, I saw in the distance
The three wheels following still, like moons on the horizon whirling,
Till, circling, they gracefully sank on the road at the side of the station.

"This is my story, sir; a trifle, indeed, I assure you.
Much more, perchance, might be said—but I hold him of all men most lightly
Who swerves from the truth in his tale. No, thank you— Well, since you *are* pressing,
Perhaps I don't care if I do: you may give me the same, Jim,—no sugar."

MISCELLANEOUS.

A Greyport Legend.

(1797.)

THEY ran through the streets of the seaport town,
They peered from the decks of the ships that lay;
The cold sea-fog that came whitening down
Was never as cold or white as they.
    "Ho, Starbuck and Pinckney and Tenterden!
    Run for your shallops, gather your men,
      Scatter your boats on the lower bay.

Good cause for fear! In the thick mid-day
The hulk that lay by the rotting pier,
Filled with the children in happy play,
Parted its moorings and drifted clear,—
    Drifted clear beyond the reach or call,—
    Thirteen children they were in all,—
      All adrift in the lower bay!

Said a hard-faced skipper, "God help us all!
She will not float till the turning tide!"
Said his wife, "My darling will hear *my* call,
Whether in sea or heaven she bide,"
    And she lifted a quavering voice and high,
    Wild and strange as a sea-bird's cry,
      Till they shuddered and wondered at her side.

The fog drove down on each labouring crew,
Veiled each from each and the sky and shore:
There was not a sound but the breath they drew,
And the lap of water and creak of oar;
    And they felt the breath of the downs, fresh blown
    O'er leagues of clover and cold grey stone,
        But not from the lips that had gone before.

They come no more. But they tell the tale,
That, when fogs are thick on the harbour reef,
The mackerel fishers shorten sail;
For the signal they know will bring relief:
    For the voices of children, still at play
    In a phantom hulk that drifts alway
        Through channels whose waters never fail.

It is but a foolish shipman's tale,
A theme for a poet's idle page;
But still, when the mists of doubt prevail,
And we lie becalmed by the shores of Age,
    We hear from the misty troubled shore
    The voice of the children gone before,
        Drawing the soul to its anchorage.

A Newport Romance.

They say that she died of a broken heart
  (I tell the tale as 'twas told to me);
But her spirit lives, and her soul is part
  Of this sad old house by the sea.

Her lover was fickle and fine and French:
  It was nearly a hundred years ago
When he sailed away from her arms—poor wench!—
  With the Admiral Rochambeau.

I marvel much what periwigged phrase
  Won the heart of this sentimental Quaker,
At what golden-laced speech of those modish days
  She listened—the mischief take her!

But she kept the posies of mignonette
  That he gave; and ever as their bloom failed
And faded (though with her tears still wet)
  Her youth with their own exhaled.

Till one night, when the sea-fog wrapped a shroud
  Round spar and spire and tarn and tree,
Her soul went up on that lifted cloud
  From this sad old house by the sea.

And ever since then, when the clock strikes two,
   She walks unbidden from room to room,
And the air is filled that she passes through
   With a subtle, sad perfume.

The delicate odour of mignonette,
   The ghost of a dead and gone bouquet,
Is all that tells of her story; yet,
   Could she think of a sweeter way?

  .   .   .   .   .   .

I sit in the sad old house to-night,—
   Myself a ghost from a farther sea;
And I trust that this Quaker woman might,
   In courtesy, visit me.

For the laugh is fled from porch and lawn,
   And the bugle died from the fort on the hill,
And the twitter of girls on the stairs is gone,
   And the grand piano is still.

Somewhere in the darkness a clock strikes two;
   And there is no sound in the sad old house,
But the long veranda dripping with dew,
   And in the wainscot a mouse.

The light of my study-lamp streams out
   From the library door, but has gone astray
In the depths of the darkened hall. Small doubt
   But the Quakeress knows the way.

Was it the trick of a sense o'erwrought
   With outward watching and inward fret?
But I swear that the air just now was fraught
   With the odour of mignonette!

A Newport Romance.

I open the window, and seem almost—
    So still lies the ocean—to hear the beat
Of its Great Gulf artery off the coast,
    And to bask in its tropic heat.

In my neighbour's windows the gas-lights flare,
    As the dancers swing in a waltz of Strauss;
And I wonder now could I fit that air
    To the song of this sad old house.

And no odour of mignonette there is
    But the breath of morn on the dewy lawn;
And mayhap from causes as slight as this
    The quaint old legend is born.

But the soul of that subtle, sad perfume,
    As the spiced embalmings, they say, outlast
The mummy laid in his rocky tomb,
    Awakens my buried past.

And I think of the passion that shook my youth,
    Of its aimless loves and its idle pains,
And am thankful now for the certain truth
    That only the sweet remains.

And I hear no rustle of stiff brocade,
    And I see no face at my library door;
For now that the ghosts of my heart are laid,
    She is viewless for evermore.

But whether she came as a faint perfume,
    Or whether a spirit in stole of white,
I feel, as I·pass from the darkened room,
    She has been with my soul to-night!

San Francisco.

(FROM THE SEA.)

SERENE, indifferent of Fate,
Thou sittest at the Western Gate;

Upon thy height, so lately won,
Still slant the banners of the sun;

Thou seest the white seas strike their tents,
O Warder of two Continents!

And, scornful of the peace that flies
Thy angry winds and sullen skies,

Thou drawest all things, small or great,
To thee, beside the Western Gate.

. . . . . .

O lion's whelp, that hidest fast
In jungle growth of spire and mast!

I know thy cunning and thy greed,
Thy hard high lust and wilful deed,

And all thy glory loves to tell
Of specious gifts material.

San Francisco.

Drop down, O Fleecy Fog, and hide
Her sceptic sneer and all her pride!

Wrap her, O Fog, in gown and hood
Of her Franciscan Brotherhood.

Hide me her faults, her sin and blame;
With thy grey mantle cloak her shame!

So shall she, cowlèd, sit and pray
Till morning bears her sins away.

Then rise, O Fleecy Fog, and raise
The glory of her coming days;

Be as the cloud that flecks the seas
Above her smoky argosies;

When forms familiar shall give place
To stranger speech and newer face;

When all her throes and anxious fears
Lie hushed in the repose of years;

When Art shall raise and Culture lift
The sensual joys and meaner thrift,

And all fulfilled the vision we
Who watch and wait shall never see,

Who, in the morning of her race,
Toiled fair or meanly in our place,

But, yielding to the common lot,
Lie unrecorded and forgot.

The Mountain Heart's-Ease.

By scattered rocks and turbid waters shining,
    By furrowed glade and dell,
To feverish men thy calm, sweet face uplifting,
    Thou stayest them to tell

The delicate thought that cannot find expression,
    For ruder speech too fair,
That, like thy petals, trembles in possession,
    And scatters on the air.

The miner pauses in his rugged labour,
    And, leaning on his spade,
Laughingly calls unto his comrade-neighbour
    To see thy charms displayed.

But in his eyes a mist unwonted rises,
    And for a moment clear
Some sweet home face his foolish thought surprises
    And passes in a tear,—

Some boyish vision of his Eastern village,
    Of uneventful toil,
Where golden harvests followed quiet tillage
    Above a peaceful soil.

One moment only, for the pick, uplifting,
    Through root and fibre cleaves,
And on the muddy current slowly drifting
    Are swept thy bruisèd leaves.

And yet, O poet, in thy homely fashion,
    Thy work thou dost fulfil,
For on the turbid current of his passion
    Thy face is shining still!

Grizzly.

Coward,—of heroic size,
In whose lazy muscles lies
Strength we fear and yet despise;
Savage,—whose relentless tusks
Are content with acorn husks;
Robber,—whose exploits ne'er soared
O'er the bee's or squirrel's hoard;
Whiskered chin and feeble nose,
Claws of steel on baby toes,—
Here, in solitude and shade,
Shambling, shuffling plantigrade,
Be thy courses undismayed!

Here, where Nature makes thy bed,
Let thy rude, half-human tread
   Point to hidden Indian springs,
Lost in ferns and fragrant grasses,
   Hovered o'er by timid wings,
Where the wood-duck lightly passes,
Where the wild bee holds her sweets,—
Epicurean retreats,
Fit for thee, and better than
Fearful spoils of dangerous man.

In thy fat-jowled deviltry
Friar Tuck shall live in thee;
Thou mayst levy tithe and dole;
   Thou shalt spread the woodland cheer,
From the pilgrim taking toll;
   Match thy cunning with his fear;
Eat, and drink, and have thy fill;
Yet remain an outlaw still!

Madroño.

Captain of the Western wood,
Thou that apest Robin Hood!
Green above thy scarlet hose,
How thy velvet mantle shows;
Never tree like thee arrayed,
Oh thou gallant of the glade!

When the fervid August sun
Scorches all it looks upon,
And the balsam of the pine
Drips from stem to needle fine,
Round thy compact shade arranged,
Not a leaf of thee is changed!

When the yellow autumn sun
Saddens all it looks upon,
Spreads its sackcloth on the hills,
Strews its ashes in the rills,
Thou thy scarlet hose dost doff,
And in limbs of purest buff
Challengest the sombre glade
For a sylvan masquerade.

Madroño.

Where, O where, shall he begin
Who would paint thee, Harlequin?
With thy waxen burnished leaf,
With thy branches' red relief,
With thy polytinted fruit,—
In thy spring or autumn suit,—
Where begin, and oh! where end,—
Thou whose charms all art transcend?

Coyote.

BLOWN out of the prairie in twilight and dew,
Half bold and half timid, yet lazy all through;
Loath ever to leave, and yet fearful to stay,
He limps in the clearing, an outcast in grey.

A shade on the stubble, a ghost by the wall,
Now leaping, now limping, now risking a fall,
Lop-eared and large jointed, but ever alway
A thoroughly vagabond outcast in grey.

Here, Carlo, old fellow,—he's one of your kind,—
Go, seek him, and bring him in out of the wind.
What! snarling, my Carlo! So even dogs may
Deny their own kin in the outcast in grey.

Well, take what you will,—though it be on the sly,
Marauding, or begging,—I shall not ask why;
But will call it a dole, just to help on his way
A four-footed friar in orders of grey!

To a Sea-Bird.

(SANTA CRUZ, 1869.)

SAUNTERING hither on listless wings,
    Careless vagabond of the sea,
Little thou heedest the surf that sings,
The bar that thunders, the shale that rings,—
    Give me to keep thy company.

Little thou hast, old friend, that's new,
    Storms and wrecks are old things to thee;
Sick am I of these changes, too;
Little to care for, little to rue,—
    I on the shore, and thou on the sea.

All of thy wanderings, far and near,
    Bring thee at last to shore and me;
All of my journeyings end them here,
This our tether must be our cheer,—
    I on the shore, and thou on the sea.

Lazily rocking on ocean's breast,
    Something in common, old friend, have we;
Thou on the shingle seek'st thy nest,
I to the waters look for rest,—
    I on the shore, and thou on the sea.

What the Chimney Sang.

Over the chimney the night-wind sang
    And chanted a melody no one knew;
And the Woman stopped, as her babe she tossed,
    And thought of the one she had long since lost,
And said, as her tear-drops back she forced,
    "I hate the wind in the chimney."

Over the chimney the night-wind sang
    And chanted a melody no one knew;
And the Children said, as they closer drew,
    "'Tis some witch that is cleaving the black night through,—
'Tis a fairy trumpet that just then blew,
    And we fear the wind in the chimney."

Over the chimney the night-wind sang
    And chanted a melody no one knew;
And the Man, as he sat on his hearth below,
    Said to himself, "It will surely snow,
And fuel is dear and wages low,
    And I'll stop the leak in the chimney."

What the Chimney Sang.

Over the chimney the night-wind sang
   And chanted a melody no one knew;
But the Poet listened and smiled, for he
   Was Man, and Woman, and Child, all three,
And said, "It is God's own harmony,
   This wind we hear in the chimney."

Dickens in Camp.

Above the pines the moon was slowly drifting,
    The river sang below;
The dim Sierras, far beyond, uplifting
    Their minarets of snow.

The roaring camp-fire, with rude humour, painted
    The ruddy tints of health
On haggard face and form that drooped and fainted
    In the fierce race for wealth;

Till one arose, and from his pack's scant treasure
    A hoarded volume drew,
And cards were dropped from hands of listless leisure
    To hear the tale anew.

And then, while round them shadows gathered faster,
    And as the firelight fell,
He read aloud the book wherein the Master
    Had writ of "Little Nell."

Perhaps 'twas boyish fancy,—for the reader
    Was youngest of them all,—
But, as he read, from clustering pine and cedar
    A silence seemed to fall;

The fir-trees, gathering closer in the shadows,
    Listened in every spray,
While the whole camp, with "Nell" on English meadows
    Wandered and lost their way.

And so in mountain solitudes—o'ertaken
    As by some spell divine—
Their cares dropped from them like the needles shaken
    From out the gusty pine.

Lost is that camp and wasted all its fire:
    And he who wrought that spell?—
Ah! towering pine and stately Kentish spire,
    Ye have one tale to tell!

Lost is that camp, but let its fragrant story
    Blend with the breath that thrills
With hop-vine's incense all the pensive glory
    That fills the Kentish hills.

And on that grave where English oak and holly
    And laurel wreaths entwine,
Deem it not all a too presumptuous folly,—
    This spray of Western pine!

JULY, 1870.

"Twenty Years."

Beg your pardon, old fellow! I think
I was dreaming just now when you spoke.
The fact is, the musical clink
Of the ice on your wine-goblet's brink
A chord of my memory woke.

And I stood in the pasture-field where
Twenty summers ago I had stood;
And I heard in that sound, I declare,
The clinking of bells in the air,
Of the cows coming home from the wood.

Then the apple-bloom shook on the hill;
And the mullein-stocks tilted each lance;
And the sun behind Rapalye's mill
Was my uttermost West, and could thrill
Like some fanciful land of romance.

Then my friend was a hero, and then
My girl was an angel. In fine,
I drank buttermilk; for at ten
Faith asks less to aid her than when
At thirty we doubt over wine.

"Twenty Years."

Ah! well, it *does* seem that I must
Have been dreaming just now when you spoke,
Or lost, very like, in the dust
Of the years that slow fashioned the crust
On that bottle whose seal you last broke.

Twenty years was its age, did you say?
Twenty years? Ah! my friend, it is true?
All the dreams that have flown since that day,
All the hopes in that time passed away,
Old friend, I've been drinking with you!

Fate.

"The sky is clouded, the rocks are bare !
The spray of the tempest is white in air ;
The winds are out with the waves at play,
And I shall not tempt the sea to-day.

" The trail is narrow, the wood is dim,
The panther clings to the arching limb ;
And the lion's whelps are abroad at play,
And I shall not join in the chase to-day."

But the ship sailed safely over the sea,
And the hunters came from the chase in glee ;
And the town that was builded upon a rock
Was swallowed up in the earthquake shock.

Grandmother Centerden.

(MASSACHUSETTS SHORE, 1800.)

I MIND it was but yesterday,—
The sun was dim, the air was chill;
Below the town, below the hill,
The sails of my son's ship did fill,—
    My Jacob, who was cast away.

He said, "God keep you, mother dear,"
But did not turn to kiss his wife;
They had some foolish, idle strife;
Her tongue was like a two-edged knife,
    And he was proud as any peer.

Howbeit that night I took no note
Of sea nor sky, for all was drear;
I marked not that the hills looked near,
Nor that the moon, though curved and clear,
    Through curd-like scud did drive and float.

For with my darling went the joy
Of autumn woods and meadows brown;
I came to hate the little town;
It seemed as if the sun went down.
    With him, my only darling boy.

It was the middle of the night,
The wind it shifted west-by-south;
It piled high up the harbour mouth;
The marshes, black with summer drouth,
    Were all abroad with sea-foam white.

It was the middle of the night,—
The sea upon the garden leapt,
And my son's wife in quiet slept,
And I, his mother, waked and wept,
    When lo! there came a sudden light.

And there he stood! his seaman's dress
All wet and dripping seemed to be;
The pale blue fires of the sea
Dripped from his garments constantly,—
    I could not speak through cowardness.

"I come through night and storm," he said;
"Through storm and night and death," said he,
"To kiss my wife, if it so be
That strife still holds 'twixt her and me,
    For all beyond is peace," he said.

"The sea is His, and He who sent
The wind and wave can soothe their strife;
And brief and foolish is our life."
He stooped and kissed his sleeping wife,
    Then sighed, and, like a dream, he went.

Now, when my darling kissed not me,
But her—his wife—who did not wake,
My heart within me seemed to break;
I swore a vow, nor thenceforth spake
    Of what my clearer eyes did see.

And when the slow weeks brought him not,
Somehow we spake of aught beside,
For she,—her hope upheld her pride;
And I,—in me all hope had died,
　And my son passed as if forgot.

It was about the next spring-tide,
She pined and faded where she stood;
Yet spake no word of ill or good;
She had the hard, cold, Edwards' blood
　In all her veins,—and so she died.

One time I thought, before she passed,
To give her peace; but ere I spake
Methought, "*He* will be first to break
The news in heaven," and for his sake
　I held mine back until the last.

And here I sit, nor care to roam;
I only wait to hear his call;
I doubt not that this day next fall
Shall see me safe in port, where all
　And every ship at last comes home.

And you have sailed the Spanish Main,
And knew my Jacob? . . . Eh! Mercy!
Ah! God of wisdom! hath the sea
Yielded its dead to humble me?
　My boy! . . . My Jacob! . . . Turn again!

Guild's Signal.

WILLIAM GUILD was engineer of the train which on the 19th of April plunged into Meadow Brook, on the line of the Stonington and Providence Railroad. It was his custom, as often as he passed his home, to whistle an "All's well" to his wife. He was found, after the disaster, dead, with his hand on the throttle-valve of his engine.

    Two low whistles, quaint and clear,
    That was the signal the engineer—
        That was the signal that Guild, 'tis said—
    Gave to his wife at Providence,
    As through the sleeping town, and thence,
           Out in the night,
           On to the light,
    Down past the farms, lying white, he sped!

    As a husband's greeting, scant, no doubt,
    Yet to the woman looking out,
        Watching and waiting, no serenade,
    Love song, or midnight roundelay
    Said what that whistle seemed to say:
           "To my trust true,
           So love to you!
    Working or waiting, good night!" it said.

Guild's Signal.

Brisk young bagmen, tourists fine,
Old commuters along the line,
  Brakemen and porters glanced ahead,
Smiled as the signal, sharp, intense,
Pierced through the shadows of Providence:
     "Nothing amiss—
     Nothing!—it is
Only Guild calling his wife," they said.

Summer and winter the old refrain
Rang o'er the billows of ripening grain,
  Pierced through the budding boughs o'erhead
Flew down the track when the red leaves burned
Like living coals from the engine spurned;
     Sang as it flew:
     "To our trust true,
First of all, duty. Good night!" it said.

And then, one night, it was heard no more
From Stonington over Rhode Island shore,
  And the folk in Providence smiled and said
As they turned in their beds, "The engineer
Has once forgotten his midnight cheer."
     One only knew,
     To his trust true,
Guild lay under his engine dead.

Aspiring Miss De Laine.

(A CHEMICAL NARRATIVE.)

CERTAIN facts which serve to explain
The physical charms of Miss Addie De Laine,
Who, as the common reports obtain,
Surpassed in complexion the lily and rose;
With a very sweet mouth and a *retroussé* nose;
A figure like Hebe's, or that which revolves
In a milliner's window, and partially solves
That question which mentor and moralist pains,
If grace may exist *minus* feeling or brains.

Of course the young lady had beaux by the score,
All that she wanted,—what girl could ask more?
Lovers that sighed, and lovers that swore,
Lovers that danced, and lovers that played,
Men of profession, of leisure, and trade;
But one, who was destined to take the high part
Of holding that mythical treasure, her heart,—
This lover—the wonder and envy of town—
Was a practising chemist,—a fellow called Brown.

I might here remark that 'twas doubted by many,
In regard to the heart, if Miss Addie had any;

But no one could look in that eloquent face,
With its exquisite outline and features of grace,
And mark, through the transparent skin, how the tide
Ebbed and flowed at the impulse of passion or pride,—
None could look who believed in the blood's circulation
As argued by Harvey, but saw confirmation
That here, at least, Nature had triumphed o'er art,
And, as far as complexion went, she had a heart.

But this *par parenthesis.* Brown was the man
Preferred of all others to carry her fan,
Hook her glove, drape her shawl, and do all that a belle
May demand of the lover she wants to treat well.
Folks wondered and stared that a fellow called Brown—
Abstracted and solemn, in manner a clown,
Ill dressed, with a lingering smell of the shop—
Should appear as her escort at party or hop.
Some swore he had cooked up some villanous charm,
Or love philter, not in the regular Pharm-
Acopœia, and thus, from pure *malice prepense,*
Had bewitched and bamboozled the young lady's sense;
Others thought, with more reason, the secret to lie
In a magical wash or indelible dye;
While Society, with its censorious eye
And judgment impartial, stood ready to damn
What wasn't improper as being a sham.

For a fortnight the townfolk had all been agog
With a party, the finest the season had seen,
To be given in honour of Miss Pollywog,
Who was just coming out as a belle of sixteen.
The guests were invited; but one night before
A carriage drew up at the modest back-door

Of Brown's lab'ratory, and, full in the glare
Of a big purple bottle, some closely-veiled fair
Alighted and entered: to make matters plain,
Spite of veils and disguises, 'twas Addie De Laine.

As a bower for true love, 'twas hardly the one
That a lady would choose to be wooed in or won:
No odour of rose or sweet jessamine's sigh
Breathed a fragrance to hallow their pledge of troth by,
Nor the balm that exhales from the odorous thyme;
But the gaseous effusions of chloride of lime,
And salts, which your chemist delights to explain
As the base of the smell of the rose and the drain.
Think of this, O ye lovers of sweetness! and know
What you smell when you snuff up Lubin or Pinaud.

I pass by the greetings, the transports and bliss,
Which, of course, duly followed a meeting like this,
And come down to business;—for such the intent
Of the lady who now o'er the crucible leant,
In the glow of a furnace of carbon and lime,
Like a fairy called up in the new pantomime,—
And give but her words as she coyly looked down,
In reply to the questioning glances of Brown:
"I am taking the drops, and am using the paste,
And the little white powders that had a sweet taste,
Which you told me would brighten the glance of my eye,
And the depilatory, and also the dye,
And I'm charmed with the trial; and now, my dear Brown,
I have one other favour,—now, ducky, don't frown,—
Only one, for a chemist and genius like you
But a trifle, and one you can easily do.

Now listen : to-morrow, you know, is the night
Of the birthday *soirée* of that Pollywog fright ;
And I'm to be there, and the dress I shall wear
Is *too* lovely; but "—" But what then, *ma chère ?* "
Said Brown, as the lady came to a full stop,
And glanced round the shelves of the little back shop.
"Well, I want—I want something to fill out the skirt
To the proper dimensions, without being girt
In a stiff crinoline, or caged in a hoop
That shows through one's skirt like the bars of a coop ;
Something light, that a lady may waltz in, or polk,
With a freedom that none but you masculine folk
Ever know. For, however poor woman aspires,
She's always bound down to the earth by these wires.

Are you listening? Nonsense ! don't stare like a spoon,
Idiotic ; some light thing, and spacious, and soon—
Something like—well, in fact—something like a balloon !"
Here she paused ; and here Brown, overcome by surprise,
Gave a doubting assent with still wondering eyes,
And the lady departed. But just at the door
Something happened,—'tis true, it had happened before
In this sanctum of science,—a sibilant sound,
Like some element just from its trammels unbound,
Or two substances that their affinities found.
The night of the anxiously-looked-for *soirée*
Had come, with its fair ones in gorgeous array ;
With the rattle of wheels and the tinkle of bells,
And the "How do ye do's," and the "Hope you are well's ; "
And the crush in the passage, and last lingering look
You give as you hang your best hat on the hook ;
The rush of hot air as the door opens wide ;
And your entry,—that blending of self-possessed pride

And humility shown in your perfect-bred stare
At the folk, as if wondering how they got there;
With other tricks worthy of Vanity Fair.
Meanwhile the safe topic, the heat of the room,
Already was loosing its freshness and bloom;
Young people were yawning, and wondering when
The dance would come off, and why didn't it then:
When a vague expectation was thrilling the crowd,
Lo! the door swung its hinges with utterance proud!
And Pompey announced, with a trumpet-like strain,
The entrance of Brown and Miss Addie De Laine.

She entered; but oh! how imperfect the verb
To express to the senses her movement superb!
To say that she "sailed in" more clearly might tell
Her grace in its buoyant and billowy swell.
Her robe was a vague circumambient space,
With shadowy boundaries made of point-lace.
The rest was but guesswork, and well might defy
The power of critical feminine eye
To define or describe: 'twere as futile to try
The gossamer web of the cirrus to trace,
Floating far in the blue of a warm summer sky.

'Midst the humming of praises and the glances of beaux,
That greet our fair maiden wherever she goes,
Brown slipped like a shadow, grim, silent, and black,
With a look of anxiety, close in her track.
Once he whispered aside in her delicate ear
A sentence of warning,—it might be of fear:
"Don't stand in a draught, if you value your life."
(Nothing more,—such advice might be given your wife
Or your sweetheart, in times of bronchitis and cough,
Without mystery, romance, or frivolous scoff.)

But hark to the music: the dance has begun.
The closely-draped windows wide open are flung;
The notes of the piccolo, joyous and light,
Like bubbles burst forth on the warm summer night.
Roundabout go the dancers; in circles they fly;
Trip, trip, go their feet as their skirts eddy by;
And swifter and lighter, but somewhat too plain,
Whisks the fair circumvolving Miss Addie De Laine.
Taglioni and Cerito well might have pined
For the vigour and ease that her movements combined;
E'en Rigelboche never flung higher her robe
In the naughtiest city that's known on the globe.
'Twas amazing, 'twas scandalous: lost in surprise,
Some opened their mouths, and a few shut their eyes.

But hark! At the moment Miss Addie De Laine,
Circling round at the outer edge of an ellipse
Which brought her fair form to the window again,
From the arms of her partner incautiously slips!
And a shriek fills the air, and the music is still,
And the crowd gather round where her partner forlorn
Still frenziedly points from the wide window-sill
Into space and the night; for Miss Addie was gone!
Gone like the bubble that bursts in the sun;
Gone like the grain when the reaper is done;
Gone like the dew on the fresh morning grass;
Gone without parting farewell; and alas!
Gone with a flavour of hydrogen gas!

. . . .

When the weather is pleasant, you frequently meet
A white-headed man slowly pacing the street;
His trembling hand shading his lack-lustre eye,
Half-blind with continually scanning the sky.

Rumour points him as some astronomical sage,
Re-perusing by day the celestial page;
But the reader, sagacious, will recognise Brown,
Trying vainly to conjure his lost sweetheart down,
And learn the stern moral this story must teach,
That Genius may lift its love out of its reach.

A Legend of Cologne.

     Above the bones
     St. Ursula owns,
And those of the virgins she *chaperones;*
     Above the boats,
     And the bridge that floats,
And the Rhine and the steamers' smoky throats;
   Above the chimneys and quaint-tiled roofs,
   Above the clatter of wheels and hoofs;
   Above Newmarket's open space,
   Above that consecrated place
Where the genuine bones of the Magi seen are,
And the dozen shops of the real Farina;
   Higher than even old *Hohestrasse,*
   Whose houses threaten the timid passer:
     Above them all,
     Through scaffolds tall
And spires like delicate limbs in splinters,
     The great Cologne's
     Cathedral stones
Climb through the storms of eight hundred winters.

     Unfinished there,
     In high mid-air
The towers halt like a broken prayer;

Through years belated,
Unconsummated,
The hope of its architect quite frustrated.
Its very youth
They say, forsooth,
With a quite improper purpose mated;
And every stone
With a curse of its own
Instead of that sermon Skakespeare stated,
Since the day its choir,
Which all admire,
By Cologne's Archbishop was consecrated.

Ah! *that* was a day,
One well might say,
To be marked with the largest, whitest stone
To be found in the towers of all Cologne!
Along the Rhine,
From old Rheinstein,
The people flowed like their own good wine.
From Rudesheim,
And Geisenheim,
And every spot that is known to rhyme;
From the famed Cat's Castle of St. Goarshausen,
To the pictured roofs of Assmannshausen,
And down the track,
From quaint Schwalbach
To the clustering tiles of Bacharach;
From Bingen, hence
To old Coblentz:
From every castellated crag,
Where the robber chieftains kept their "swag,"
The folk flowed in, and Ober-Cassel
Shone with the pomp of knight and vassal;

A Legend of Cologne.

And pouring in from near and far,
As the Rhine to its bosom draws the Ahr,
Or takes the arm of the sober Mosel,
So in Cologne, knight, squire, and losel,
Choked up the city's gates with men
From old St. Stephen to *Zint Märjen*.

What had they come to see? Ah me!
I fear no glitter of pageantry,
  Nor sacred zeal
  For Church's weal,
Nor faith in the virgins' bones to heal;
 Nor childlike trust in frank confession
 Drew these, who, dyed in deep transgression,
  Still in each nest
  On every crest
Kept stolen goods in their possession;
  But only their *gout*
  For something new,
More rare than the "roast" of a wandering Jew;
  Or—to be exact—
  To see—in fact—
A Christian soul, in the very act
Of being damned, *secundum artem*,
By the devil, before a soul could part 'em.

  For a rumour had flown
  Throughout Cologne,
That the church, in fact, was the devil's own;
  That its architect
  (Being long "suspect")
Had confessed to the bishop that he had wreckt
 Not only his *own* soul, but had lost
 The *very first Christian soul* that crossed

The sacred threshold ; and all, in fine,
For that very beautiful design
  Of the wonderful choir
  They were pleased to admire.
And really, he must be allowed to say—
To speak in a purely business way—
That, taking the ruling market prices
Of souls and churches, in such a crisis
  It would be shown—
  And his Grace must own—
It was really a *bargain* for Cologne!

  Such was the tale
  That turned cheeks pale
With the thought that the enemy might prevail,
  And the church doors snap
  With a thunder-clap
On a Christian soul in that devil's trap.
  But a wiser few,
  Who thought that they knew
Cologne's Archbishop, replied, " Pooh, pooh !
  Just watch him and wait,
  And as sure as fate,
You'll find that the Bishop will give checkmate."

  One here might note
  How the popular vote,
As shown in all legends and anecdote,
  Declares that a breach
  Of trust to o'erreach
The devil is something quite proper for each.
  And, really, if you
  Give the devil his due
In spite of the proverb—it's something you'll rue.

But to lie and deceive him,
To use and to leave him,
From Job up to Faust is the way to receive him,
Though no one has heard
It ever averred
That the "Father of Lies" ever yet broke *his* word,
But has left this position,
In every tradition,
To be taken alone by the "truth-loving" Christian!

Bom! from the tower!
It is the hour!
The host pours in, in its pomp and power
Of banners and pyx,
And high crucifix,
And crosiers and other processional sticks,
And no end of Marys
In quaint reliquaries;
To gladden the souls of all true antiquaries;
And an *Osculum Pacis*—
(A myth to the masses
Who trusted their bones more to mail and cuirasses),
All borne by the throng
Who are marching along
To the square of the Dom with processional song,
With the flaring of dips,
And bending of hips,
And the chanting of hundred perfunctory lips;
And some good little boys
Who had come up from Neuss
And the *Quirinuskirche* to show off their voice:
All march to the square
Of the great Dom, and there
File right and left, leaving alone and quite bare

A covered sedan,
Containing—so ran
The rumour—the victim to take off the ban.

They have left it alone,
They have sprinkled each stone
Of the porch with a sanctified *Eau de Cologne*,
Guaranteed in this case
To disguise every trace
Of a sulphurous presence in that sacred place.
Two Carmelites stand
On the right and left hand
Of the covered sedan chair, to wait the command
Of the prelate to throw
Up the cover and show
The form of the victim in terror below.
There's a pause and a prayer,
Then the signal, and there—
Is a *woman !*—by all that is good and is fair !

A woman ! and known
To them all—one must own
Too well known to the many, to-day to be shown
As a martyr, or e'en
As a Christian ! A queen
Of pleasaunce and revel, of glitter and sheen ;
So bad that the worst
Of Cologne spake up first,
And declared 'twas an outrage to suffer one **curst**,
And already a fief
Of the Satanic chief,
To martyr herself for the Church's relief.

A Legend of Cologne.

But in vain fell their sneer
On the mob, who I fear
On the whole felt a strong disposition to cheer.

A woman! and there
She stands in the glare
Of the pitiless sun and their pitying stare—
A woman still young,
With garments that clung
To a figure, though wasted with passion and wrung
With remorse and despair,
Yet still passing fair,
With jewels and gold in her dark shining hair,
And cheeks that are faint
'Neath her dyes and her paint—
A woman most surely—but hardly a saint!

She moves. She has gone
From their pity and scorn;
She has mounted alone
The first step of stone,
And the high swinging doors she wide open has thrown,
Then pauses and turns,
As the altar blaze burns
On her cheeks, and with one sudden gesture she spurns
Archbishop and Prior,
Knight, ladye, and friar,
And her voice rings out high from the vault of the choir.

"Oh, men of Cologne!
What I *was* ye have known;
What I *am*, as I stand here, One knoweth alone.
If it be but His will
I shall pass from Him still,

Lost, curst, and degraded, I reckon no ill;
    If still by that sign
    Of His anger divine
One soul shall be saved, He hath blessed more than mine.
    Oh, men of Cologne!
    Stand forth if ye own
A faith like to this, or more fit to atone,
    And take ye my place,
    And God give you grace
To stand and confront Him, like me, face to face!"

    She paused. Yet aloof
    They all stand. No reproof
Breaks the silence that fills the celestial roof.
    One instant—no more—
    She halts at the door,
Then enters! . . . A flood from the roof to the floor
    Fills the church rosy red.
    She is gone!
        But instead,
Who is this leaning forward with glorified head
    And hands stretched to save?
    Sure this is no slave
Of the Powers of Darkness, with aspect so brave!

    They press to the door,
    But too late! All is o'er.
Nought remains but a woman's form prone on the floor.
    But they still see a trace
    Of that glow in her face
That they saw in the light of the altar's high blaze
    On the image that stands
    With the babe in its hands
Enshrined in the churches of all Christian lands.

A Legend of Cologne.

   A *Te Deum* sung,
   A censer high swung,
With praise, benediction, and incense wide-flung,
   Proclaim that the *curse*
   Is removed—and no worse
Is the Dom for the trial—in fact, the *reverse;*
   For instead of their losing
   A soul in abusing
The Evil One's faith, they gained one of his choosing.

   Thus the legend is told:
   You will find in the old
Vaulted aisles of the Dom, stiff in marble or cold
   In iron and brass,
   In gown and cuirass,
The knights, priests, and bishops who came to that Mass;
   And high o'er the rest,
   With her babe at her breast,
The image of Mary Madonna the blest.
   But you look round in vain,
   On each high pictured pane,
For the woman most worthy to walk in her train.

   Yet, standing to-day
   O'er the dust and the clay,
'Midst the ghosts of a life that has long passed away,
   With the slow-sinking sun
   Looking softly upon
That stained-glass procession, I scarce miss the one
   That it does not reveal,
   For I know and I feel
That these are but shadows—the woman was real!

The Tale of a Pony.

NAME of my heroine, simply "Rose;"
Surname, tolerable only in prose;
Habitat, Paris,—that is where
She resided for change of air;
Ætat. twenty; complexion fair,
Rich, good-looking, and *débonnaire*,
Smarter than Jersey-lightning—There!
That's her photograph, done with care.

In Paris, whatever they do besides,
EVERY LADY IN FULL DRESS RIDES!
Moiré antiques you never meet
Sweeping the filth of a dirty street;
But every woman's claim to *ton*
    Depends upon
The team she drives, whether phaeton,
Landau, or britzka. Hence it's plain
That Rose, who was of her toilet vain,
Should have a team that ought to be
Equal to any in all *Paris!*

"Bring forth the horse!" The *commissaire*
Bowed, and brought Miss Rose a pair
Leading an equipage rich and rare.
Why doth that lovely lady stare?

The Tale of a Pony.

Why? The tail of the off grey mare
Is bobbed, by all that's good and fair!
Like the shaving-brushes that soldiers wear,
Scarcely showing as much back-hair
As Tam O'Shanter's "Meg,"—and there,
Lord knows, she'd little enough to spare.

That stare and frown the Frenchman knew,
But did as well-bred Frenchmen do:
Raised his shoulders above his crown,
Joined his thumbs with the fingers down,
And said, "Ah Heaven!"—then, "Mademoiselle
Delay one minute, and all is well!"
He went—returned; by what good chance
These things are managed so well in France
I cannot say,—but he made the sale
And the bob-tailed mare had a flowing tail.

All that is false in this world below
Betrays itself in a love of show;
Indignant Nature hides her lash
In the purple-black of a dyed mustache;
The shallowest fop will trip in French,
The would-be critic will misquote Trench;
In short, you're always sure to detect
A sham in the things folks most affect;
Bean-pods are noisiest when dry,
And you always wink with your weakest eye:
And that's the reason the old grey mare
Forever had her tail in the air,
With flourishes beyond compare,
    Though every whisk
    Incurred the risk
Of leaving that sensitive region bare,—

She did some things that you couldn't but feel
She wouldn't have done had her tail been real.

Champs Elysées : Time, past five ;
There go the carriages,—look alive !
Everything that man can drive,
Or his inventive skill contrive,—
Yankee buggy or English "chay,"
Dog-cart, droschky, and smart coupé,
A *désobligeante* quite bulky
(French idea of a Yankee *sulky*) ;
Band in the distance playing a march,
Footmen standing stiff as starch ;
Savans, lorettes, deputies, Arch-
Bishops, and there together range
Sous-lieutenants and *cent*-gardes (strange
Way these soldier-chaps make change),
Mixed with black-eyed Polish dames,
With unpronounceable awful names ;
Laces tremble and ribbons flout,
Coachmen wrangle and gendarmes shout,—
Bless us ! what is the row about ?
Ah ! here comes Rosy's new turn-out !
Smart ! You bet your life 'twas that !
Nifty ! (short for *magnificat*).
Mulberry panels,—heraldic spread,—
Ebony wheels picked out with red,
And two grey mares that were thorough-bred ;
No wonder that every dandy's head
Was turned by the turn-out,—and 'twas said
That Caskowhisky (friend of the Czar),
A very good *whip* (as Russians are),
Was tied to Rosy's triumphal car,

The Tale of a Pony.

Entranced, the reader will understand,
By "ribbons" that graced her head and hand.

Alas! the hour you think would crown
Your highest wishes should let you down!
Or Fate should turn, by your own mischance,
Your victor's car to an ambulance;
From cloudless heavens her lightnings glance,
(And these things happen, even in France).
And so Miss Rose, as she trotted by,
The cynosure of every eye,—
Saw to her horror the off mare shy,—
Flourish her tail so exceedingly high
That, disregarding the closest tie,
And without giving a reason why,
She flung that tail so free and frisky
Off in the face of Caskowhisky.

Excuses, blushes, smiles : in fine,
End of the pony's tail, and mine!

On a Cone of the Big Trees.

(SEQUOIA GIGANTEA.)

BROWN foundling of the Western wood,
    Babe of primeval wildernesses!
Long on my table thou hast stood
    Encounters strange and rude caresses;
Perchance contented with thy lot,
    Surroundings new and curious faces,
As though ten centuries were not
    Imprisoned in thy shining cases.

Thou bring'st me back the halcyon days
    Of grateful rest, the week of leisure,
The journey lapped in autumn haze,
    The sweet fatigue that seemed a pleasure,
The morning ride, the noonday halt,
    The blazing slopes, the red dust rising,
And then the dim, brown, columned vault,
    With its cool, damp, sepulchral spicing.

Once more I see the rocking masts
    That scrape the sky, their only tenant
The jay-bird, that in frolic casts
    From some high yard his broad blue pennant.

On a Cone of the Big Trees.

I see the Indian files that keep
   Their places in the dusty heather,
Their red trunks standing ankle-deep
   In moccasins of rusty leather.

I see all this, and marvel much
   That thou, sweet woodland waif, art able
To keep the company of such
   As throng thy friend's—the poet's—table:
The latest spawn the press hath cast,—
   The "modern Pope's" "the later Byron's,"—
Why e'en the best may not outlast
   Thy poor relation,—*Sempervirens.*

Thy sire saw the light that shone
   On Mohammed's uplifted crescent,
On many a royal gilded throne
   And deed forgotten in the present;
He saw the age of sacred trees
   And Druid groves and mystic larches;
And saw from forest domes like these
   The builder bring his Gothic arches.

And must thou, foundling, still forego
   Thy heritage and high ambition,
To lie full lowly and full low,
   Adjusted to thy new condition?
Not hidden in the drifted snows,
   But under ink-drops idly spattered,
And leaves ephemeral as those
   That on thy wooldand tomb were scattered?

Yet lie thou there, O friend ! and speak
    The moral of thy simple story :
Though life is all that thou dost seek,
    And age alone thy crown of glory,—
Not thine the only germs that fail
    The purpose of their high creation,
If their poor tenements avail
    For worldly show and ostentation.

Lone Mountain.

(CEMETERY, SAN FRANCISCO.)

This is that hill of awe
That Persian Sindbad saw,—
    The mount magnetic;
And on its seaward face,
Scattered along its base,
    The wrecks prophetic.

Here come the argosies
Blown by each idle breeze,
    To and fro shifting;
Yet to the hill of Fate
All drawing, soon or late,—
    Day by day drifting;—

Drifting forever here
Barks that for many a year
    Braved wind and weather;
Shallops but yesterday
Launched on yon shining bay,—
    Drawn all together.

This is the end of all :
Sun thyself by the wall,
   O poorer Hindbad !
Envy not Sindbad's fame :
Here come alike the same
   Hindbad and Sindbad.

Alnaschar.

Here's yer toy balloons! All sizes!
Twenty cents for that. It rises
Jest as quick as that 'ere, Miss,
Twice as big. Ye see it is
Some more fancy. Make it square
Fifty for 'em both. That's fair.

That's the sixth I've sold since noon.
Trade's reviving. Just as soon
As this lot's worked off, I'll take
Wholesale figgers. Make or break,
That's my motto! Then I'll buy
In some first-class lottery
One half ticket, numbered right—
As I dreamed about last night.

That'll fetch it. Don't tell me!
When a man's in luck, you see,
All things help him. Every chance
Hits him like an avalanche.
Here's your toy balloons, Miss. Eh?
You won't turn your face this way?
Mebbe you'll be glad some day

With that clear ten thousand prize
This 'yer trade I'll drop, and rise
Into wholesale. No! I'll take
Stocks in Wall Street. Make or break,
That's my motto! With my luck,
Where's the chance of being stuck?
Call it sixty thousand, clear,
Made in Wall Street in one year.

Sixty thousand! Umph! Let's see!
Bond and mortgage'll do for me.
Good! That gal that passed me by
Scornful like—why, mebbe I
Some day'll hold in pawn—why not?
All her father's prop. She'll spot
What's my little game, and see
What I'm after's *her*. He! he!

He! he! When she comes to sue—
Let's see! What's the thing to do?
Kick her? No! There's the perliss!
Sorter throw her off like this.
Hello! Stop! Help! Murder! Hey!
There's my whole stock got away,
Kiting on the house-tops! Lost!
All a poor man's fortin! Cost?
Twenty dollars! Eh! What's this?
Fifty cents! God bless ye, Miss!

The Two Ships.

As I stand by the cross on the lone mountain's crest,
    Looking over the ultimate sea;
In the gloom of the mountain a ship lies at rest,
    And one sails away from the lea:
One spreads its white wings on a far-reaching track,
    With pennant and sheet flowing free;
One hides in the shadow with sails laid aback,—
    The ship that is waiting for me!

But lo! in the distance the clouds break away,
    The Gate's glowing portals I see;
And I hear from the outgoing ship in the bay
    The song of the sailors in glee.
So I think of the luminous footprints that bore
    The comfort o'er dark Galilee,
And wait for the signal to go to the shore,
    To the ship that is waiting for me.

Address.

(OPENING OF THE CALIFORNIA THEATRE, SAN FRANCISCO,
JANUARY 19, 1870).

Brief words, when actions wait, are well:
The prompter's hand is on his bell;
The coming heroes, lovers, kings,
Are idly lounging at the wings;
Behind the curtain's mystic fold
The glowing future lies unrolled,—
And yet, one moment for the Past;
One retrospect,—the first and last.

"The world's a stage," the Master said.
To-night a mightier truth is read:
Not in the shifting canvas screen,
The flash of gas or tinsel sheen;
Not in the skill whose signal calls
From empty boards baronial halls;
But, fronting sea and curving bay,
Behold the players and the play.

Ah, friends! beneath your real skies
The actor's short-lived triumph dies:
On that broad stage of empire won,
Whose footlights were the setting sun.

Whose flats a distant background rose
In trackless peaks of endless snows;
Here genius bows, and talent waits
To copy that but One creates.

Your shifting scenes: the league of sand,
An avenue by ocean spanned;
The narrow beach of straggling tents,
A mile of stately monuments;
Your standard, lo! a flag unfurled,
Whose clinging folds clasp half the world,—
This is your drama, built on facts,
With "twenty years between the acts."

One moment more: if here we raise
The oft-sung hymn of local praise,
Before the curtain facts must sway:
Here waits the moral of your play.
Glassed in the poet's thought, you view
What *money* can yet cannot do;
The faith that soars, the deeds that shine,
Above the gold that builds the shrine.

And oh! when others take our place,
And Earth's green curtain hides our face,
Ere on the stage, so silent now,
The last new hero makes his bow:
So may our deeds, recalled once more
In Memory's sweet but brief encore,
Down all the circling ages run,
With the world's plaudit of "Well done!"

Dolly Varden.

Dear 'Dolly! who does not recall
The thrilling page that pictured all
Those charms that held our sense in thrall.
   Just as the artist caught her—
As down that English lane she tripped,
In bowered chintz, hat sideways tipped,
Trim-bodiced, bright-eyed, roguish-lipped—
   The locksmith's pretty daughter?

Sweet fragment of the Master's art!
O simple faith! O rustic heart!
O maid that hath no counterpart
   In life's dry, dog-eared pages!
Where shall we find thy like? Ah, stay!
Methinks I saw her yesterday
In chintz that flowered, as one might say,
   Perennial for ages.

Her father's modest cot was stone,
Five stories high; in style and tone
Composite, and, I frankly own,
   Within its walls revealing
Some certain novel, strange ideas:
A Gothic door with Roman piers,
And floors removed some thousand years
   From their Pompeiian ceiling.

The small *salon* where she received
Was Louis Quatorze, and relieved
By Chinese cabinets, conceived
   Grotesquely by the heathen;
The sofas were a classic sight—
The Roman bench (*sedilia* hight);
The chairs were French in gold and white,
   And one Elizabethan.

And she, the goddess of that shrine,
Two ringed fingers placed in mine—
The stones were many carats fine,
   And of the purest water—
Then dropped a curtesy, far enough
To fairly fill her *cretonne* puff
And show the petticoat's rich stuff
   That her fond parent bought her.

Her speech was simple as her dress—
Not French the more, but English less,
She loved; yet sometimes, I confess,
   I scarce could comprehend her.
Her manners were quite far from shy:
There was a quiet in her eye
Appalling to the Hugh who'd try
   With rudeness to offend her.

"But whence," I cried, "this masquerade?
Some figure for to-night's charade—
A Watteau shepherdess or maid?"
   She smiled and begged my pardon:
"Why, surely you must know the name—
That woman who was Shakespeare's flame
Or Byron's—well, it's all the same:
   Why, Lord! I'm Dolly Varden!"

Telemachus versus Mentor.

Don't mind me, I beg you, old fellow,—I'll do very well here alone ;
You must not be kept from your "German" because I've dropped in like a stone :
Leave all ceremony behind you, leave all thought of aught but yourself;
And leave, if you like, the Madeira, and a dozen cigars on the shelf.

As for me, you will say to your hostess—well, I scarcely need give you a cue.
Chant my praise ! All will list to Apollo, though Mercury pipe to a few.
Say just what you please, my dear boy; there's more eloquence lies in youth's rash
Outspoken heart-impulse than ever growled under this grizzling mustache.

Go, don the dress coat of our tyrant—youth's panoplied armour for fight,
And tie the white neckcloth that rumples, like pleasure, and lasts but a night.
And pray the Nine Gods to avert you what time the Three Sisters shall frown,
And you'll lose your high-comedy figure, and sit more at ease in your gown

He's off! There's his foot on the staircase. By Jove what
    a bound! Really now
Did *I* ever leap like this springald, with Love's chaplet
    green on my brow?
Was *I* such an ass? No, I fancy. Indeed I remember
    quite plain
A gravity mixed with my transports, a cheerfulness softened
    my pain. '

He's gone! There's the slam of his cab door, there's the
    clatter of hoofs and the wheels;
And while he the light toe is tripping in this arm-chair I'll
    tilt up my heels.
He's gone, and for what? For a tremor from a waist like
    a teetotum spun;
For a rosebud that's crumpled by many before it is gathered
    by one.

Is there naught in the halo of youth but the glow of a
    passionate race—
'Midst the cheers and applause of a crowd—to the goal
    of a beautiful face?
A race that is not to the swift, a prize that no merits
    enforce,
But is won by some *fainéant* youth, who shall simply walk
    over the course?

Poor boy! shall I shock his conceit? When he talks of her
    cheek's loveliness,
Shall I say 'twas the air of the room, and was due to carbonic
    excess?

That when waltzing she drooped on his breast, and the
    veins of her eyelids grew dim,
'Twas oxygen's absence she felt, but never the presence of
    him?

Shall I tell him first love is a fraud, a weakling that's
    strangled in birth,
Recalled with perfunctory tears, but lost in unsanctified
    mirth?
Or shall I go bid him believe in all womankind's charm,
    and forget
In the light ringing laugh of the world the rattlesnake's gay
    castanet?

Shall I tear out a leaf from my heart, from that book that
    forever is shut
On the past? Shall I speak of my first love—Augusta—
    my Lalage? But
I forget. Was it really Augusta? No. 'Twas Lucy! No.
    Mary! No. Di!
Never mind! they were all first and faithless, and yet—I've
    forgotten just why.

No, no! Let him dream on and ever. Alas! he will
    waken too soon;
And it doesn't look well for October to always be preaching
    at June.
Poor boy! All his fond foolish trophies pinned yonder—a
    bow from *her* hair,
A few *billets-doux*, invitations, and—what's this? My name,
    I declare!

Humph! "You'll come, for I've got you a prize, with
   beauty and money no end;
You know her, I think; 'twas *on dit* she once was engaged
   to your friend;
But she says that's all over." Ah, is it? Sweet Ethel!
   incomparable maid!
Or—what if the thing were a trick?—this letter so freely
   displayed!—

My opportune presence! No! nonsense! Will nobody
   answer the bell?
Call a cab! Half past ten. Not too late yet. Oh,
   Ethel! Why don't you go! Well?
"Master said you would wait—" Hang your master!
   "Have I ever a message to send?"
Yes, tell him I've gone to the German to dance with the
   friend of his friend.

What the Wolf really said to Little Red Riding-Hood.

WONDERING maiden, so puzzled and fair,
Why dost thou murmur and ponder and stare?
"Why are my eyelids so open and wild?"—
Only the better to see with, my child!
Only the better and clearer to view
Cheeks that are rosy and eyes that are blue.

Dost thou still wonder, and ask why these arms
Fill thy soft bosom with tender alarms,
Swaying so wickedly?—are they misplaced
Clasping or shielding some delicate waist:
Hands whose coarse sinews may fill you with fear
Only the better protect you, my dear!

Little Red Riding-Hood, when in the street,
Why do I press your small hand when we meet?
Why, when you timidly offered your cheek,
Why did I sigh, and why didn't I speak?
Why, well: you see—if the truth must appear—
I'm not your grandmother, Riding-Hood, dear!

Half-an-Hour before Supper.

"So she's here, your unknown Dulcinea—the lady you met on the train—
And you really believe she would know you if you were to meet her again?"

"Of course," he replied, "she would know me; there never was womankind yet
Forgot the effect she inspired. She excuses, but does not forget."

"Then you told her your love?" asked the elder; the younger looked up with a smile:
"I sat by her side half an hour—what else was I doing the while?

"What, sit by the side of a woman as fair as the sun in the sky,
And look somewhere else lest the dazzle flash back from your own to her eye?

"No, I hold that the speech of the tongue be as frank and as bold as the look,
And I held up herself to herself,—that was more than she got from her book."

"Young blood!" laughed the elder; "no doubt you are
 voicing the mode of To-Day:
But then we old fogies at least gave the lady some chance
 for delay.

"There's my wife—(you must know)—we first met on the
 journey from Florence to Rome:
It took me three weeks to discover who was she and where
 was her home;

"Three more to be duly presented; three more ere I saw
 her again;
And a year ere my romance *began* where yours ended that
 day on the train."

"Oh, that was the style of the stage-coach; we travel to-day
 by express;
Forty miles to the hour," he answered, "won't admit of a
 passion that's less."

"But what if you make a mistake?" quoth the elder. The
 younger half sighed:
"What happens when signals are wrong or switches
 misplaced?" he replied.

"Very well, I must bow to your wisdom," the elder returned,
 "but submit
Your chances of winning this woman your boldness has
 bettered no whit.

"Why, you do not at best know her name. And what if I try your ideal
With something, if not quite so fair, at least more *en règle* and real?

"Let me find you a partner. Nay, come, I insist—you shall follow—this way.
My dear, will you not add your grace to entreat Mr. Rapid to stay?

"My wife, Mr. Rapid—Eh, what! Why, he's gone—yet he said he would come.
How rude! I don't wonder, my dear, you are properly crimson and dumb!"

What the Bullet Sang.

O joy of creation
        To be!
O rapture to fly
        And be free!
Be the battle lost or won,
Though its smoke shall hide the sun,
I shall find my love—the one
        Born for me!

I shall know him where he stands,
        All alone,
With the power in his hands
        Not o'erthrown;
I shall know him by his face,
By his god-like front and grace;
I shall hold him for a space,
        All my own!

It is he—O my love!
        So bold!
It is I—All thy love
        Foretold!
It is I. O love! what bliss!
Dost thou answer to my kiss?
O sweetheart! what is this
        Lieth there so cold?

PARODIES, ETC.

Before the Curtain.

BEHIND the footlights hangs the rusty baize,
A trifle shabby in the upturned blaze
Of flaring gas and curious eyes that gaze.

The stage, methinks, perhaps is none too wide,
And hardly fit for royal Richard's stride,
Or Falstaff's bulk, or Denmark's youthful pride.

Ah, well! no passion walks its humble boards;
O'er it no king nor valiant Hector lords:
The simplest skill is all its space affords.

The song and jest, the dance and trifling play,
The local hit at follies of the day,
The trick to pass an idle hour away,—

For these no trumpets that announce the Moor,
No blast that makes the hero's welcome sure,—
A single fiddle in the overture!

To the Pliocene Skull.

(A GEOLOGICAL ADDRESS.)

"Speak, O man, less recent! Fragmentary fossil!
Primal pioneer of pliocene formation,
Hid in lowest drifts below the earliest stratum
    Of volcanic tufa!

"Older than the beasts, the oldest Palæotherium;
Older than the trees, the oldest Cryptogami;
Older than the hills, those infantile eruptions
    Of earth's epidermis!

"Eo—Mio—Plio—whatsoe'er the 'cene' was
That those vacant sockets filled with awe and wonder,—
Whether shores Devonian or Silurian beaches,—
    Tell us thy strange story!

"Or has the professor slightly antedated
By some thousand years thy advent on this planet,
Giving thee an air that's somewhat better fitted
    For cold-blooded creatures?

"Wert thou true spectator of that mighty forest
When above thy head the stately Sigillaria
Reared its columned trunks in that remote and distant
    Carboniferous epoch?

To the Pliocene Skull.

"Tell us of that scene,—the dim and watery woodland,
Songless, silent, hushed, with never bird or insect,
Veiled with spreading fronds and screened with tall club-
    mosses,
    Lycopodiacea,—

"When beside thee walked the solemn Plesiosaurus,
And around thee crept the festive Ichthyosaurus,
While from time to time above thee flew and circled
    Cheerful Pterodactyls.

"Tell us of thy food,—those half-marine refections,
Crinoids on the shell and Brachipods *au natural*,—
Cuttlefish to which the *pieuvre* of Victor Hugo
    Seems a periwinkle.

"Speak, thou awful vestige of the earth's creation,—
Solitary fragment of remains organic!
Tell the wondrous secret of thy past existence,—
    Speak! thou oldest primate!"

Even as I gazed, a thrill of the maxilla,
And a lateral movement of the condyloid process,
With post-pliocene sounds of healthy mastication,
    Ground the teeth together.

And, from that imperfect dental exhibition,
Stained with express juices of the weed Nicotian,
Came these hollow accents, blent with softer murmurs
    Of expectoration:

"Which my name is Bowers, and my crust was busted
Falling down a shaft in Calaveras County,
But I'd take it kindly if you'd send the pieces
    Home to old Missouri!"

The Ballad of Mr. Cooke.

(A LEGEND OF THE CLIFF HOUSE, SAN FRANCISCO.)

WHERE the sturdy ocean breeze
Drives the spray of roaring seas,
That the Cliff-House balconies
    Overlook:
There, in spite of rain that balked,
With his sandals duly chalked,
Once upon a tight-rope walked
    Mr. Cooke.

But the jester's lightsome mien,
And his spangles and his sheen,
All had vanished when the scene
    He forsook.
Yet in some delusive hope,
In some vague desire to cope,
One still came to view the rope
    Walked by Cooke.

 • • • • • •

Amid Beauty's bright array,
On that strange eventful day,
Partly hidden from the spray,
    In a nook,

The Ballad of Mr. Cooke.

Stood Florinda Vere de Vere;
Who, with wind-dishevelled hair,
And a rapt, distracted air,
     Gazed on Cooke,

Then she turned, and quickly cried
To her lover at her side,
While her form with love and pride
     Wildly shook :
"Clifford Snook! oh, hear me now!
Here I break each plighted vow ;
There's but one to whom I bow,
     And that's Cooke!"

Haughtily that young man spoke :
"I descend from noble folk;
'Seven Oaks,' and then 'Se'nnoak,'
     Lastly Snook,
Is the way my name I trace.
Shall a youth of noble race
In affairs of love give place
     To a Cooke?"

"Clifford Snook, I know thy claim
To that lineage and name,
And I think I've read the same
     In Horne Tooke;
But I swear, by all divine,
Never, never, to be thine,
Till thou canst upon yon line
     Walk like Cooke."

Though to that gymnastic feat
He no closer might compete
Than to strike a *balance*-sheet
    In a book;
Yet thenceforward, from that day,
He his figure would display
In some wild athletic way,
    After Cooke.

On some household eminence,
On a clothes-line or a fence,
Over ditches, drains, and thence
    O'er a brook,
He, by high ambition led,
Ever walked and balancèd,
Till the people, wondering, said,
    "How like Cooke!"

Step by step did he proceed,
Nerved by valour, not by greed,
And at last the crowning deed
    Undertook.
Misty was the midnight air,
And the cliff was bleak and bare,
When he came to do and dare,
    Just like Cooke.

Through the darkness, o'er the flow,
Stretched the line where he should go,
Straight across as flies the crow
    Or the rook:

One wild glance around he cast;
Then he faced the ocean blast,
And he strode the cable last
              Touched by Cooke.

Vainly roared the angry seas,
Vainly blew the ocean breeze;
But, alas! the walker's knees
              Had a crook;
And before he reached the rock
Did they both together knock,
And he stumbled with a shock—
              Unlike Cooke!

Downward dropping in the dark,
Like an arrow to its mark,
Or a fish-pole when a shark
              Bites the hook,
Dropped the pole he could not save,
Dropped the walker, and the wave
Swift engulfed the rival brave
              Of J. Cooke!

Came a roar across the sea
Of sea-lions in their glee,
In a tongue remarkably
              Like Chinook;
And the maddened sea-gull seemed
Still to utter, as he screamed,
"Perish thus the wretch who deemed
              Himself Cooke!"

But on misty moon-lit nights
Comes a skeleton in tights,
Walks once more the giddy heights
     He mistook;
And, unseen to mortal eyes,
Purged of grosser earthly ties
Now at last in spirit guise
     Outdoes Cooke.

 . . . . . .

Still the sturdy ocean breeze
Sweeps the spray of roaring seas,
Where the Cliff-house balconies
     Overlook;
And the maidens in their prime,
Reading of this mournful rhyme,
Weep where, in the olden time,
     Walked J. Cooke.

The Ballad of the Emeu.

O SAY, have you seen at the Willows so green,—
  So charming and rurally true,—
A singular bird, with a manner absurd,
  Which they call the Australian Emeu?
               Have you
  Ever seen this Australian Emeu?

It trots all around with its head on the ground,
  Or erects it quite out of your view;
And the ladies all cry, when its figure they spy,
  "Oh! what a sweet pretty Emeu!
               Oh! do
  Just look at that lovely Emeu!"

One day to this spot, when the weather was hot,
  Came Matilda Hortense Fortescue;
And beside her there came a youth of high name,—
  Augustus Florell Montague:
               The two
  Both loved that wild, foreign Emeu.

With two loaves of bread then they fed it, instead
  Of the flesh of the white cockatoo,

Which once was its food in that wild neighbourhood
  Where ranges the sweet Kangaroo,
                   That too
  Is game for the famous Emeu!

Old saws and gimlets but its appetite whets,
  Like the world-famous bark of Peru;
There's nothing so hard that the bird will discard,
  And nothing its taste will eschew,
                   That you
  Can give that long-legged Emeu!

The time slipped away in this innocent play
  When up jumped the bold Montague:
"Where's that specimen pin that I gayly did win
  In raffle, and gave unto you,
                   Fortescue?"
  No word spoke the guilty Emeu!

"Quick! tell me his name whom thou gavest that same,
  Ere these hands in thy blood I embrue!"
"Nay, dearest," she cried, as she clung to his side,
  "I'm innocent as that Emeu!"
                   "Adieu!"
He replied, "Miss M. H. Fortescue!"

Down she dropped at his feet, all as white as a sheet,
  As wildly he fled from her view;
He thought 'twas her sin,—for he knew not the pin
  Had been gobbled up by the Emeu;
                   All through
  The voracity of that Emeu!

Mrs. Judge Jenkins.

(BEING THE ONLY GENUINE SEQUEL TO "MAUD MÜLLER.")

Maud Müller all that summer day
Raked the meadow sweet with hay;

Yet, looking down the distant lane,
She hoped the Judge would come again.

But when he came, with smile and bow,
Maud only blushed, and stammered, "Ha-ow?"

And spoke of her "pa," and wondered whether
He'd give consent they should wed together.

Old Müller burst in tears, and then
Begged that the Judge would lend him "ten;"

For trade was dull, and wages low,
And the "craps," this year, were somewhat slow.

And ere the languid summer died,
Sweet Maud became the Judge's bride.

But, on the day that they were mated,
Maud's brother Bob was intoxicated;

And Maud's relations, twelve in all,
Were very drunk at the Judge's hall.

And when the summer came again,
The young bride bore him babies twain;

And the Judge was blest, but thought it strange
That bearing children made such a change.

For Maud grew broad and red and stout,
And the waist that his arm once clasped about.

Was more than he now could span; and he
Sighed as he pondered, ruefully,

How that which in Maud was native grace
In Mrs. Jenkins was out of place;

And thought of the twins, and wished that they
Looked less like the man who raked the hay

On Müller's farm, and dreamed with pain
Of the day he wandered down the lane.

And, looking down that dreary track,
He half regretted that he came back.

For, had he waited, he might have wed
Some maiden fair and thoroughbred;

For there be women fair as she,
Whose verbs and nouns do more agree.

Alas for maiden! alas for judge!
And the sentimental,—that's one-half "fudge;"

For Maud soon thought the Judge a bore,
With all his learning and all his lore;

And the Judge would have bartered Maud's fair face
For more refinement and social grace.

If, of all words of tongue and pen,
The saddest are, "It might have been,"

More sad are these we daily see:
"It is, but hadn't ought to be."

A Geological Madrigal.

I HAVE found out a gift for my fair;
  I know where the fossils abound,
Where the footprints of *Aves* declare
  The birds that once walked on the ground;
Oh, come, and—in technical speech—
  We'll walk this Devonian shore,
Or on some Silurian beach
  We'll wander, my love, evermore.

I will show thee the sinuous track
  By the slow-moving annelid made,
Or the Trilobite that, farther back,
  In the old Potsdam sandstone was laid;
Thou shalt see, in his Jurassic tomb,
  The Plesiosaurus embalmed;
In his Oolitic prime and his bloom,
  Iguanodon safe and unharmed!

You wished—I remember it well,
  And I loved you the more for that wish—
For a perfect cystedian shell
  And a *whole* holocephalic fish.
And oh, if Earth's strata contains
  In its lowest Silurian drift,
Or palæozoic remains
  The same,—'tis your lover's free gift!

A Geological Madrigal.

Then come, love, and never say nay,
    But calm all your maidenly fears;
We'll note, love, in one summer's day
    The record of millions of years;
And though the Darwinian plan
    Your sensitive feelings may shock,
We'll find the beginning of man,—
    Our fossil ancestors, in rock!

Avitor.

(AN AËRIAL RETROSPECT.)

WHAT was it filled my youthful dreams,
In place of Greek or Latin themes,
Or beauty's wild, bewildering beams?
      Avitor!

What visions and celestial scenes
I filled with aerial machines,
Montgolfier's and Mr. Green's!
      Avitor!

What fairy tales seemed things of course!
The roc that brought Sindbad across,
The Calendar's own wingèd-horse!
      Avitor!

How many things I took for facts,—
Icarus and his conduct lax,
And how he sealed his fate with wax!
      Avitor!

The first balloons I sought to sail,
Soap-bubbles fair, but all too frail,
Or kites,—but thereby hangs a tail.
      Avitor!

Avitor.

What made me launch from attic tall
A kitten and a parasol,
And watch their bitter, frightful fall?
      Avitor!

What youthful dreams of high renown
Bade me inflate the parson's gown,
That went not up, nor yet came down?
      Avitor!

My first ascent I may not tell;
Enough to know that in that well
My first high aspirations fell.
      Avitor!

My other failures let me pass:
The dire explosions, and, alas!
The friends I choked with noxious gas.
      Avitor!

For lo! I see perfected rise
The vision of my boyish eyes,
The messenger of upper skies.
      Avitor!

The Willows.

(AFTER EDGAR ALLAN POE.)

The skies they were ashen and sober,
   The streets they were dirty and drear;
It was night in the month of October,
   Of my most immemorial year.
Like the skies, I was perfectly sober,
   As I stopped at the mansion of Shear,—
At the Nightingale,—perfectly sober,
   And the willowy woodland down here.

Here, once in an alley Titanic
   Of Ten-pins,—I roamed with my soul,—
   Of Ten-pins,—with Mary, my soul;
They were days when my heart was volcanic,
   And impelled me to frequently roll,
   And made me resistlessly roll,
Till my ten-strikes created a panic
   In the realms of the Boreal pole,
Till my ten-strikes created a panic
   With the monkey atop of his pole.

I repeat, I was perfectly sober,
   But my thoughts they were palsied and sear,—
   My thoughts were decidedly queer;
For I knew not the month was October,

And I marked not the night of the year;
I forgot that sweet *morceau* of Auber
　　That the band oft performèd down here,
And I mixed the sweet music of Auber
　　With the Nightingale's music by Shear.

And now as the night was senescent,
　　And star-dials pointed to morn,
　　And car-drivers hinted of morn,
At the end of the path a liquescent
　　And bibulous lustre was born ;
'Twas made by the bar-keeper present,
　　Who mixèd a duplicate horn,—
His two hands describing a crescent
　　Distinct with a duplicate horn.

And I said : " This looks perfectly regal,
　　For it's warm, and I know I feel dry,
　　I am confident that I feel dry ;
We have come past the emeu and eagle,
　　And watched the gay monkey on high ;
Let us drink to the emeu and eagle,—
　　To the swan and the monkey on high,
　　To the eagle and monkey on high ;
For this bar-keeper will not inveigle,—
　　Bully boy with the vitreous eye ;
He surely would never inveigle,—
　　Sweet youth with the crystalline eye."

But Mary, uplifting her finger,
　　Said, "Sadly this bar I mistrust,—
　　I fear that this bar does not trust.
Oh, hasten ! oh, let us not linger
　　Oh, fly,—let us fly,—ere we must !"

In terror she cried, letting sink her
    Parasol till it trailed in the dust,—
In agony sobbed, letting sink her
    Parasol till it trailed in the dust,—
    Till it sorrowfully trailed in the dust.

Then I pacified Mary and kissed her,
    And tempted her into the room,
    And conquered her scruples and gloom;
And we passed to the end of the vista,
    But were stopped by the warning of doom,—
    By some words that were warning of doom.
And I said, "What is written, sweet sister,
    At the opposite end of the room?"
She sobbed, as she answered, "All liquors
    Must be paid for ere leaving the room."

Then my heart it grew ashen and sober,
    As the streets were deserted and ear,—
    For my pockets were empty and drear;
And I cried, "It was surely October,
    On this very night of last year,
    That I journeyed—I journeyed down here,—
    That I brought a fair maiden down here,
    On this night of all nights in the year.
    Ah! to me that inscription is clear;
Well I know now, I'm perfectly sober,
    Why no longer they credit me here,—
Well I know now that music of Auber,
    And this Nightingale, kept by one Shear.

North Beach.

(AFTER SPENSER.)

Lo! where the castle of bold Pfeiffer throws
Its sullen shadow on the rolling tide,—
No more the home where joy and wealth repose,
But now where wassailers in cells abide;
See yon long quay that stretches far and wide,
Well known to citizens as wharf of Meiggs;
There each sweet Sabbath walks in maiden pride
Then pensive Margaret, and brave Pat, whose legs
Encased in broadcloth oft keep time with Peg's.

Here cometh oft the tender nursery-maid,
While in her ear her love his tale doth pour;
Meantime her infant doth her charge evade,
And rambleth sagely on the sandy shore,
Till the sly sea-crab, low in ambush laid,
Seizeth his leg and biteth him full sore.
Ah me! what sounds the shuddering echoes bore
When his small treble mixed with Ocean's roar.

Hard by there stands an ancient hostelrie,
And at its side a garden, where the bear,
The stealthy catamount, and coon agree
To work deceit on all who gather there;
And when Augusta—that unconscious fair—
With nuts and apples plieth Bruin free,
Lo! the green parrot claweth her back hair,
And the grey monkey grabbeth fruits that she
On her gay bonnet wears, and laugheth loud in glee!

The Lost Tails of Miletus.

High on the Thracian hills, half hid in the billows of clover,
Thyme, and the asphodel blooms, and lulled by Pactolian streamlet,
She of Miletus lay, and beside her an aged satyr
Scratched his ear with his hoof, and playfully mumbled his chestnuts.

Vainly the Mænid and the Bassarid gambolled about her,
The free-eyed Bacchante sang, and Pan—the renowned, the accomplished—
Executed his difficult solo. In vain were their gambols and dances:
High o'er the Thracian hills rose the voice of the shepherdess, wailing.

"Ai! for the fleecy flocks,—the meek-nosed, the passionless faces;
Ai! for the tallow-scented, the straight-tailed, the high-stepping;
Ai! for the timid glance, which is that which the rustic, sagacious,
Applies to him who loves but may not declare his passion!"

Her then Zeus answered slow: "O daughter of song and sorrow,—
Hapless tender of sheep,—arise from thy long lamentation!
Since thou canst not trust fate, nor behave as becomes a Greek maiden,
Look and behold thy sheep."—And lo! they returned to her tailless!

The Ritualist.

BY A COMMUNICANT OF "ST. JAMES'S."

He wore, I think, a chasuble, the day when first we met;
A stole and snowy alb likewise: I recollect it yet.
He called me "daughter," as he raised his jewelled hand to bless;
And then, in thrilling undertones, he asked, "Would I confess?"

O mother dear! blame not your child, if then on bended knees
I dropped, and thought of Abélard, and also Eloise;
Or when, beside the altar high, he bowed before the pyx,
I envied that seraphic kiss he gave the crucifix.

The cruel world may think it wrong, perhaps may deem me weak,
And, speaking of that sainted man, may call his conduct "cheek;"
And, like that wicked barrister whom Cousin Harry quotes,
May term his mixèd chalice "grog," his vestments "petticoats:"

But, whatsoe'er they do or say, I'll build a Christian's hope
On incense and on altar-lights, on chasuble and cope.
Let others prove, by precedent, the faith that they profess:
"His can't be wrong" that's symbolised by such becoming dress.

A Moral Vindicator.

If Mr. Jones, Lycurgus B.,
Had one peculiar quality,
'Twas his severe advocacy
Of conjugal fidelity.

His views of heaven were very free;
His views of life were painfully
Ridiculous; but fervently
He dwelt on marriage sanctity.

He frequently went on a spree;
But in his wildest revelry,
On this especial subject he
Betrayed no ambiguity.

And though at times Lycurgus B.
Did lay his hands not lovingly
Upon his wife, the sanctity
Of wedlock was his guaranty.

But Mrs. Jones declined to see
Affairs in the same light as he,
And quietly got a decree
Divorcing her from that L. B.

And what did Jones, Lycurgus B.,
With his known idiosyncrasy?
He smiled,—a bitter smile to see,—
And drew the weapon of Bowie.

He did what Sickles did to Key,—
What Cole on Hiscock wrought, did he;
In fact, on persons twenty-three
He proved the marriage sanctity.

The counsellor who took the fee,
The witnesses and referee,
The Judge who granted the decree,
Died in that wholesale butchery.

And then when Jones, Lycurgus B.,
Had wiped the weapon of Bowie,
Twelve jurymen did instantly
Acquit and set Lycurgus free.

California Madrigal.

(ON THE APPROACH OF SPRING.)

OH come, my beloved! from thy winter abode,
From thy home on the Yuba, thy ranch overflowed:
For the waters have fallen, the winter has fled,
And the river once more has returned to its bed.

Oh, mark how the spring in its beauty is near!
How the fences and tules once more reappear!
How soft lies the mud on the banks of yon slough
By the hole in the levee the waters broke through!

All nature, dear Chloris, is blooming to greet
The glance of your eye and the tread of your feet;
For the trails are all open, the roads are all free,
And the highwayman's whistle is heard on the lea.

Again swings the lash on the high mountain trail,
And the pipe of the packer is scenting the gale;
The oath and the jest ringing high o'er the plain,
Where the smut is not always confined to the grain.

Once more glares the sunlight on awning and roof,
Once more the red clay's pulverised by the hoof,

Once more the dust powders the "outsides" with red,
Once more at the station the whisky is spread.

Then fly with me, love, ere the summer's begun,
And the mercury mounts to one hundred and one;
Ere the grass now so green shall be withered and sear,
In the spring that obtains but one month in the year.

What the Engines Said.

(OPENING OF THE PACIFIC RAILROAD.)

WHAT was it the Engines said,
Pilots touching,—head to head
Facing on the single track,
Half a world behind each back?
This is what the Engines said,
Unreported and unread.

With a prefatory screech,
In a florid Western speech,
Said the Engine from the WEST:
"I am from Sierra's crest;
And, if altitude's a test,
Why, I reckon, it's confessed
That I've done my level best."

Said the Engine from the EAST:
"They who work best talk the least.
S'pose you whistle down your brakes;
What you've done is no great shakes,—
Pretty fair,—but let our meeting
Be a different kind of greeting.

Let these folks with champagne stuffing,
Not their Engines, do the *puffing*.
Listen! Where Atlantic beats
Shores of snow and summer heats;
Where the Indian autumn skies
Paint the woods with wampum dyes,—
I have chased the flying sun,
Seeing all he looked upon,
Blessing all that he has blest,
Nursing in my iron breast
All his vivifying heat,
All his clouds about my crest;
And before my flying feet
Every shadow must retreat."

Said the Western Engine, "Phew!"
And a long low whistle blew.
"Come now, really that's the oddest
Talk for one so very modest.
You brag of your East! *You* do?
Why, *I* bring the East to *you!*
All the Orient, all Cathay,
Find through me the shortest way;
And the sun you follow here
Rises in my hemisphere.
Really,—if one must be rude,—
Length, my friend, ain't longitude."

Said the Union, "Don't reflect, or
I'll run over some Director."
Said the Central, "I'm Pacific;
But, when riled, I'm quite terrific.
Yet to-day we shall not quarrel,
Just to show these folks this moral,

How two Engines—in their vision—
Once have met without collision."
That is what the Engines said,
Unreported and unread;
Spoken slightly through the nose,
With a whistle at the close.

The Legends of the Rhine.

Beetling walls with ivy grown,
Frowning heights of mossy stone;
Turret, with its flaunting flag
Flung from battlemented crag;
Dungeon-keep and fortalice
Looking down a precipice
O'er the darkly glancing wave
By the Lurline-haunted cave;
Robber haunt and maiden bower,
Home of Love and Crime and Power,—
That's the scenery, in fine,
Of the Legends of the Rhine.

One bold baron, double-dyed
Bigamist and parricide,
And, as most the stories run,
Partner of the Evil One;
Injured innocence in white,
Fair but idiotic quite,
Wringing of her lily hands;
Valour fresh from Paynim lands,
Abbot ruddy, hermit pale,
Minstrel fraught with many a tale,—
Are the actors that combine
In the Legends of the Rhine.

Bell-mouthed flagons round a board;
Suits of armour, shield, and sword;
Kerchief with its bloody stain;
Ghosts of the untimely slain;
Thunder-clap and clanking chain;
Headsman's block and shining axe;
Thumb-screw, crucifixes, racks;
Midnight-tolling chapel bell,
Heard across the gloomy fell,—
These and other pleasant facts
Are the properties that shine
In the Legends of the Rhine.

Maledictions, whispered vows
Underneath the linden boughs;
Murder, bigamy, and theft;
Travellers of goods bereft;
Rapine, pillage, arson, spoil,—
Everything but honest toil,
Are the deeds that best define
Every Legend of the Rhine.

That Virtue always meets reward,
But quicker when it wears a sword;
That Providence has special care
Of gallant knight and lady fair;
That villains, as a thing of course,
Are always haunted by remorse,—
Is the moral, I opine,
Of the Legends of the Rhine.

Songs without Sense,

FOR THE PARLOUR AND PIANO.

I.—THE PERSONIFIED SENTIMENTAL.

Affection's charm no longer gilds
    The idol of the shrine;
But cold Oblivion seeks to fill
    Regret's ambrosial wine.
Though Friendship's offering buried lies
    'Neath cold Aversions snow,
Regard and Faith will ever bloom
    Perpetually below.

I see thee whirl in marble halls,
    In Pleasure's giddy train;
Remorse is never on that brow,
    Nor Sorrow's mark of pain.
Deceit has marked thee for her own;
    Inconstancy the same;
And Ruin wildly sheds its gleam
    Athwart thy path of shame.

II.—THE HOMELY PATHETIC.

The dews are heavy on my brow;
    My breath comes hard and low;
Yet, mother dear, grant one request,
    Before your boy must go.
Oh! lift me ere my spirit sinks,
    And ere my senses fail:

Place me once more, O mother dear!
   Astride the old fence-rail.

The old fence-rail, the old fence-rail!
   How oft these youthful legs,
With Alice' and Ben Bolt's, were hung
   Across those wooden pegs.
'Twas there the nauseating smoke
   Of my first pipe arose:
O mother dear! these agonies
   Are far less keen than those.

I know where lies the hazel dell,
   Where simple Nellie sleeps;
I know the cot of Nettie Moore,
   And where the willow weeps.
I know the brook side and the mill,
   But all their pathos fails
Beside the days when once I sat
   Astride the old fence-rails.

III.—SWISS AIR.

I'M a gay tra, la, la,
With my fal, lal, la, la,
And my bright—
And my light—
   Tra, la, le.   [Repeat.]

Then laugh, ha, ha, ha,
And ring, ting, ling, ling,
And sing fal, la, la,
   La, la, le.   [Repeat.]

LITTLE POSTERITY.

Master Johnny's Next=Door Neighbour.

It was spring the first time that I saw her, for her papa and mamma moved in
Next door, just as skating was over, and marbles about to begin,
For the fence in our back-yard was broken, and I saw as I peeped through the slat,
There were " Johnny Jump-ups " all around her, and I knew it was spring just by that.

I never knew whether she saw me—for she didn't say nothing to me,
But " Ma! here's a slat in the fence broke, and the boy that is next door can see."
But the next day I climbed on our wood-shed, as you know mamma says I've a right,
And she calls out, " Well, peekin is manners!" and I answered her, " Sass is perlite!"

But I wasn't a bit mad, no, Papa, and to prove it, the very next day,
When she ran past our fence in the morning I happened to get in her way,

For you know I am "chunkèd" and clumsy, as she says
  are all boys of my size,
And she nearly upset me, she did, Pa, and laughed till tears
  came in her eyes.

And then we were friends from that moment, for I knew
  that she told Kitty Sage,
And she wasn't a girl that would flatter, "that she thought
  I was tall for my age."
And I gave her four apples that evening, and took her to
  ride on my sled,
And—"What am I telling you this for?" Why, Papa, my
  neighbour is *dead!*

You don't hear one-half I am saying—I really do think
  it's too bad!
Why, you might have seen crape on her door-knob, and
  noticed to-day I've been sad.
And they've got her a coffin of rosewood, and they say they
  have dressed her in white,
And I've never once looked through the fence, Pa, since
  she died—at eleven last night.

And Ma says it's decent and proper, as I was her neigh
  bour and friend,
That I should go there to the funeral, and she thinks that
  you ought to attend;
But I am so clumsy and awkward, I know I shall be in the
  way,
And suppose they should speak to me, Papa, I wouldn't
  know just what to say.

So I think I will get up quite early, I know I sleep late, but I know
I'll be sure to wake up if our Bridget pulls the string that I'll tie to my toe ;
And I'll crawl through the fence and I'll gather the "Johnny Jump-ups" as they grew
Round her feet the first day that I saw her, and, Papa, I'll give them to you.

For you're a big man, and you know, Pa, can come and go just where you choose,
And you'll take the flowers into her, and surely they'll never refuse ;
But, Papa, don't *say* they're from Johnny ; *they* won't understand, don't you see ?
But just lay them down on her bosom, and, Papa, *she'll* know they're from Me.

Miss Edith's Modest Request.

My papa knows you, and he says you're a man who makes
    reading for books;
But I never read nothing you wrote, nor did papa—I know
    by his looks.
So I guess you're like me when I talk, and I talk, and I
    talk all the day,
And they only say: "Do stop that child!" or, "Nurse, take
    Miss Edith away."

But papa said if I was good I could ask you—alone by
    myself—
If you wouldn't write me a book like that little one up on
    the shelf.
I don't mean the pictures, of course, for to make *them*
    you've got to be smart;
But the reading that runs all around them, you know—
    just the easiest part.

You needn't mind what it's about, for no one will see it but
    me
And Jane—that's my nurse—and John—he's the coach-
    man—just only us three.
You're to write of a bad little girl, that was wicked and
    bold and all that;
And then you are to write, if you please, something good
    —very good—of a cat!

Miss Edith's Modest Request.

This cat she was virtuous and meek, and kind to her parents
 and mild,
And careful and neat in her ways, though her mistress was
 such a bad child;
And hours she would sit and would gaze when her mistress
 —that's me—was so bad,
And blink, just as if she would say: "O Edith! you make
 my heart sad."

And yet, you would scarcely believe it, that beautiful angelic
 cat
Was blamed by the servants for stealing whatever, they said,
 she'd get at.
And when John drank my milk—don't you tell me!—I
 know just the way it was done—
They said 'twas the cat—and she sitting and washing her
 face in the sun!

And then there was Dick, my canary. When I left its cage
 open one day,
They all made believe that she ate it, though I know that
 the bird flew away.
And why? Just because she was playing with a feather
 she found on the floor,
As if cats couldn't play with a feather without people thinking 'twas more.

Why, once we were romping together, when I knocked down
 a vase from the shelf,
That cat was as grieved and distressed as if she had done it
 herself;

And she walked away sadly and hid herself, and never came
    out until tea—
So they say, for they sent *me* to bed, and she never came
    even to me.

No matter whatever happened, it was laid at the door of
    that cat.
Why, once when I tore my apron—she was wrapped in it,
    and I called " Rat !"—
Why, they blamed that on *her*. I shall never—no, not to
    my dying day—
Forget the pained look that she gave me when they slapped
    me and took me away.

Of course, you know just what comes next, when a child is
    as lovely as that :
She wasted quite slowly away—it was goodness was killing
    that cat.
I know it was nothing she ate, for her taste was exceedingly
    nice ;
But they said she stole Bobby's ice cream, and caught a bad
    cold from the ice.

And you'll promise to make me a book like that little one
    up on the shelf,
And you'll call her " Naomi," because it's a name that she
    just gave herself;
For she'd scratch at my door in the morning, and whenever I'd call out, " Who's there ?"
She would answer, "Naomi ! Naomi !" like a Christian I
    vow and declare.

And you'll put me and her in a book. And, mind, you're
    to say I was bad;
And I might have been badder than that but for the
    example I had.
And you'll say that she was a Maltese, and—what's that
    you asked? "Is she dead?"
Why, please, sir, *there ain't any cat!* You're to make one
    up out of your head!

Miss Edith makes it Pleasant for Brother Jack.

"CRYING!" of course I am crying, and I guess you would be crying too
If people were telling such stories as they tell about me, about *you*.
Oh yes, you can laugh, if you want to, and smoke as you didn't care how,
And get your brains softened like uncle's.—Dr. Jones says you're gettin' it now.

Why don't you say "stop!" to Miss Ilsey? she cries twice as much as I do,
And she's older and cries just from meanness—for a ribbon or anything new.
Ma says it's her "sensitive nature." Oh my! No. I shan't stop my talk!
And I don't want no apples nor candy, and I don't want to go take a walk!

I know why you're mad? Yes, I do, now! You think that Miss Ilsey likes *you*,
And I've heard her *repeatedly* call you the bold-facest boy that she knew;
And she'd "like to know where you learnt manners." Oh yes! Kick the table—that's right!
Spill the ink on my dress, and go then round telling Ma that I look like a fright!

What stories?   Pretend you don't know that they're
    saying I broke off the match
'Twixt old Money-grubber and Mary, by saying she called
    him "Crosspatch!"
When the only allusion I made him about sister Mary was
    she
Cared more for his cash than his temper, and you know,
    Jack, *you* said that to me.

And it's true!   But it's *me*, and I'm scolded, and Pa says if
    I keep on I might
By and by get my name in the papers!   Who cares?   Why,
    'twas only last night
I was reading how Pa and the sheriff were selling some lots,
    and it's plain
If it's awful to be in the papers why Papa would go and
    complain.

You think it ain't true about Ilsey?   Well, I guess I know
    girls—and I say
There's nothing I see about Ilsey to show she likes you
    anyway!
I know what it means when a girl who has called her cat
    after one boy
Goes and changes its name to another's.   And she's done
    it—and I wish you joy!

Miss Edith makes Another Friend.

OH, you're the girl lives on the corner? Come in—if you
    want to—come quick!
There's no one but me in the house and the cook—but she's
    only a stick.
Don't try the front way but come over the fence—through
    the window—that's how.
Don't mind the big dog—he won't bite you—just see him
    obey me! there now!

What's your name, "Mary Ellen?" How funny, mine's
    Edith—it's nicer, you see,
But yours does for you, for you're plainer, though maybe
    you're gooder than me,
For Jack says I'm sometimes a devil, but Jack, of all folks,
    needn't talk,
For I don't call the seamstress an angel 'til Ma says the
    poor thing must "walk."

Come in! It's quite dark in the parlour, for sister will
    keep the blinds down,
For you know her complexion is sallow like yours, but she
    isn't as brown;
Though Jack says that isn't the reason she likes to sit here
    with Jim Moore.
Do you think that he meant that she kissed him? Would
    you—if your lips wasn't sore?

If you like, you can try our piano. 'Taint ours. A man
    left it here
To rent by the month, although Ma says he hasn't been
    paid for a year.
Sister plays—oh, such fine variations!—why, I once heard
    a gentleman say
That she didn't mind *that* for the music—in fact, it was just
    in her way!

Ain't I funny? And yet it's the queerest of all, that what-
    ever I say,
One-half of the folks die a-laughing, and the rest they all
    look t'other way.
And some say, "That child!" Do they ever say that to such
    people as you?
Though maybe you're naturally silly, and that makes your
    eyes so askew.

Now stop—don't you dare to be crying! Just as sure as
    you live, if you do,
I'll call in my big dog to bite you, and I'll make my Papa
    kill you too!
And then where'll you be? So play pretty. There's my
    doll, and a nice piece of cake.
You don't want it—you think it is poison! Then *I'll* eat
    it, dear, just for your sake!

On the Landing.

(AN IDYL OF THE BALUSTERS.)

BOBBY, *ætat.* 3½.   JOHNNY, *ætat.* 4½.

BOBBY.

Do you know why they've put us in that back room,
Up in the attic, close against the sky,
And made believe our nursery's a cloak-room?
    Do you know why?

JOHNNY.

No more I don't, nor why that Sammy's mother
What Ma thinks horrid, 'cause he bunged my eye,
Eats an ice cream, down there, like any other—
    No more don't I!

BOBBY.

Do you know why Nurse says it isn't manners
For you and me to ask folks twice for pie,
And no one hits that man with two bananas?
    Do you know why?

JOHNNY.

No more I don't, nor why that girl, whose dress is
Off of her shoulders, don't catch cold and die,
When you and me gets croup when *we* undresses!
    No more don't I!

BOBBY.

Perhaps she ain't as good as you and I is,
And God don't want her up there in the sky,
And lets her live—to come in just when pie is—
        Perhaps that's why?

JOHNNY.

Do you know why that man that's got a cropped head
Rubbed it just now as if he felt a fly?
Could it be, Bobby, something that I dropped?
        And is that why?

BOBBY.

Good boys behaves, and so they don't get scolded,
Nor drop hot milk on folks as they pass by.

JOHNNY [*piously*].

Marbles would bounce on Mr. Jones' bald head—
        But *I* shan't try!

BOBBY.

Do you know why Aunt Jane is always snarling
At you and me because we tells a lie,
And she don't slap that man that called her darling?
        Do you know why?

JOHNNY.

No more I don't, nor why that man with Mamma
Just kissed her hand.

BOBBY.

She hurt it—and that's why,
He made it well, the very way that Mamma
Does do to I.

JOHNNY.

I feel so sleepy. . . . Was that Papa kissed us?
What made him sigh, and look up to the sky?

BOBBY.

We wer'n't downstairs, and he and God had missed us,
And that was why!

DRAMA.

TWO MEN OF SANDY BAR.

Dramatis Personæ.

"SANDY"	Son of Alexander Morton, sen.	*The Prodigals.*
JOHN OAKHURST	His former partner, personating the prodigal son, Sandy.	
COL. STARBOTTLE	Alexander Morton, sen.'s legal adviser.	
OLD MORTON	Alexander Morton, sen.	
DON JOSÉ	Father of Jovita Castro.	
CAPPER	A detective.	
CONCHO	Major-domo of Don José's rancho.	
YORK	An old friend of Oakhurst.	
PRITCHARD	An Australian convict.	
SOAPY / SILKY	His pals.	
JACKSON	Confidential clerk of Alexander Morton, jun., and confederate of Pritchard.	
HOP SING	A Chinese laundryman.	

SERVANT of Alexander Morton, sen.—POLICEMEN.

MISS MARY MORRIS	The schoolmistress of Red Gulch, in love with Sandy, and cousin of Alexander Morton, sen.
DOÑA JOVITA CASTRO	In love with John Oakhurst, and daughter of Don José.
THE DUCHESS	Wife of Pritchard, illegally married to Sandy, and former "flame" of John Oakhurst.
MANUELA	Servant of Castro, and maid to Doña Jovita.

ACT I.
THE RANCHO OF THE BLESSED INNOCENTS, AND HOUSE OF DON JOSÉ CASTRO.

ACT II.
RED GULCH.

ACT III.
THE BANKING-HOUSE OF MORTON & SON, SAN FRANCISCO.

ACT IV.
THE VILLA OF ALEXANDER MORTON, SEN., SAN FRANCISCO.

COSTUMES.

ALEXANDER MORTON ("Sandy").—First dress: Mexican *vaquero:* black velvet trousers open from knee, over white trousers; laced black velvet jacket, and broad white *sombrero:* large silver spurs. Second dress: miner's white duck jumper, and white duck trousers; (sailor's) straw hat. Third dress: fashionable morning costume. Fourth dress: full evening dress.

JOHN OAKHURST.—First dress: riding-dress, black, elegantly fitting. Second and third dress: fashionable. Fourth dress: full evening dress.

COL. STARBOTTLE.—First dress: blue double-breasted frock, and white "strapped" trousers; white hat. Second dress: same coat, blue trousers, and black broad-brimmed felt hat; cane, *semper;* ruffles, *semper.* Third dress: the same. Fourth dress: the same, with pumps.

YORK.—Fashionable morning dress.

JACKSON.—Business suit.

CONCHO.—First dress: *vaquero's* dress. Second dress: citizen's dress.

HOP SING.—Dress of Chinese coolie: dark-blue blouse, and dark-blue drawers gathered at ankles; straw conical hat, and wooden *sabots.*

DON JOSÉ.—First dress: *serapé,* black, with gold embroidery. Second dress: fashionable black suit, with broad-brimmed black stiff *sombrero.*

OLD MORTON.—First, second, third, and fourth dress: black, stiff, with white cravat.

CAPPER.—Ordinary dress of period.

MISS MARY.—First dress: tasteful calico morning dress. Second and third dress: lady's walking-costume—fashionable. Fourth dress: full dress.

DOÑA JOVITA.—First dress: handsome Spanish dress, with *manta.* Second dress: more elaborate, same quality.

THE DUCHESS.—First dress: elaborate but extravagant fashionable costume. Second dress: travelling dress.

MANUELA.—The *saya y manta;* white waist, and white or black skirt, with flowers.

Two Men of Sandy Bar.

ACT I.

SCENE I.—*Courtyard and Corridors of the Rancho.*

Manuela [*arranging supper-table in corridor*, L., *solus*]. There! Tortillas, chocolate, olives, and—the whisky of the Americans! And supper's ready. But why Don José chooses to-night, of all nights, with this heretic fog lying over the Mission Hills like a wet *serapé*, to take his supper out here, the saints only know. Perhaps it's some distrust of his madcap daughter, the Doña Jovita; perhaps to watch her—who knows? And now to find Diego. Ah, here he comes. So! The old story. He is getting Doña Jovita's horse ready for another madcap journey. Ah! [*Retires to table.*]

Enter cautiously from corridor, L., Sandy Morton, *carrying lady's saddle and blanket; starts on observing* Manuela, *and hastily hides saddle and blanket in recess.*

Sandy [*aside*]. She's alone. I reckon the old man's at his siesta yet. Ef he'll only hang onto that snooze ten minutes longer, I'll manage to let that gal Jovita slip out to that yer fandango, and no questions asked.

Manuela [*calling* Sandy]. Diego!

Sandy [*aside, without heeding her*]. That's a sweet voice for a serenade. Round, full, high-shouldered, and calkilated to fetch a man every time. Only thar ain't, to my sartain knowledge, one o' them chaps within a mile of the rancho. [*Laughs.*]

Manuela. Diego!

Sandy [*aside*]. Oh, go on! That's the style o' them Greasers. They'll stand rooted in their tracks, and yell for a chap without knowin' whether he's in sight or sound.

Manuela [*approaching Sandy impatiently*]. Diego!

Sandy [*starting, aside*]. The devil! Why, that's *me* she's after. [*Laughs.*] I clean disremembered that when I kem yer I tole those chaps my name was James,—James Smith [*laughs*], and thet they might call me "Jim." And De-a-go's their lingo for Jim. [*Aloud.*] Well, my beauty, De-a-go it is. Now, wot's up?

Manuela. Eh? no sabe!

Sandy. Wot's your little game? [*Embraces her.*]

Manuela [*aside, and recoiling coquettishly*]. Mother of God! He must be drunk again. These Americans have no time for love when they are sober. [*Aloud and coquettishly.*] Let me go, Diego. Don José is coming. He has sent for you. He takes his supper to-night on the corridor. Listen, Diego. He must not see you thus. You have been drinking again. I will keep you from him. I will say you are not well.

Sandy. Couldn't you, my darling, keep him from *me?* Couldn't you make him think *he* was sick? Couldn't you say he's exposin' his precious health by sittin' out thar to-night; thet ther's chills and fever in every breath? [*Aside.*] Ef the old Don plants himself in that chair, that gal's chances for goin' out to-night is gone up.

Manuela. Never. He would suspect at once. Listen, Diego. If Don José does not know that his daughter steals away with you to meet some *caballero*, some *lover*,—you understand, Diego,—it is because he does not know, or would not *seem* to know, what every one else in the rancho knows. Have a care, foolish Diego! If Don José is old and blind, look you, friend, we are *not*. You understand?

Sandy [aside]. What the devil does she expect?—money? No! [*Aloud.*] Look yer, Manuela, you ain't goin' to blow on that young gal! [*Putting his arm around her waist.*] Allowin' that she hez a lover, thar ain't nothin' onnateral in thet, bein' a purty sort o' gal. Why, suppose somebody should see you and me together like this, and should just let on to the old man.

Manuela. Hush! [*Disengaging herself.*] Hush! He is coming. Let me go, Diego. It is Don José!

Enter DON JOSÉ, *who walks gravely to the table, and seats himself.* MANUELA *retires to table.*

Sandy [aside]. I wonder if he saw us. I hope he did: it would shut that Manuela's mouth for a month of Sundays. [*Laughs.*] God forgive me for it! I've done a heap of things for that young gal Doña Jovita; but this yer gittin' soft on the Greaser maid-servant to help out the misses, is a little more than Sandy Morton bargained fur.

Don José [*to* MANUELA]. You can retire. Diego will attend me. [*Looks at* DIEGO *attentively.*]

[*Exit* MANUELA.

Sandy [aside]. Diego will attend him! Why, blast his yeller skin, does he allow that Sandy Morton hired out as a purty waiter-gal? Because I calkilated to feed his horses, it ain't no reason thet my dooty to animals don't stop thar. Pass his hash! [*Turns to follow* MANUELA, *but stops.*] Hello, Sandy! wot are ye doin', eh? You ain't going back on Miss Jovita, and jest spile that gal's chances to git out to-night, on'y to teach that God-forsaken old gov'ment mule manners? No! I'll humour the old man, and keep one eye out for the gal. [*Comes to table, and leans familiarly over the back of* DON JOSÉ'S *chair.*]

Don José [*aside*]. He seems insulted and annoyed. His manner strengthens my worst suspicions. He has not expected this. [*Aloud.*] Chocolate, Diego.

Sandy [*leaning over table carelessly*]. Yes, I reckon it's somewhar thar.

Don José [*aside*]. He is unused to menial labour. If I should be right in my suspicions! if he really were Doña Jovita's secret lover! This gallantry with the servants only a deceit! *Bueno!* I will watch him. [*Aloud.*] Chocolate, Diego!

Sandy [*aside*]. I wonder if the old fool reckons I'll pour it out. Well, seein's he's the oldest. [*Pours chocolate awkwardly, and spills it on the table and* DON JOSÉ.]

Don José [*aside*]. He *is* embarrassed. I am right. [*Aloud.*] Diego!

Sandy [*leaning confidentially over* DON JOSÉ'S *chair*]. Well, old man?

Don José. Three months ago my daughter the Doña Jovita picked you up, a wandering vagabond, in the streets of the Mission. [*Aside.*] He does not seem ashamed. [*Aloud.*] She—she—ahem! The *aguardiente*, Diego.

Sandy [*aside*]. That means the whisky. It's wonderful how quick a man learns Spanish. [*Passes the bottle, fills* DON JOSÉ'S *glass, and then his own.* DON JOSÉ *recoils in astonishment.* I looks toward ye, ole man. [*Tosses off liquor.*]

Don José [*aside*]. This familiarity! He *is* a gentleman. *Bueno!* [*Aloud.*] She was thrown from her horse; her skirt caught in the stirrup; she was dragged; you saved her life. You——

Sandy [*interrupting, confidentially drawing a chair to the table, and seating himself*]. Look yer! I'll tell you all about it. It wasn't that gal's fault, ole man. The hoss shied at me, lying drunk in a ditch, you see; the hoss backed, the girth broke; it warn't in human natur for her to keep her seat, and that gal rides like an angel; but the mustang throwed her. Well, I sorter got in the way o' thet hoss, and it stopped. Hevin' bin the cause o' the hoss shyin', for I reckon I didn't look much like an angel lyin' in that ditch, it was about the only squar thing for me to waltz in and help the gal. Thar, thet's about the way the thing pints. Now, don't you go and hold that agin her!

Don José. Well, well! She was grateful. She has a strange fondness for you Americans; and at her solicitation I gave you—*you*, an unknown vagrant—employment here as groom. You comprehend, Diego. I, Don José Castro, proprietor of this rancho, with an hundred idle *vaqueros* on my hands,—I made a place for you.

Sandy [meditatively]. Umph.

Don José. You said you would reform. How have you kept your word? You were drunk last Wednesday.

Sandy. Thet's so.

Don José. And again last Saturday.

Sandy [slowly]. Look yer, ole man, don't ye be too hard on me: that was the same old drunk.

Don José. I am in no mood for trifling. Hark ye, friend Diego. You have seen, perhaps,—who has not?— that I am a fond, an indulgent father. But even my consideration for my daughter's strange tastes and follies has its limit. Your conduct is a disgrace to the rancho. You must go.

Sandy [meditatively]. Well, I reckon, perhaps I'd better.

Don José [aside]. His coolness is suspicious. Can it be that he expects the girl will follow him? Mother of God! perhaps it has been already planned between them. Good! Thank Heaven I can end it here. [*Aloud.*] Diego.

Sandy. Old man.

Don José. For my daughter's sake, you understand,—for her sake,—I am willing to try you once more. Hark ye! My daughter is young, foolish, and romantic. I have reason to believe, from her conduct lately, that she has contracted an intimacy with some Americaño, and that in her ignorance, her foolishness, she has allowed that man to believe that he might aspire to her hand. Good! Now listen to me. You shall stay in her service. You shall find out,—you are in her confidence,—you shall find out this American, this adventurer, this lover if you please, of the Doña Jovita my daughter; and you will tell him this,—you will tell him that a union with him is impossible, forbidden; that the hour she attempts it, without my consent, she is *penniless;* that this estate, this rancho, passes into the hands of the Holy Church, where even your laws cannot reach it.

Sandy [*leaning familiarly over the table*]. But suppose that he sees that little bluff, and calls ye.

Don José. I do not comprehend you [*coldly*].

Sandy. Suppose he loves that gal, and will take her as she stands, without a cent, or hide or hair of yer old cattle.

Don José [*scornfully*]. Suppose—a miracle! Hark ye, Diego! It is now five years since I have known your countrymen, these smart Americaños. I have yet to know when love, sentiment, friendship, was worth any more than a money value in your market.

Sandy [*truculently and drunkenly*]. You hev, hev ye? Well, look yar, ole man. Suppose I *refuse.* Suppose I'd rather go than act as a spy on that young gal your darter! Suppose that—hic—allowin' she's my friend, I'd rather starve in the gutters of the Mission than stand between her and the man she fancies. Hey? Suppose I would—damn me! Suppose I'd see you and your derned old rancho in

—t'other place—hic—damn me. You hear me, ole man! That's the kind o' man I am—damn me.

Don José [*aside, rising contemptuously*]. It is as I suspected. Traitor. Ingrate! Satisfied that his scheme has failed, he is ready to abandon her. And this—*this* is the man for whom she has been ready to sacrifice everything,—her home, her father! [*Aloud, coldly*]. Be it so, Diego: you shall go.

Sandy [*soberly and seriously, after a pause*]. Well, I reckon I had better. [*Rising.*] I've a few duds, old man, to put up. It won't take me long. [*Goes to* L., *and pauses.*]

Don José [*aside*]. Ah! he hesitates! He is changing his mind. [SANDY *returns slowly to table, pours out a glass of liquor, nods to* DON JOSÉ, *and drinks.*] I look towards ye, ole man. *Adios!* [*Exit* SANDY.

Don José. His coolness is perfect. If these Americans are cayotes in their advances, they are lions in retreat! *Bueno!* I begin to respect him. But it will be just as well to set Concho to track him to the Mission; and I will see that he leaves the rancho alone. [*Exit* JOSÉ.

Enter hurriedly JOVITA CASTRO, *in riding habit, with whip.*

So! Chiquita not yet saddled, and that spy Concho haunting the plains for the last half-hour. What an air of mystery! Something awful, something deliciously dreadful, has happened! Either my amiable drunkard has forgotten to despatch Concho on his usual fool's errand, or he is himself lying helpless in some ditch. Was there ever a girl so persecuted? With a father wrapped in mystery, a lover nameless and shrouded in the obscurity of some Olympian height, and her only confidant and messenger a Bacchus instead of a Mercury! Heigh ho And in another hour Don Juan—he told me I might call him John—will be waiting for me outside the convent wall! What if Diego fails me? To go there alone would be madness! Who else would be as charmingly unconscious and inattentive as this American vagabond! [*Goes to* L.] Ah, my saddle and blanket hidden! He *has* been interrupted! Some one has been watching. This freak of my father's means something. And to-night, of all nights, the night that Oakhurst was to disclose himself, and tell me all! What is to be done? Hark! [DIEGO, *without, singing.*]

"Oh, here's your *aguardiente*.
Drink it down!"

Jovita. It is Diego; and, Mother of God! drunk again!
Enter SANDY, *carrying pack, intoxicated; staggers to centre, and, observing* JOVITA, *takes off his hat respectfully.*

Jovita [*shaking him by the shoulders passionately*]. Diego! How dare you! And at such a time!

Sandy [*with drunken solemnity*]. Miss Jovita, did ye ever know me to be drunk afore at such a time?

Jovita. No.

Sandy. Zactly so. It's abnormal. And it means—the game's up.

Jovita. I do not understand. For the love of God, Diego, be plain!

Sandy [*solemnly and drunkenly*]. When I say your game's up, I mean the old man knows it all. You're blowed upon. Hearken, miss! [*seriously and soberly*]. Your father knows all that I know; but, as it wasn't my business to interfere with, I hev sorter helped along. He knows that you meet a stranger, an American, in these rides with me.

Jovita [*passionately*]. Ingrate! You have not dared to tell him! [*Seizing him by the collar, and threatening him with the horsewhip.*]

Sandy [*rising with half-drunken, half-sober solemnity*]. One minit, miss! one minit! Don't ye! don't ye do that! Ef ye forget (and I don't blame ye for it), ef ye forget that I'm a man, don't ye, don't ye forget that you're a woman! Sit ye down, sit ye down, so! Now, ef ye'll kindly remember, miss, I never saw this yer man, yer lover. Ef ye'll recollect, miss, whenever you met him, I allers hung back and waited round in the mission or in the fields beyond for ye, and allowed ye to hev yer own way, it bein' no business o' mine. Thar isn't a man on the ranch, who, ef he'd had a mind to watch ye, wouldn't hev known more about yer lover than I do.

Jovita [*aside*]. He speaks truly. He always kept in the background. Even Don Juan never knew that I had an attendant until I told him. [*Aloud.*] I made a mistake, Diego. I was hasty. What am I to do? He is waiting for me even now.

Sandy. Well [*with drunken gravity*], ef ye can't go to him, I reckon it's the squar thing for him to come to ye.

Jovita. Recollect yourself, Diego. Be a man!

Sandy. Thash jus war I say. Let him be a man, and come to ye here. Let him ride up to this ranch like a man, and call out to yer father that he'll take ye jist as ye are, without the land. And if the old man allows, rather than hev ye marry that stranger, he'll give this yer place to the Church, why, let him do it, and be damned.

Jovita [*recoiling, aside*]. So! That is their plan. Don José has worked on the fears or the cupidity of this drunken ingrate.

Sandy [*with drunken submission*]. Ye was speaking to me, miss. Ef ye'll take my advice,—a drunken man's advice, miss,—ye'll say to that lover of yours, ef he's afeard to come for ye here, to take ye as ye stand, he ain't no man for ye. And, ontil he does, ye'll do as the old man says. Fur ef

I do say it, miss,—and thar ain't no love lost between us,—he's a good father to ye. It ain't every day that a gal kin afford to swap a father like that, as she *does know*, fur the husband that she *don't!* He's a proud old fool, miss; but to ye, to ye, he's clar grit all through.

Jovita [*passionately, aside*]. Tricked, fooled, like a child! and through the means of this treacherous, drunken tool. [*Stamping her foot.*] Ah! we shall see! You are wise, you are wise, Don José; but your daughter is not a novice, nor a helpless creature of the Holy Church. [*Passionately.*] I'll—I'll become a Protestant to-morrow!

Sandy [*unheeding her passion, and becoming more earnest and self-possessed*]. Ef ye hed a father, miss, ez instead o' harkinin' to your slightest wish, and surroundin' ye with luxury, hed made your infancy a struggle for life among strangers, and your childhood a disgrace and a temptation; ef he had left ye with no company but want, with no companions but guilt, with no mother but suffering; ef he had made your home, this home, so unhappy, so vile, so terrible, so awful, that the crowded streets and gutters of a great city was something to fly to for relief; ef he had made his presence, his very name,—your name, miss, allowin' it was your father,—ef he had made that presence so hateful, that name so infamous, that exile, that flyin' to furrin' parts, that wanderin' among strange folks ez didn't know ye, was the only way to make life endurable; and ef he'd given ye,—I mean this good old man Don José, miss,—ef he'd given ye as part of yer heritage a taint, a weakness in yer very blood, a fondness for a poison, a poison that soothed ye like a vampire bat and sucked yer life-blood [*seizing her arm*] ez it soothed ye; ef this curse that hung over ye dragged ye down day by day, till hating him, loathing him, ye saw yerself day by day becoming more and more like him, till ye knew that his fate was yours, and yours his,—why then,

Miss Jovita [*rising with an hysterical, drunken laugh*], why then, I'd run away with ye myself,—I would, damn me!

Jovita [*who has been withdrawing from him scornfully*]. Well acted, Diego. Don José should have seen his pupil. Trust me, my father will reward you. [*Aside.*] And yet there were tears in his drunken eyes. Bah! it is the liquor; he is no longer sane. And, either hypocrite or imbecile, he is to be trusted no longer. But where and why is he going? [*Aloud.*] You are leaving us, Diego.

Sandy [*quietly*]. Well, the old man and me don't get on together.

Jovita [*scornfully*]. Bueno! I see. Then you abandon me?

Sandy [*quickly*] To the old man, miss,—not the young one. [*Walks to the table and begins to pour out liquor.*]

Jovita [*angrily*]. You would not dare to talk to me thus if John Oakhurst—ah! [*Checking herself.*]

Sandy [*drops glass on table, hurries to centre, and seizes* DOÑA JOVITA]. Eh! Wot? Wot name did you say? [*Looks at her amazed and bewildered.*]

Jovita [*terrified, aside*]. Mother of God! what have I done? Broken my sacred pledge to keep his name secret. No! no! Diego did not hear me! Surely this wretched drunkard does not know him. [*Aloud.*] Nothing. I said nothing: I mentioned no name.

Sandy [*still amazed, frightened, and bewildered, passing his hand over his forehead slowly*]. Ye mentioned no name? Surely I am wild, crazed. Tell me, miss—ye didn't,—I know ye didn't, but I thought it sounded like it—ye didn't mention the name of—of—of—John Oakhurst?

Jovita [*hurriedly*]. No, of course not. You terrify me, Diego. You are wild.

Sandy [*dropping her hand with a sigh of relief*]. No, no! In course ye didn't. I was wild, miss, wild; this drink has confused me 'yer. [*Pointing to his head.*] There are times when I hear that name, miss,—times when I see his face. [*Sadly.*] But is when I've took too much— too much. I'll drink no more—no more!—to-night—to-night! [*Drops his head slowly in his hands.*]

Jovita [*looking at* DIEGO, *aside*]. Really I'm feeling very uncomfortable. I'd like to ask a question of this maniac. But nonsense! Don Juan gave me to understand Oakhurst wasn't his real name; that is, he intimated there was something dreadful and mysterious about it that mustn't be told,—something that would frighten people. *Holy Virgin!* it has! Why, this reckless vagabond here is pale and agitated. Don Juan shall explain this mystery to-night. But then, how shall I see him? Ah! I have it. The night of the last *festa*, when I could not leave the rancho, he begged me to show a light from the flat roof of the upper corridor, that he might know I was thinking of him, —dear fellow! He will linger to-night at the Mission; he will see the light; he will know that I have not forgotten. He will approach the rancho; I shall manage to slip away at midnight to the ruined Mission. I shall—ah! it is my father! Holy Virgin, befriend me now with self-possession.

[*Stands quietly at* L., *looking toward* SANDY, *who still remains buried in thought, as—*

Enter DON JOSÉ; *regards his daughter and* DIEGO *with a sarcastic smile.*

Don José [*aside*]. *Bueno!* It is as I expected,—an explanation, an explosion, a lovers' quarrel, an end to romance. From his looks I should say she has been teaching the adventurer a lesson. Good! I could embrace her. [*Crosses to* SANDY—*aloud.*] You still here!

Sandy [*rising with a start*]. Yes! I—a—I was only

taking leave of Miss Jovita that hez bin kind to me. She's a good gal, ole man, and won't be any the worse when I'm gone.—Good-by, Miss Jovita [*extending his hand*]. I wish ye luck.

Jovita [*coldly*]. Adios, friend Diego. [*Aside, hurriedly.*] You will not expose my secret?

Sandy [*aside*]. It ain't in me, miss. [*To* DON JOSÉ, *going.*] Adios, ole man. [*Shouldering his pack.*]

Don José. Adios, friend Diego. [*Formally.*] May good luck attend you! [*Aside.*] You understand, on your word as—as—as—*a gentleman!*—you have no further communication with this rancho, or aught that it contains.

Sandy [*gravely*]. I hear ye, ole man. Adios. [*Goes to gateway, but pauses at table, and begins to fill a glass of aguardiente.*]

Don José [*aside, looking at his daughter*]. I could embrace her now. She is truly a Castro. [*Aloud to* JOVITA.] Hark ye, little one! I have news that will please you, and—who knows? perhaps break up the monotony of the dull life of the rancho. To-night come to me two famous *caballeros Americanos,* you understand: they will be here soon, even now. Retire, and make ready to receive them. [*Exit* JOVITA.]

Don José [*aside, looking at* SANDY]. He lingers. I shall not be satisfied until Concho has seen him safely beyond the Mission wall.

Enter CONCHO.

Concho. Two *caballeros* have dismounted in the corral, and seek the honour of Don José's presence.

Don José. Bueno! [*Aside.*] Follow that fellow beyond the Mission. [*Aloud.*] Admit the strangers. Did they give their names?

Concho. They did, Don José,—Col. Culpepper Starbottle and the Don Alexandro Morton.

Sandy [*dropping glass of aguardiente, and staggering stupidly to the centre, confronting* DON JOSÉ *and* CONCHO, *still holding bottle*]. Eh! Wot? Wot name did you say? [*Looks stupidly and amazedly at* CONCHO *and* DON JOSÉ, *and then slowly passes his hand over his forehead. Then slowly and apologetically.*] I axes your pardon, Don José, and yours, sir [*to* CONCHO], but I thought ye called me. No!—that ez—I mean—I mean—I'm a little off color here [*pointing to his head*]. I don't follow suit—I—eh—eh! Oh!—ye'll pardon me, sir, but thar's names—perhaps yer darter will remember that I was took a bit ago on a name—thar's names sortir hangin' round me 'yer [*pointing to his head*], that I thinks I hear—but bein' drunk—I hopes ye'll excoos me. Adios. [*Staggers to gateway,* CONCHO *following.*]

Concho [*aside*]. There is something more in this than Don José would have known. I'll watch Diego, and keep an eye on Miss Jovita too.

[*Exit, following* SANDY, *who, in exit, jostles against* COL. STARBOTTLE *entering, who stops and leans exhaustedly at the wall to get his breath; following him closely, and oblivious of* SANDY MORTON, ALEXANDER MORTON, sen. *Enter* COL. STARBOTTLE *and* ALEXANDER MORTON, sen.

SCENE 2.—*The Same.*

Col. Starbottle [*entering, to* DON JOSÉ]. Overlooking the insult of—er—inebriated individual, whose menial position in this—er—er—household precludes a demand for personal satisfaction, sir, I believe I have the honour of addressing Don José Castro. Very good, sir. Permit me, sir, to introduce myself as Col. Culpepper Starbottle—demn me!

the legal adviser of Mr. Alexander Morton, sen., and I may add, sir, the friend of that gentleman, and as such, sir—er—er—personally—personally responsible.

Alexander Morton [*puritanically and lugubriously*]. As a God-fearing and forgiving Christian, Mr. Castro, I trust you will overlook the habitual profanity of the erring but well-meaning man, who, by the necessities of my situation, accompanies me. I am the person—a helpless sinner—mentioned in the letters which I believe have preceded me. As a professing member of the Cumberland Presbyterian Church, I have ventured, in the interest of works rather than faith, to overlook the plain doctrines of the Church in claiming sympathy of a superstitious Papist.

Starbottle [*interrupting, aside to* ALEXANDER MORTON]. Ahem! ahem! [*Aloud to* DON JOSÉ.] My friend's manner, sir, reminds me of—er—er—Ram Bootgum Sing, first secretary of Turkish legation at Washington in '45; most remarkable man—demn me—most remarkable—and warm personal friend. Challenged Tod Robinson for putting him next to Hebrew banker at dinner, with remark—demn me—that they were both believers in the profit!—he, he! Amusing, perhaps; irreverent, certainly. Fought with cimeters. Second pass, Ram divided Tod in two pieces—fact, sir—just here [*pointing*] in—er—er—regions of moral emotions. Upper half called to me,—said to me warningly—last words—never forget it,—" Star,"—always called me Star,—" Respect man's religious convictions." Legs dead; emotion confined to upper part of body—pathetic picture. Ged, sir, something to be remembered!

Don José [*with grave Spanish courtesy*]. You are welcome, gentlemen, to the rancho of the Blessed Fisherman. Your letters, with their honourable report, are here. Believe me, señores, in your modesty you have forgotten to mention your strongest claim to the hospitality of my house,—the royal right of strangers.

Morton. Angels before this have been entertained as strangers, says the Good Book; and that, I take it, is your authority for this ceremoniousness, which else were but lip-service and Papist airs. But I am here in the performance of a duty, Mr. Castro,—the duty of a Christian father. I am seeking a prodigal son. I am seeking him in his wine-husks and among his harl—

Starbottle [interrupting]. A single moment. [*To* DON JOSÉ.] Permit me to—er—er—explain. As my friend Mr. Morton states, we are, in fact, at present engaged in—er—er—quest—er—pilgrimage that possibly to some, unless deterred by considerations of responsibility—personal responsibility—sir—Ged, sir, might be looked upon as visionary, enthusiastic, sentimental, fanatical. We are seeking a son, or, as my friend tersely and scripturally expresses it—er—er—prodigal son. I say scripturally, sir, and tersely, but not, you understand it, literally, not, I may add, sir, legally. Ged, sir, as a precedent, I admit we are wrong. To the best of my knowledge, sir, the—er—Prodigal Son sought his own father. To be frank, sir,—and Ged, sir, if Culpepper Starbottle has a fault, it is frankness, sir. As Nelse Buckthorne said to me in Nashville in '47, "You would infer, Col. Starbottle, that I equivocate." I replied, "I do, sir; and permit me to add that equivocation has all the guilt of a lie with cowardice superadded." The next morning at nine o'clock, Ged, sir, he gasped to me—he was lying on the ground, hole through his left lung just here [*illustrating with* DON JOSÉ'S *coat*],—he gasped, "If you have a merit, Star, above others, it is frankness!" his last words, sir,—demn me. . . . To be frank, sir, years ago, in the wild exuberance of youth, the son of this gentleman left his—er—er—er—boyhood's home, owing to an innocent but natural misunderstanding with the legal protector of his youth—

Morton [*interrupting gravely and demurely*]. Driven from home by my own sinful and then unregenerate hand—

Starbottle [*quickly*]. One moment, a simple moment. We will not weary you with—er—er—history, or the vagaries of youth. He—er—came to California in '49. A year ago, touched by—er—er—parental emotion and solicitude, my friend resolved to seek him here. Believing that the—er—er—lawlessness of—er—er—untrammelled youth and boyish inexperience might have led him into some trifling indiscretion, we have sought him successively in hospitals, almshouses, reformatories, State's prisons, lunatic and inebriate asylums, and—er—er—even on the monumental inscriptions of the—er—er—country churchyards. We have thus far, I grieve to say, although acquiring much and valuable information of a varied character and interest, as far as the direct matter of our search,—we have been, I think I may say, unsuccessful. Our search has been attended with the—er—disbursement of some capital under my—er—er—direction, which, though large, represents quite inadequately the—er—er—earnestness of our endeavours.

Enter MANUELA.

Manuela [*to* DON JOSÉ]. The Doña Jovita is waiting to receive you.

Don José [*to* MORTON]. You shall tell me further of your interesting pilgrimage hereafter. At present, my daughter awaits us to place this humble roof at your disposal. I am a widower, Don Alexandro, like yourself. When I say that, like you, I have an only child, and that I love her, you will understand how earnest is my sympathy. This way, gentlemen. [*Leading to door in corridor, and awaiting them.*]

Starbottle [*aside*]. Umph! An interview with lovely woman means—er—intoxication, but—er—er—no liquor. It's evident that the Don doesn't drink, Eh! [*Catches sight of table in corridor, and bottle.*] Oh, he does, but some absurd Spanish formality prevents his doing the polite thing before dinner. [*Aloud to* DON JOSÉ.] One moment, sir, one moment. If you will—er—er—pardon the—er—seeming discourtesy, for which I am, I admit—er—personally responsible, I will for a few moments enjoy the—er—er—delicious air of the courtyard and the beauties of Nature as displayed in the—er—sunset. I will—er—rejoin you and the—er—er—ladies a moment later.

Don José. The house is your own, señor: do as you will. This way, Don Alexandro.

[*Exit, in door* L., DON JOSE *and* MORTON, SEN.

Starbottle. "Do as you will." Well, I don't understand Spanish ceremony, but that's certainly good English. [*Going to table.*] Eh! [*Smelling decanter.*] Robinson County whisky! Umph! I have observed that the spirit of American institutions, sir, are already penetrating the —er—er—superstitions of—er—foreign and effete civilisations. [*Pours out glass of whisky and drinks; pours again, and observes* MANUELA *watching him respectfully.*] What the devil is that girl looking at? Eh! [*Puts down glass.*]

Manuela [*aside*]. He is fierce and warlike. Mother of God! But he is not so awful as that grey-haired *caballero*, who looks like a fasting St. Anthony. And he loves *aguardiente:* he will pity poor Diego the more. [*Aloud.*] Ahem! Señor. [*Courtesies coquettishly.*]

Col. Starbottle [*aside*]. Oh, I see. Ged! not a bad-looking girl,—a trifle dark, but Southern, and—er—tropical. Ged, Star, Star, this won't do, sir; no, sir. The filial affections of Æneas are not to be sacrificed through the blandishments of—er—Dodo—I mean a Dido.

Manuela. O señor, you are kind, you are good! You are an Americano, one of a great nation. You will feel sympathy for a poor young man,—a mere *muchaco*,—one of your own race, who was a *vaquero* here, señor. He has been sent away from us here, disgraced, alone, hungry, perhaps penniless. [*Wipes her eyes.*]

Col. Starbottle. The devil! Another prodigal. [*Aloud.*] My dear, the case you have just stated would appear to be the—er—er—normal condition of the—er—youth of America. But why was he discharged? [*Pouring out liquor.*]

Manuela [*demurely glancing at the Colonel*]. He was drunk, señor.

Starbottle [*potently*]. Drunkenness, my child, which is— er—weakness in the—er—er—gentleman, in the subordinate is a crime. What—er—excites the social impulse and exhilarates the fancy of the—er—master of the house, in the performance of his duty, renders the servant unfit for his. Legally it is a breach of contract. I should give it as my opinion,—for which I am personally responsible,—that your friend Diego could not recover. Ged! [*aside.*] I wonder if this scapegoat could be our black sheep?

Manuela. But that was not all, señor. It was an excuse only. He was sent away for helping our young lady to a cavalier. He was discharged because he would not be a traitor to her. He was sent away because he was too good, too honourable—too— [*Bursts out crying.*]

Starbottle [*aside*]. Oh, the devil! *this* is no Sandy Morton. [*Coming forward gravely.*] I have never yet analysed the— er—er—character of the young gentleman I have the honour to assist in restoring to his family and society; but judging— er—calmly—er—dispassionately, from my knowledge of his own father—from what the old gentleman must have been in his unregenerate state, and knowing what he is now in his present reformed Christian condition, I should say calmly and deliberately that the son must be the most infernal and accomplished villain unhung. Ged, I have a thought, an inspiration. [*To* MANUELA, *tapping her under the chin.*] I see, my dear; a lover, ha, ha! Ah, you rogue! Well, well, we will talk of this again. I will—er—er—interest myself in this Diego. [*Exit* MANUELA.]

Starbottle [*solus*]. How would it do to get up a prodigal? Umph! Something must be done soon: the old man grows languid in his search. My position as a sinecure is—er—in peril. A prodigal ready-made! But could I get a scoundrel bad enough to satisfy the old man? Ged, that's serious. Let me see: he admits that he is unable to recognise his own son in face, features, manner, or speech. Good! If I could pick up some rascal whose—er—irregularities didn't quite fill the bill, and could say—Ged!—that he was reforming. Reforming! Ged, Star! That very defect would show the hereditary taint, demn me! I must think of this seriously. Ged, Star, the idea is—an inspiration of humanity and virtue. Who knows? it might be the saving of the vagabond,—a crown of glory to the old man's age. Inspiration, did I say? Ged, Star, it's a *duty*,—a sacred, solemn duty, for which you are responsible,—personally responsible.

[*Lights down half. Enter from corridor* L., MORTON, DON JOSÉ, *the* DOÑA JOVITA, *and* MANUELA.

Doña Jovita [*stepping forward with exaggerated Spanish courtesy*]. A thousand graces await your Excellency, Commander Don—Don—

Starbottle [*bowing to the ground with equal delight and exaggerated courtesy*]. Er—Coolpepero!

Doña Jovita. Don Culpepero! If we throw ourselves unasked at your Excellency's feet [*courtesy*], if we appear unsought before the light of your Excellency's eyes [*courtesy*], if we err in maidenly decorum in thus seeking unbidden your Excellency's presence [*courtesy*], believe us, it is the fear of some greater, some graver indecorum in our conduct that has withdrawn your Excellency's person from us since you have graced our roof with your company. We know, Señor Commander, how superior are the charms of the American ladies. It is in no spirit of rivalry with them, but to show—Mother of God!—that we are not absolutely ugly, that we intrude upon your Excellency's solitude. [*Aside.*] I shall need the old fool, and shall use him.

Col. Starbottle [*who has been bowing and saluting with equal extravagance during this speech—aside*]. Ged! she *is* beautiful! [*Aloud.*] Permit me—er—er—Doña Jovita, to correct—Ged, I must say it, correct erroneous statements. The man who should—er—utter in my presence remarks disparaging those—er—charms it is my privilege to behold, I should hold responsible,—Ged! personally responsible. You—er—remind me of—er—incident, trifling perhaps, but pleasing—Charleston in '52—a reception at John C. Calhoun's. A lady, one of the demnedest beautiful women you ever saw, said to me, "Star!"—she always called me Star,—"you've avoided me, you have, Star! I fear you are no longer my friend."—"Your friend, madam," I said. "No, I've avoided you because I am your lover." Ged, Miss Jovita, a fact—demn me. Sensation. Husband heard garbled report. He was old friend, but jealous, rash, indiscreet. Fell at first fire—umph—January 5th. Lady —beautiful woman—never forgave—went into convent. Sad affair. And all a mistake—demn me,—all a mistake, through perhaps extravagant gallantry and compliment. I lingered here, oblivious perhaps of—er—beauty, in the enjoyment of Nature.

Doña Jovita. Is there enough for your Excellency to

share with me, since it must be my rival? See, the fog is clearing away: we shall have moonlight. [DON JOSÉ *and* MORTON *seat themselves at table.*] Shall we not let these venerable *caballeros* enjoy their confidences and experiences together? [*Aside.*] Don José watches me like a fox, does not intend to lose sight of me. How shall I show the light three times from the courtyard roof? I have it! [*Takes* STARBOTTLE'S *arm.*] It is too pleasant to withdraw. There is a view from the courtyard wall your Excellency should see. Will you accompany me? The ascent is easy.

Starbottle [*bowing*]. I will ascend, although, permit me to say, Doña Jovita, it would be—er—impossible for me to be nearer—er—heaven, than—er—at present.

Doña Jovita. Flatterer! Come, you shall tell me about this sad lady who died. Ah! Don Culpepero, let me hope all your experiences will not be so fatal to us! [*Exeunt* DOÑA JOVITA *and* STARBOTTLE.]

Morton [*aside*]. A froward daughter of Baal, and, if I mistake not, even now concocting mischief for this foolish, indulgent, stiff-necked father. [*Aloud.*] Your only daughter, I presume.

Don José. My darling, Don Alexandro. Motherless from her infancy. A little wild, and inclined to gaiety, but I hope not seeking for more than these walls afford. I have checked her but seldom, Don Alexandro, and then I did not let her see my hand on the rein that held her back. I do not ask her confidence always: I only want her to know that when the time comes it can be given to me without fear.

Morton. Umph!

Don José [*leaning forward confidentially*]. To show that you have not intrusted your confidence regarding your wayward son—whom may the saints return to you!—to unsympathetic or inexperienced ears, I will impart a secret.

A few weeks ago I detected an innocent intimacy between this foolish girl and a vagabond *vaquero* in my employ. You understand, it was on her part romantic, visionary: on his, calculating, shrewd, self-interested, for he expected to become my heir. I did not lock her up. I did not tax her with it. I humoured it. To-day I satisfied the lover that his investment was not profitable, that a marriage without my consent entailed the loss of the property, and then left them together. They parted in tears, think you, Don Alexandro? No, but mutually hating each other. The romance was over. An American would have opposed the girl, have driven her to secrecy, to an elopement perhaps. Eh?

Morton [*scornfully*]. And you believe that they have abandoned their plans?

Don José. I am sure—hush! she is here!

  Enter on roof of corridor STARBOTTLE *and* JOVITA.

Col. Starbottle. Really a superb landscape! An admirable view of the—er—fog—rolling over the Mission Hills, the plains below, and the—er—er—single figure of—er—motionless horseman—

Doña Jovita [*quickly*]. Some belated *vaquero.* Do you smoke, Señor Commander?

Starbottle. At times.

Doña Jovita. With me. I will light a cigarette for you: it is the custom.

  [COL. STARBOTTLE *draws match from his pocket and
   is about to light, but is stopped by* DOÑA JOVITA.

Doña Jovita. Pardon, your Excellency, but we cannot endure your American matches. There is a taper in the passage.

  [COL. STARBOTTLE *brings taper.* DOÑA JOVITA *turns
   to light cigarette, but manages to blow out candle.*

Doña Jovita. I must try your gallantry again. That is once I have failed. [*Significantly.*]

[COL. STARBOTTLE *relights candle, business, same results.*]

Doña Jovita. I am stupid and nervous to-night. I have failed *twice.* [*With emphasis.*]

[COL. STARBOTTLE *repeats business with candle.* DOÑA JOVITA *lights cigarette, hands it to the Colonel.*]

Doña Jovita. Thrice, and I have succeeded. [*Blows out candle.*]

Col. Starbottle. A thousand thanks! There is a—er—er—light on the plain.

Doña Jovita [*hastily*]. It is the *vaqueros* returning. My father gives a *festa* to peons in honour of your arrival. There will be a dance. You have been patient, Señor Commander; you shall have my hand for a waltz.

Enter vaqueros, their wives and daughters. A dance, during which the " sembi canca" is danced by COL. STARBOTTLE *and* DOÑA JOVITA. *Business, during which the bell of Mission Church, faintly illuminated beyond the wall, strikes twelve. Dancers withdraw hurriedly, leaving alone* MANUELA, DOÑA JOVITA, COL. STARBOTTLE, DON JOSÉ *and* CONCHO. CONCHO *formally hands keys to* DON JOSÉ.

Don José [*delivering keys to* MORTON *with stately impressiveness*]. Take them, Don Alexandro Morton, and with them all that they unlock for bliss or bale. Take them, noble guest, and with them the homage of this family,—to-night, Don Alexandro, your humble servants. Good-night, gentlemen. May a thousand angels attend you, O Don Alexandro and Don Culpepero!

Doña Jovita. Good-night, Don Alexandro. May your dreams to-night see all your wishes fulfilled! Good-night,

O Señor Commander. May she you dream of be as happy as you!

Manuela and Concho [*together*]. Good-night, O señores and illustrious gentlemen! May the Blessed Fisherman watch over you! [*Both parties retreat into opposite corridors, bowing.*]

| MANUELA. | CONCHO. | MORTON. |
| DON JOSÉ. | JOVITA. | STARBOTTLE. |

SCENE 3.—*The same. Stage darkened. Fog passing beyond wall outside, and occasionally obscuring moonlit landscape beyond. Enter* JOVITA *softly from corridor* L. *Her face is partly hidden by Spanish mantilla.*

Jovita. All quiet at last; and, thanks to much *aguardiente*, my warlike admirer snores peacefully above. Yet I could swear I heard the old Puritan's door creak as I descended! Pshaw! What matters? [*Goes to gateway and tries gate.*] Locked! *Carramba!* I see it now. Under the pretext of reviving the old ceremony, Don José has locked the gates and placed me in the custody of his guests. Stay! There is a door leading to the corral from the passage by Concho's room. *Bueno!* Don José shall see! [*Exit* R.]

Enter cautiously R. OLD MORTON.

Old Morton. I was not mistaken! It was the skirt of that Jezebel daughter that whisked past my door a moment ago, and her figure that flitted down that corridor. So! The lover driven out of the house at four P.M., and at twelve o'clock at night the young lady trying the gate secretly. This may be Spanish resignation and filial submission, but it looks very like Yankee disobedience and forwardness. Perhaps it's well that the keys are in my pocket. This fond confiding Papist may find the heretic American father of some service. [*Conceals himself behind pillar of corridor.*]

[*After a pause the head of* JOHN OAKHURST *appears over the wall of corridor: he climbs up to roof of corridor, and descends very quietly and deliberately to stage.*]

Oakhurst [*dusting his clothing with his handkerchief*]. I never knew before why these Spaniards covered their adobe walls with whitewash. [*Leans against pillar in shadow.*]

Re-enter JOVITA *hastily.*

Jovita. All is lost! The corral door is locked, the key is outside, and Concho is gone,—gone where? *Madre di Dios!* to discover, perhaps to kill him.

Oakhurst [*approaching her*]. No!

Jovita. Juan! [*embracing him.*] But how did you get here? This is madness!

Oakhurst. As you did not come to the Mission, I came to the rancho. I found the gate locked—by the way, is not that a novelty here?—I climbed the wall. But you, Miss Castro, you are trembling! Your little hands are cold!

Jovita [*glancing around*]. Nothing! nothing! But you are running a terrible risk. At any moment we may be discovered.

Oakhurst. I understand you: it would be bad for the discoverer. Never fear, I will be patient.

Jovita. But I feared that you might meet Concho.

Oakhurst. Concho—Concho [*meditatively*]. Let me see,—tall, dark, long in the arm, weighs about one hundred and eighty, and active.

Jovita. Yes, tell me! You have met him?

Oakhurst. Possibly, possibly! Was he a friend of yours?

Jovita. No!

Oakhurst. That's better. Are his pursuits here sedentary or active?

Jovita. He is my father's major-domo.

Oakhurst. I see: a sinecure. [*Aside.*] Well, if he has to lay up for a week or two, the rancho won't suffer.

Jovita. Well?

Oakhurst. Well!

Jovita [*passionately*]. There! having scaled the wall, at the risk of being discovered—this is all you have to say! [*Turning away.*]

Oakhurst [*quietly*]. Perhaps, Jovita [*taking her hand with grave earnestness*], to a clandestine intimacy like ours there is but one end. It is not merely elopement, not merely marriage, it is exposure! Sooner or later you and I must face the eyes we now shun. What matters if to-night or later?

Jovita [*quickly*]. I am ready. It was you who—

Oakhurst. It was I who first demanded secrecy; but it was I who told you when we last met that I would tell you why to-night.

Jovita. I am ready; but hear me, Juan. Nothing can change my faith in you.

Oakhurst [*sadly*]. You know not what you say. Listen, my child. I am a gambler. Not the man who lavishes his fortune at the gaming-table for excitement's sake; not the fanatic who stakes his own earnings—perhaps the confided earnings of others—on a single *coup*. No, he is the man who loses,—whom the world deplores, pities, and forgives. I am the man who wins—whom the world hates and despises.

Jovita. I do not understand you, Juan.

Oakhurst. So much the better, perhaps. But you must hear me. I make a profession—an occupation more exacting, more wearying, more laborious, than that of your meanest herdsman—of that which others make a dissipation of the senses. And yet, Jovita, there is not the meanest *vaquero* in this ranch, who, playing against me, winning or losing, is not held to be my superior. I have no friends— only confederates. Even the woman who dares to pity me must do it in secret.

Jovita. But you will abandon this dreadful trade. As the son of the rich Don José, no one dare scorn you. My father will relent. I am his heiress.

Oakhurst. No more, Jovita, no more. If I were the man who could purchase the world's respect through a woman's weakness for him, I should not be here to-night. I am not here to sue your father's daughter with hopes of forgiveness, promises of reformation. Reformation, in a man like me, means cowardice or self-interest. [OLD MORTON, *becoming excited, leans slowly out from the shadow of the pillar, listening intently.*] I am here to take, by force if necessary, a gambler's wife,—the woman who will share my fortunes, my disgrace, my losses; who is willing to leave her old life of indulgence, of luxury, of respectability, for mine. You are frightened, little dove: compose yourself [*soothing her tenderly and sadly*]; you are frightened at the cruel hawk who has chosen you for a mate.

Old Morton [*aside*]. God in heaven! This is like HIM! like me!—like me before the blessed Lord lifted me into regeneration. If it should be! [*Leans forward anxiously from pillar*].

Oakhurst [*aside*]. Still silent? Poor dove! I can hear her foolish heart flutter against mine. Another moment decides our fate. Another moment: John Oakhurst and freedom, or Red Gulch and—she is moving. [*To* JOVITA.] I am harsh, little one, and cold. Perhaps I have had much to make me so. But when [*with feeling*] I first met you; when, lifting my eyes to the church-porch, I saw your beautiful face; when, in sheer recklessness and bravado, I raised my hat to you; when you—you, Jovita—lifted your brave eyes to mine, and there, there in the sanctuary, returned my salute,—the salutation of the gambler, the outcast, the reprobate,—then, then I swore that you should be mine, if I tore you from the sanctuary. Speak now, Jovita: if it was coquetry, speak now; I forgive you: if it was sheer wantonness, speak now; I shall spare you: but if—

Jovita [*throwing herself in his arms*]. Love, Juan! I am yours, now and for ever. [*Pause.*] But you have not told me all. I will go with you to-night—now. I leave behind me all,—my home, my father, my—[*pause*]—my name. You have forgotten, Juan, you have not told me what I change *that* for: you have not told me *yours*.

[OLD MORTON, *in eager excitement, leans beyond shadow of pillar.*

Oakhurst [*embracing her tenderly, with a smile*]. If I have not told you who I am, it was because, darling, it was more important that you should know what I am. Now that you know that—why—[*embarrassedly*]—I have nothing more to tell. I did not wish you to repeat the name of Oakhurst, because—[*aside*]—how the devil shall I tell her that Oakhurst was my real name after all, and that I only feared she might divulge it?—[*aloud*]—because—because—[*determinedly*]—I doubted your ability to keep a secret. My real name is—[*looks up, and sees* MORTON *leaning beyond pillar*]—is a secret. [*Pause, in which* OAKHURST *slowly recovers his coolness.*] It will be given to the good priest who to-night joins our fate forever, Jovita,—forever, in spite of calumny, opposition, or *spies!*—the *padre* whom we shall reach, if enough life remains in your pulse and mine to clasp these hands together. [*After a pause.*] Are you content?

Jovita. I am.

Oakhurst. Then there is not a moment to lose. Retire and prepare yourself for a journey. I will wait here.

Jovita. I am ready now.

Oakhurst [*looking toward pillar*]. Pardon, my darling: there was a bracelet—a mere trifle—I once gave you. It is not on your wrist. I am a trifle superstitious, perhaps: it was my first gift. Bring it with you. I will wait. Go! [*Exit* JOVITA.]

> [OAKHURST *watches her exit, lounges indifferently toward gate; when opposite pillar, suddenly seizes* MORTON *by the throat and drags him noiselessly to centre.*

Oakhurst [*hurriedly*]. One outcry,—a single word,—and it is your last. I care not who *you* may be!—who I am,—you have heard enough to know, at least, that you are in the grip of a desperate man. [*Keys fall from* MORTON'S *hand.* OAKHURST *seizes them.*] Silence! on your life.

Morton [*struggling*]. You would not dare! I command you—

Oakhurst [*dragging him to gateway*]. Out you must go.

Morton. Stop, I command you. *I* never turned *my* father out of doors!

Oakhurst [*gazing at* MORTON]. It is an *old* man! I release you. Do as you will, only remember that that girl is mine forever, that there is no power on earth will keep me from her.

Morton. On conditions.

Oakhurst. Who are you that make conditions? You are not—her father?

Morton. No, but I am *yours!* Alexander Morton, **I** charge you to hear me.

Oakhurst [starting in astonishment, aside]. Sandy Morton, my lost partner's father! This is fate.

Morton. You are astonished; but I thought so. Ay, you will hear me now! I am your father, Alexander Morton, who drove you, a helpless boy, into disgrace and misery. I know your shameless life: for twenty years it was mine, and worse, until, by the grace of God, I reformed, as you shall. I have stopped you in a disgraceful act. Your mother—God forgive me!—left *her* house, for *my* arms, as wickedly, as wantonly, as shamelessly—

Oakhurst. Stop, old man, stop! Another word [*seizing him*], and I may forget your years.

Morton. But not your blood. No, Alexander Morton, I have come thousands of miles for one sacred purpose,— to save you; and I shall, with God's will, do it now. Be it so, on one condition. You shall have this girl; but lawfully, openly, with the sanction of Heaven and your parents.

Oakhurst [aside]. I see a ray of hope. This is Sandy's father: the cold, insensate brute who drove him into exile, the one bitter memory of his life. Sandy disappeared irreclaimable, or living alone, hating irrevocably the author of his misery; why should not I—

Morton [continuing]. On one condition. Hear me, Alexander Morton. If within a year, you, abandoning your evil practices, your wayward life, seek to reform beneath my roof, I will make this proud Spanish Don glad to accept you as the more than equal of his daughter.

Oakhurst [aside]. It would be an easy deception. Sandy has given me the details of his early life. At least, before the imposition was discovered I shall be—[*Aloud.*] I—I [*Aside.*] Perdition! *she* is coming! There is a light moving in the upper chamber. Don José is awakened. [*Aloud.*] I—I—accept.

Morton. It is well. Take these keys, open yonder gate and fly! [*As* OAKHURST *hesitates.*] Obey me. I will meet your sweetheart and explain all. You will come here at daylight in the morning and claim admittance, not as a vagabond, a housebreaker, but as my son. You hesitate. Alexander Morton, I, your father, command you. Go!

[OAKHURST *goes to the gate, opens it, as the sound of* DIEGO'S *voice, singing in the fog, comes faintly in.*

O yer's your Sandy Morton,
    Drink him down!
O yer's your Sandy Morton,
    Drink him down!
O yer's your Sandy Morton,
For he's drunk and goin' a-courtin'.'
O yer's your Sandy Morton,
    Drink him down!

[OAKHURST *recoils against gate;* MORTON *hesitates, as window in corridor opens and* DON JOSÉ *calls from upper corridor.*

Don José. Concho! [*Pause.*] 'Tis that vagabond Diego, lost his way in the fog. Strange that Concho should have overlooked him. I will descend.

Morton [*to* OAKHURST]. Do you hear?

[*Exit* OAKHURST *through gateway.* MORTON *closes gate and returns to centre.— Enter* JOVITA *hurriedly.*

Jovita. I have it here. Quick! there is a light in Don José's chamber; my father is coming down. [*Sees* MORTON *and screams.*]

Morton [*seizing her*]. Hush, for your own sake, for *his*, control yourself. He is gone, but he will return. [*To* JOVITA, *still struggling.*] Hush, I beg, Miss Jovita. I beg, I command you, my daughter, hush!

Jovita [*whispering*]. His voice has changed. What does this mean? [*Aloud.*] Where has he gone? and why are *you* here?

Morton [*slowly and seriously*]. He has left me here to answer the unanswered question you asked him. [*Enter* Don José *and* Col. Starbottle r. *and* l.] I am here to tell you that I am his father, and that he is Alexander Morton.

TABLEAU.

Curtain.

END OF ACT I.

ACT II.

SCENE 1.—*Red Gulch. Cañon of river, and distant view of Sierras, snow-ravined. Schoolhouse of logs in right middle distance. Ledge of rocks in centre. On steps of schoolhouse two large bunches of flowers. Enter* STARBOTTLE, *slowly climbing rocks* L., *panting and exhausted. Seats himself on rock, foreground, and wipes his face with his pockethandkerchief.*

Starbottle. This is evidently the—er—locality. Here are the—er—groves of Academus—the heights of—er—Ida! I should say that the unwillingness which the—er—divine Shakespeare points out in the—er—"whining schoolboy" is intensified in—er—climbing this height, and the—er—alacrity of his departure must be in exact ratio to his gravitation. Good idea. Ged! say it to schoolma'am. Wonder what she's like? Humph! the usual thin, weazened, hatchet-faced Yankee spinster, with an indecent familiarity with Webster's Dictionary! And this is the woman, Star, you're expected to discover, and bring back to affluence and plenty. This is the new fanaticism of Mr. Alexander Morton, sen. Ged! not satisfied with dragging his prodigal son out of merited obscurity, this miserable old lunatic commissions *me* to hunt up another of his abused relatives; some forty-fifth cousin, whose mother he had frozen, beaten, or starved to death. And all this to please his prodigal! Ged! if that prodigal hadn't presented himself that morning, I'd have

picked up—er—some—er—reduced gentleman—Ged! that
knew how to spend the old man's money to better advantage. [*Musing.*] If this schoolmistress were barely good-
looking, Star,—and she's sure to have fifty thousand from
the old man—Ged! you might get even with Alexander, sen.
for betrothing his prodigal to Doña Jovita, in spite of the
—er—evident preference that the girl showed for you.
Capital idea! If she's not positively hideous I'll do it! Ged!
I'll reconnoitre first! [*Musing.*] I could stand one eye;
yes—er—single eye would not be positively objectionable in
the—er—present experiments of science toward the—er—
the substitution of glass. Red hair, Star, is—er—Venetian
—the beauty of Giorgione. [*Goes up to schoolhouse window,
and looks in.*] Too early! Seven empty benches; seven
desks splashed with ink. The—er—rostrum of the awful
Minerva empty, but—er—adorned with flowers, nosegays—
demn me! And here, here on the—er—very threshold
[*looking down*], floral tributes. The—er—conceit of these
New England schoolma'ams, and their—er—evident Jesuiti-
cal influence over the young, is fraught, sir, fraught with—
er—darkly political significance. Eh, Ged! there's a carica-
ture on the blackboard. [*Laughing.*] Ha, ha! Absurd
chalk outline of ridiculous fat person. Evidently the schoolma'am's admirer. Ged! immensely funny! Ah! boys will
be boys. Like you, Star, just like you,—always up to tricks
like that. A sentence scrawled below the figure seems to be
—er—explanation. Hem! [*Takes out eyeglass.*] Let's see
[*reading.*] "This is old"—old—er—old—demme, sir!
—"Starbottle!" This is infamous. I haven't been forty-
eight hours in the place, and to my certain knowledge
haven't spoken to a child. Ged! sir, it's the—er—posting
of a libel! The woman, the—er—female, who permits this
kind of thing should be made responsible—er—personally

responsible. Eh, hush! What have we here? [*Retires to ledge of rock.*]

Enter MISS MARY, L., *reading letter.*

Miss Mary. Strange! Is it all a dream? No! here are the familiar rocks, the distant snow-peaks, the school-house, the spring below. An hour ago I was the poor schoolmistress of Red Gulch, with no ambition nor hope beyond this mountain wall; and now—oh, it must be a dream! But here is the letter. Certainly this is no delusion: it is too plain, formal, business-like. [*Reads.*]

MY DEAR COUSIN,—I address the only surviving child of my cousin Mary and her husband John Morris, both deceased. It is my duty as a Christian relative to provide you with a home,—to share with you that wealth and those blessings that a kind Providence has vouchsafed me. I am aware that my conduct to your father and mother, while in my sinful and unregenerate state, is no warrant for my present promise; but my legal adviser, Col. Starbottle, who is empowered to treat with you, will assure you of the sincerity of my intention, and my legal ability to perform it. He will conduct you to my house; you will share its roof with me and my prodigal son Alexander, now by the grace of God restored, and mindful of the error of his ways. I enclose a draft for one thousand dollars: if you require more, draw upon me for the same.
     Your cousin,
       ALEXANDER MORTON, SEN.

My mother's cousin—so! Cousin Alexander! a rich man, and reunited to the son he drove into shameful exile. Well, we will see this confidential lawyer; and until then—until then—why, we are the schoolmistress of Red Gulch, and responsible for its youthful prodigals. [*Going to schoolhouse door.*]

Miss Mary [*stopping to examine flowers*]. Poor, poor Sandy! Another offering, and, as he fondly believes, unknown and anonymous! As if he were not visible in every petal and leaf! The *mariposa* blossom of the plain. The snow flower I longed for, from those cool snow-drifts beyond the ridge. And I really believe he was sober when he arranged them. Poor fellow! I begin to think that the dissipated portion of this community are the most interesting. Ah! some one behind the rock,—Sandy, I'll wager. No! a stranger!

Col. Starbottle [*aside, and advancing*]. If I could make her think I left those flowers! [*Aloud.*] When I state that —er—I am perhaps—er—stranger—

Miss Mary [*interrupting him coldly*]. You explain, sir, your appearance on a spot which the rude courtesy of even this rude miners' camp has preserved from intrusion.

Starbottle [*slightly abashed, but recovering himself*]. Yes —Ged!—that is, I—er—saw you admiring—er—tribute —er—humble tribute of flowers. I am myself passionately devoted to flowers. Ged! I've spent hours—in—er—bending over the—er—graceful sunflower, in—er—plucking the timid violet from the overhanging but reluctant bough, in collecting the—er—er—*fauna*—I mean the—er—*flora*—of this—er—district.

Miss Mary [*who has been regarding him intently*]. Permit me to leave you uninterrupted admiration of them. [*Handing him flowers.*] You will have ample time in your journey down the gulch to indulge your *curiosity!*

[*Hands* STARBOTTLE *flowers, enters schoolhouse, and quietly closes door on* STARBOTTLE *as* SANDY MORTON *enters cautiously and sheepishly from left*. SANDY *stops in astonishment on observing* STARBOTTLE, *and remains by wing left.*

Starbottle [*smelling flowers, and not noticing* MISS MARY'S *absence*]. Beautiful—er—exquisite. [*Looking up at closed door.*] Ged! most extraordinary disappearance! [*Looks around, and discovers* SANDY; *examines him for a moment through his eyeglass, and then, after a pause, inflates his chest, turns his back on* SANDY, *and advances to schoolhouse door.* SANDY *comes quickly, and, as* STARBOTTLE *raises his cane to rap on door, seizes his arm. Both men, regarding each other fixedly, holding each other, retreat slowly and cautiously to centre. Then* STARBOTTLE *disengages his arm.*]

Sandy [*embarrassedly but determinedly*]. Look 'yer, stranger. By the rules of this camp, this place is sacred to the school-ma'am and her children.

Starbottle [*with lofty severity*]. It is! Then—er—permit me to ask, sir, what *you* are doing here.

Sandy [*embarrassed, and dropping his head in confusion*]. I was passing. There is no school to-day.

Starbottle. Then, sir, Ged! permit me to—er—*demand*—*demand*, sir, an apology. You have laid, sir, your hand upon my person—demn me! Not the first time, sir, either; for, if I am not mistaken, you are—er—inebriated menial, sir, who two months ago jostled me, sir—demn me—as I entered the rancho of my friend Don José Castro.

Sandy [*starting aside*]. Don José! [*Aloud.*] Hush, hush! She will hear you. No—that is—[*stops confused and embarrassed. Aside.*] She will hear of my disgrace. He will tell her the whole story.

Starbottle. I shall await your apology one hour. At the end of that time, if it is not forthcoming, I shall—er—er—waive your menial antecedents, and expect the—er—satisfaction of a gentleman. Good-morning, sir. [*Turns to schoolhouse.*]

Sandy. No, no! you shall not go!

Starbottle. Who will prevent me?

Sandy [*grappling him.*] *I* will. [*Appealingly.*] Look 'yer, stranger; don't provoke me, I, a desperate man, desperate and crazed with drink,—don't ye, don't ye do it! For God's sake, take your hands off me! Ye don't know what ye do. Ah! [*Wildly holding* STARBOTTLE *firmly, and forcing him backward to precipice beyond ledge of rocks.*] Hear me. Three years ago, in a moment like this, I dragged a man—my friend—to this precipice. I—I—no, no :—don't anger me now! [SANDY'S *grip on* STARBOTTLE *relaxes slightly and his head droops.*]

Starbottle [*coolly*]. Permit me to remark, sir, that any reminiscence of your—er—friend—or any other man, is—er —at this moment irrelevant and impertinent. Permit me to point out the—er—fact, sir, that your hand is pressing heavily, demned heavily, on my shoulder.

Sandy [*fiercely*]. You shall not go!

Starbottle [*fiercely*]. Shall not?

> [*Struggle.* STARBOTTLE *draws derringer from his breast-pocket, and* SANDY *seizes his arm. In this position both parties struggle to ledge of rocks, and* COL. STARBOTTLE *is forced partly over.*]

Miss Mary [*opening schoolhouse-door*]. I thought I heard voices. [*Looking toward ledge of rocks, where* COL. STARBOTTLE *and* SANDY *are partly hidden by trees. Both men relax grasp of each other at* MISS MARY'S *voice.*]

Col. Starbottle [*aloud, and with voice slightly raised, to* SANDY]. By—er—leaning over this way a moment, a single moment, you will—er—perceive the trail I speak of. It follows the cañon to the right. It will bring you to—er—the settlement in an hour. [*To* MISS MARY, *as if observing her for the first time.*] I believe I am—er—right; but, being —er—more familiar with the locality, you can direct the gentleman better.

> [SANDY *slowly sinks on his knees beside rock, with his face averted from schoolhouse, as* COL. STAR-BOTTLE *disengages himself, and advances jauntily and gallantly to schoolhouse.*

Col. Starbottle. In—er—er—showing the stranger the—er—way, I perhaps interrupted our interview. The—er—observances of—er—civility and humanity must not be foregone, even for—er—the ladies. I—er—believe I address Miss Mary Morris. When I—er—state that my name is Col. Starbottle, charged on mission of—er—delicate nature, I believe I—er—explain *my* intrusion.

> [MISS MARY *bows, and motions to schoolhouse-door;* COL. STARBOTTLE, *bowing deeply, enters; but* MISS MARY *remains standing by door, looking toward trees that hide* SANDY.

MISS MARY [*aside*]. I am sure it was Sandy's voice! But why does he conceal himself?

Sandy [*aside, rising slowly to his feet, with his back to schoolhouse-door*]. Even this conceited bully overcomes me, and shames me with his readiness and tact. He was quick to spare her—a stranger—the spectacle of two angry men. I—I—must needs wrangle before her very door! Well, well! better out of her sight forever, than an object of pity or terror. [*Exit slowly, and with downcast eyes, right.*]

Miss Mary [*watching the trail*]. It *was* Sandy! and this concealment means something more than bashfulness. Perhaps the stranger can explain. [*Enters schoolhouse and closes door.*]

SCENE 2.—*The same. Enter* CONCHO, *lame, cautiously, from* R. *Pauses at* R., *and then beckons to* HOP SING, *who follows* R.

Concho [*impatiently*]. Well, you saw him?
Hop Sing. Me see him.
Concho. And you recognised him?
Hop Sing. No shabe likoquise.
Concho [*furiously*]. You knew him, eh? *Carramba!* you *knew* him?
Hop Sing [*slowly and sententiously*]. Me shabe man you callee Diego. Me shabbee Led Gulchee call Sandy. Me shabbee man Poker Flat callee Alexandlee Molton. Allee same, John! Allee same!
Concho [*rubbing his hands.*] *Bueno!* Good John! good John! And you knew he was called Alexander Morton? And go on—good John—go on!
Hop Sing. Me plentee washee shirtee—Melican man Poker Flat. Me plentee washee shirt Alexandlee Molton. Always litee, litee on shirt allee time. [*Pointing to tail of his blouse, and imitating writing with finger.*] Alexandlee Molton. Melican man tellee me—shirt say Alexandlee Molton—shabbee?
Concho. *Bueno!* Excellent John. Good John. His linen marked Alexander Morton. The proofs are gathering. [*Crosses to* C.] The letter I found in his pack, addressed to Alexander Morton, Poker Flat, which first put me on his track; the story of his wife's infidelity, and her flight with his partner to Red Gulch, the quarrel and fight that separated them, his flight to San José, his wanderings to the

mission of San Carmel, to the rancho of the Holy Fisherman. The record is complete!

Hop Sing. Alexandlee Molton—

Concho [*hurriedly returning to* HOP SING]. Yes! good John; yes, good John—go on. Alexander Morton—

Hop Sing. Alexandlee Molton. Me washee shirt, Alexandlee Molton; he no pay washee. Me washee flowty dozen hep—four bittie dozen—twenty dollar hep. Alexandlee Molton no payee. He say, "Go to hellee!" You pay me [*extending his hand*].

Concho. Car—! [*checking himself.*] *Poco tiempo,* John! In good time, John. Forty dollar—yes. Fifty dollar! Tomorrow, John.

Hop Sing. Me no likee "to-mollow!" Me no likee "nex time, John!" Allee time Melican man say, "Chalkee up, John," "No smallee change, John." Umph! Plenty foolee me!

Concho. You shall have your money, John; but go now—you comprehend. *Carramba!* go! [*Pushes* HOP SING *to wing.*]

Hop Sing [*expostulating*]. Flowty dozen, hep, John! twenty dollar, John. Sabe. Flowty—twenty—[*gesticulating with fingers.*]

[*Exit* HOP SING, *pushed off by* CONCHO.

Concho. The pagan dolt! But he is important. Ah! if he were wiser, I should not rid myself of him so quickly! And now for the schoolmistress,—the sweetheart of Sandy. If these men have not lied, he is in love with her; and if he is, he has told her his secret before now; and she will be swift to urge him to his rights. If he has not told her—umph! [*laughing*] it will not be a *day*—an *hour*—before she will find out if her lover is Alexander Morton, the rich man's son, or "Sandy," the unknown vagabond. Eh, friend Sandy! It was a woman that locked up your secret: it shall be a woman, *Madre di Dios!* who shall unlock it. Ha! [*Goes to door of schoolhouse as door opens, and appears* COL. STAR-BOTTLE.]

Concho [*aside*]. A thousand devils! the lawyer of the old man Morton. [*Aloud.*] Pardon, pardon! I am a stranger. I have lost my way on the mountain. I am seeking a trail. Senor, pardon!

Starbottle [*aside*]. Another man seeking the road! Ged! I believe he's lying too. [*Aloud.*] It is before you, sir, *down,*—down the mountain.

Concho. A thousand thanks, senor. [*Aside.*] Perdition catch him! [*Aloud.*] Thanks, senor. [*Exit* R.

Starbottle. Ged! I've seen that face before. Ged! it's Castro's major-domo. Demn me, but I believe all his domestics have fallen in love with the pretty schoolma'am.

Enter MISS MARY *from schoolhouse.*

Miss Mary [*slowly refolding letter*]. You are aware, then, of the contents of this note; and you are the friend of Alexander Morton, sen.?

Col. Starbottle. Permit me a moment, a single moment, to—er—er—explain. I am Mr. Morton's legal adviser. There is—er—sense of—er—responsibility,—er—personal responsibility, about the term "friend," that at the—er—er —present moment I am not—er—prepared to assume. The substance of the letter is before you. I am here to—er— express its spirit. I am here [*with great gallantry*] to express the—er—yearnings of cousinly affection. I am aware—er— that *our* conduct,—if I may use the—er—the plural of advocacy,—I am aware that—er—*our* conduct has not in the past years been of—er—er—exemplary character. I am aware that the—er—death of our lamented cousin, your sainted mother, was—er—hastened—I may—er—say—pre-cipi-

VOL. I.   Z

tated—by our—er—indiscretion. But we are here to—er—confess judgment—with—er—er—costs.

Miss Mary [*interrupting*]. In other words, your client, my cousin, having ruined my father, having turned his own widowed relation out of doors, and sent me, her daughter, among strangers to earn her bread; having seen my mother sink and die in her struggle to keep her family from want,—this man now seeks to condone his offences—pardon me, sir, if I use your own legal phraseology—by offering me a home; by giving me part of his ill-gotten wealth, the association of his own hypocritical self, and the company of his shameless, profligate son—

Starbottle [*interrupting*]. A moment, Miss Morris,—a single moment! The epithets you have used, the—er—vigorous characterisation of our—er—conduct, is—er—within the—er—strict rules of legal advocacy, correct. We are—er—rascals! we are—er—scoundrels! we are—er—well, I am not—er—prepared to say that we are not—er—demn me—hypocrites! But the young man you speak of —our son, whose past life (speaking as Col. Starbottle) no one more sincerely deprecates than myself,—that young man has reformed; has been for the past few months a miracle of sobriety, decorum, and industry; has taken, thanks to the example of—er—friends, a position of integrity in his father's business, of filial obedience in his father's household; is, in short, a paragon; and, demn me, I doubt if he's his father's son.

Miss Mary. Enough, sir! You are waiting for my answer. There is no reason why it should not be as precise, as brief, and as formal as your message. Go to my cousin; say that you saw the person he claims as his relation; say that you found her a poor schoolmistress in a mining-camp, dependent for her bread on the scant earnings of already impoverished men, dependent for her honour on the rude chivalry of outcasts and vagabonds; and say that then and there she repudiated your kinship, and respectfully declined your invitation.

Starbottle [*aside*]. Ged! Star, this is the—er—female of your species! This is the woman—the—er—one woman—for whom you are responsible, sir—personally responsible!

Miss Mary [*coldly*]. You have my answer, sir.

Col. Starbottle. Permit me—er—single moment—a single moment! Between the—er—present moment and that of my departure there is an—er—interval of twelve hours. May I, at the close of that interval, again present myself, without prejudice, for your final answer?

Miss Mary [*indifferently*]. As you will, sir. I shall be here.

Col. Starbottle. Permit me. [*Takes her hand gallantly.*] Your conduct and manner, Miss Morris, remind me—er—singularly of—er—beautiful creature—one of the—er—first families. [*Observing* MISS MARY *regarding him amusedly, becomes embarrassed.*] That is—er—I mean—er—er—good morning, Miss Morris! [*Passes by schoolhouse-door retreating and bowing, and picks up flowers from door-step.*] Good morning!

Miss Mary. Excuse me, Col. Starbottle [*with winning politeness*], but I fear I must rob you of those flowers. I recognise them now as the offering of one of my pupils. I fear I must revoke my gift [*taking flowers from astonished Colonel's hand*], all except a single one for your buttonhole. Have you any choice, or shall I [*archly*] choose for you? Then it shall be this. [*Begins to place flowers in buttonhole,* COL. STARBOTTLE *exhibiting extravagant gratitude in dumb show. Business prolonged through* MISS MARY'S *speech.*] If I am not wrong, Colonel, the gentleman to whom you so kindly pointed out the road this morning was not a stranger to you. Ah! I am right. There,—one moment,—a sprig of green, a single leaf, would set off the pink nicely. Here he is known only as " Sandy." You know the absurd habits of this camp. Of course he has another name. There! [*releasing the Colonel*]—it is much prettier now.

Col. Starbottle. Ged, madam! The rarest exotic—the Victoria Regina—is not as—er—graceful—er—tribute!

Miss Mary. And yet you refuse to satisfy my curiosity?

Col. Starbottle [*with great embarrassment, which at last resolves itself into increased dignity of manner*]. What you ask is—er—er—impossible! You are right: the—er—gentleman you allude to is known to me under—er—er—another name. But honour—Miss Morris, honour!—seals the lips of Col. Starbottle. [*Aside.*] If she should know he was a menial! No! the position of the man you have challenged, Star, must be equal to your own. [*Aloud.*] Anything, Miss Morris, but—er—that!

Miss Mary [*smiling*]. Be it so. *Adios*, Col. Starbottle.

Col. Starbottle [*gallantly*]. *Au revoir*, Miss Morris.

[*Exit, impressively, left.*

Miss Mary. So Sandy conceals another name, which he withholds from Red Gulch. Well! pshaw! What is that to me? The camp is made up of refugees,—men who perhaps have good reason to hide a name that may be infamous, the name that would publish a crime. Nonsense! Crime and Sandy! No! Shame and guilt do not hide themselves in those honest but occasionally somewhat bloodshot eyes. Besides, goodness knows! the poor fellow's weakness is palpable enough. No, that is not the reason; it is no guilt that keeps his name hidden,—at least, not his. [*Seating herself and arranging flowers in her lap.*] Poor Sandy! he must have climbed the eastern summit to get this. See, the rosy sunrise still lingers in its very petals; the dew is fresh upon it. Dear little mountain baby! I really believe that fellow got up before daylight to climb that giddy height and secure its virgin freshness. And to think in a moment of spite I'd have given it to that bombastic warrior! [*Pause.*] That was a fine offer you refused just now, Miss Mary. Think of it; a home of luxury, a position of assured respect and homage; the life I once led, with all its difficulties smoothed away, its uncertainty dispelled,—think of it! My poor mother's dream fulfilled,—I, her daughter, the mistress of affluence, the queen of social power! What a temptation! Ah! Miss Mary, *was* it a temptation? Was there nothing in your free life here that stiffened your courage, that steeled the adamant of your refusal? or was it only the memory of your mother's wrongs? Luxury and wealth! Could you command a dwelling more charming than this? Position and respect! Is not the awful admiration of these lawless men more fascinating than the perilous flattery of gentlemen like Col. Starbottle? Is not the devotion of these outcasts more complimentary than the lip-service of perfumed gallantry? [*Pause.*] It's very odd he doesn't come. I wonder if that conceited old fool said anything to him. [*Rises, and then seats herself smiling.*] He *has* come. He is dodging in and out of the manganita bushes below the spring. I suppose he imagines my visitor still here. The bashful fool! If anybody should see him, it would be enough to make a petty scandal! I'll give him a talking-to. [*Pause.*] I wonder if the ridiculous fool has gone to sleep in those bushes. [*Rises.*] Well, let him: it will help him to recover his senses from last night's dissipation; and you, Miss Mary, it is high time you were preparing the lessons for to-morrow. [*Goes to schoolhouse, enters door, and slams it behind her; after a moment reappears with empty bucket.*] Of course there's no water, and I am dying of thirst. [*Goes slowly to left, and pauses embarrassedly and bashfully, presently laughs, suddenly frowns and assumes an appearance of indignation.*] Miss Mary Morris, have you become such an egregious fool that you dare not satisfy the ordinary cravings of human nature, just because an idle, dissipated, bashful blockhead—nonsense !

[*Exit, brandishing pail.*

SCENE 3.—*The same.*

[*A pause.* SANDY'S *voice without.*] This way, miss: the trail is easier.

[MISS MARY'S *voice without.*] Never mind me : look after the bucket.

Enter SANDY, *carrying bucket with water, followed by* MISS MARY. SANDY *sets bucket down.*

Miss Mary. There ! you've spilt half of it. If it had been whisky, you'd have been more careful.

Sandy [*submissively*]. Yes, miss.

Miss Mary [*aside*]. "Yes, miss!" The man will drive me crazy with his saccharine imbecility. [*Aloud.*] I believe you would assent to anything, even if I said you were an impostor !

Sandy [*amazedly*]. An impostor, Miss Mary?

Miss Mary. Well, I don't know what other term you use in Red Gulch to express a man who conceals his real name under another.

Sandy [*embarrassed, but facing* MISS MARY]. Has anybody been tellin' ye I was an impostor, miss? Has that derned old fool that I saw you with——

Miss Mary. "That old fool," as you call him, was too honourable a gentleman to disclose your secret, and too loyal a friend to traduce you by an epithet. Fear nothing, Mr. "Sandy." If you have limited your confidence to *one* friend, it has not been misplaced. But, dear me, don't think *I* wish to penetrate your secret. No! The little I learned was accidental. Besides, his business was with me: perhaps, as his friend, you already know it.

Sandy [*meekly*]. Perhaps, miss, he was too honourable a gentleman to disclose *your* secret. His business was with me.

Miss Mary [*aside*]. He has taken a leaf out of my book! He is not so stupid, after all. [*Aloud.*] *I* have no secret. Col. Starbottle came here to make me an offer.

Sandy [*recoiling*]. An offer!

Miss Mary. Of a home and independence. [*Aside.*] Poor fellow! how pale he looks! [*Aloud.*] Well you see, I am more trustful than you. I will tell you *my* secret, and you shall aid me with your counsel. [*They sit on ledge of rocks.*] Listen! My mother had a cousin once,—a cousin cruel, cowardly, selfish, and dissolute. She loved him, as women are apt to love such men,—loved him so that she beguiled her own husband to trust his fortunes in the hands of this wretched profligate. The husband was ruined, disgraced. The wife sought her cousin for help for her necessities. He met her with insult, and proposed that she should fly with him.

Sandy. One moment, miss: it wasn't his partner,—his partner's wife—eh?

Miss Mary [*impatiently*]. It was the helpless wife of his own blood, I tell you. The husband died broken-hearted. The wife, my mother, struggled in poverty, under the shadow of a proud name, to give me an education, and died while I was still a girl. To-day this cousin,—this more than murderer of my parents,—old, rich, self-satisfied, *reformed*, invites me, by virtue of that kinship he violated and despised, to his home, his wealth, his—his family roof-tree! The man you saw was his agent.

Sandy. And you—

Miss Mary. Refused.

Sandy [*passing his hand over his forehead*]. You did wrong, Miss Mary.

Miss Mary. Wrong, sir? [*Rising.*]

Sandy [*humbly but firmly*]. Sit ye down, Miss Mary. It ain't for ye to throw your bright young life away 'yer in this place. It ain't for such as ye to soil your fair young hands by raking in the ashes to stir up the dead embers of a family wrong. It ain't for ye—ye'll pardon me, Miss Mary, for sayin' it—it ain't for ye to allow when it's *too* late fur a man to reform or to go back of his reformation. Don't ye do it, miss, fur God's sake,—don't ye do it! Harken, Miss Mary. If ye'll take my advice—a fool's advice, maybe— ye'll go. And when I tell ye that that advice, if ye take it, will take the sunshine out of these hills, the colour off them trees, the freshness outer them flowers, the heart's blood outer me,—ye'll know that I ain't thinkin' o' myself, but of ye. And I wouldn't say this much to ye, Miss Mary, but you're goin' away. There's a flower, miss, you're wearin' in your bosom,—a flower I picked at daybreak this morning, five miles away in the snow. The wind was blowing chill around it, so that my hands that dug for it were stiff and cold; but the roots were warm, Miss Mary, as they are now in your bosom. Ye'll keep that flower, Miss Mary, in remembrance of my love for ye, that kept warm and blossomed through the snow. And, don't start, Miss Mary,—for ye'll leave behind ye, as I did, the snow and rocks through which it bloomed. I axes your pardin, miss—I'm hurtin' yer feelins, sure.

Miss Mary [*rising with agitation.*] Nothing,—nothing; but climbing these stupid rocks has made me giddy: that's all. Your arm. [*To* SANDY *impatiently.*] Can't you give me your arm? [SANDY *supports* MISS MARY *awkwardly toward schoolhouse. At door* MISS MARY *pauses.*] But if this reformation is so easy, so acceptable, why have you not profited by it? Why have you not reformed? Why have I found you here, a disgraced, dissipated, anonymous outcast, whom an honest girl dare not know? Why do you presume to preach to me? Have you a father?

Sandy. Hush! Miss Mary, hush! I had a father. Harken! All that you have suffered from a kinship even so far removed, I have known from the hands of one who should have protected me. *My* father was—but no matter. You, Miss Mary, came out of your trials like gold from the washing. I was only the dirt and gravel to be thrown away. It is too late, Miss Mary, too late. My father has never sought me, would turn me from his doors had I sought him. Perhaps he is only right.

Miss Mary. But why should he be so different from others? Listen! This very cousin whose offer I refused had a son,—wild, wayward, by all report the most degraded of men. It was part of my cousin's reformation to save this son, and, if it were possible, snatch him from that terrible fate which seemed to be his only inheritance.

Sandy [*eagerly*]. Yes, miss.

Miss Mary. To restore him to a regenerated home. With this idea he followed his prodigal to California. I, you understand, was only an after-thought consequent upon his success. He came to California upon this pilgrimage two years ago. He had no recollection, so they tell me, by which he could recognise this erring son; and at first his search was wild, profitless, and almost hopeless. But by degrees, and with a persistency that seemed to increase with his hopelessness, he was rewarded by finding some clue to him at—at—at—

Sandy [*excitedly*]. At Poker Flat?

Miss Mary. Ah! perhaps you know the story,—at Poker Flat. He traced him to the Mission of San Carmel—

Sandy. Yes, miss; go on.

Miss Mary. He was more successful than he deserved, perhaps. He found him. I see you know the story.

Sandy. Found him! found him! Miss, did you say found him?

Miss Mary. Yes, found him. And to-day Alexander Morton, the reclaimed prodigal, is part of the household I am invited to join. So you see, Mr. Sandy, there is still hope. What has happened to him is only a promise to you. Eh! Mr. Sandy—what is the matter? Are you ill? Your exertion this morning, perhaps. Speak to me! Gracious heavens, he is going mad! No! no! Yes—it cannot be—it is—he *has* broken his promise: he is drunk again.

Sandy [*rising, excited and confused*]. Excuse me, miss, I am a little onsartain here [*pointing to his head*]. I can't—I disremember—what you said just now: ye mentioned the name o' that prodigal that was found.

Miss Mary. Certainly: compose yourself,—my cousin's son, Alexander Morton. Listen, Sandy: you promised *me*, you know, you said for *my* sake you would not touch a drop.

[*Enter cautiously toward schoolhouse the* DUCHESS; *stops on observing* SANDY, *and hides behind rock.*

Sandy [*still bewildered and incoherent*]. I reckon. Harken, miss; is that thar thing [*pointing towards rock where* DUCHESS *is concealed*]—is that a tree, or—or—a woman? Is it sorter movin' this way?

Miss Mary [*laying her hand on* SANDY'S]. Recover your senses, for heaven's sake, Sandy,—for *my* sake! It is only a tree.

Sandy [*rising*]. Then, miss, I've broke my word with ye: I'm drunk. P'r'aps I'd better be a-goin' [*lookin' round confusedly*] till I'm sober.   [*Going toward* L.

Miss Mary [*seizing his hand*]. But you'll see me again, Sandy: you'll come here—before—before—I go?

Sandy. Yes, miss,—before ye go. [*Staggers stupidly toward* L. *Aside.*] Found him! found Alexander Morton! It's a third time, Sandy, the third time: it means—it means you're mad! [*Laughs wildly, and exit* L.]

Miss Mary [*springing to her feet*]. There is a mystery behind all this, Mary Morris, that you—you—must discover. That man was *not* drunk: he *had not* broken his promise to me. What does it all mean? I have it. I will accept the offer of this Alexander Morton. I will tell him the story of this helpless man, this poor, poor, reckless Sandy. With the story of his own son before his eyes, he cannot but interest himself in his fate. He is rich: he will aid me in my search for Sandy's father, for Sandy's secret. At the worst, I can only follow the advice of this wretched man,— an advice so generous, so kind, so self-sacrificing. Ah!—

SCENE 4.—*The same. Enter the* DUCHESS, *showily and extravagantly dressed. Her manner at first is a mixture of alternate shyness and bravado.*

The Duchess. I heerd tell that you was goin' down to 'Frisco to-morrow, for your vacation; and I couldn't let ye go till I came to thank ye for your kindness to my boy,— little Tommy.

Miss Mary [*aside, rising abstractedly, and recalling herself with an effort.*] I see,—a poor outcast, the mother, of my anonymous pupil. [*Aloud.*] Tommy! a good boy, —a dear, good little boy.

The Duchess. Thankee, miss, thankee. If I am his mother, thar ain't a sweeter, dearer, better boy lives than him. And, if I ain't much as says it, thar ain't a sweeter, dearer, angeler teacher than he's got. It ain't for you to be complimented by me, miss; it ain't for such as me to be comin' here in broad day to do it, neither; but I come to ask a favour,—not for me, miss, but for the darling boy.

Miss Mary [aside, abstractedly]. This poor, degraded creature will kill me with her wearying gratitude. Sandy will not return, of course, while she is here. [*Aloud.*] Go on. If I can help you or yours, be assured I will.

The Duchess. Thankee, miss. You see, thar's no one the boy has any claim on but me, and I ain't the proper person to bring him up. I did allow to send him to 'Frisco last year; but when I heerd talk that a schoolma'am was comin' up, and you did, and he sorter tuk to ye natril from the first, I guess I did well to keep him 'yer. For O miss, he loves ye so much; and, if you could hear him talk in his purty way, ye wouldn't refuse him anything.

Miss Mary [with fatigued politeness and increasing impatience.] I see, I see—pray go on.

The Duchess [with quiet persistency]. It's natril he should take to ye, miss; for his father, when I first knowed him, miss, was a gentleman like yourself; and the boy must forget me sooner or later—and I ain't goin' to cry about *that.*

Miss Mary [impatiently]. Pray tell me how I can serve you.

The Duchess. Yes, miss; you see, I came to ask you to take my Tommy,—God bless him for the sweetest, bestest boy that lives—to take him with you. I've money plenty; and it's all yours and his. Put him in some good school, whar ye kin go and see, and sorter help him to—forget—his mother. Do with him what you like. The worst you can do will be kindness to what he would learn with me. You will—I know you will, won't you? You will make him as pure and as good as yourself; and when he has grown up, and is a gentleman, you will tell him his father's name,—the name that hasn't passed my lips for years,—the name of Alexander Morton.

Miss Mary [*aside*]. Alexander Morton! The prodigal! Ah! I see,—the ungathered husks of his idle harvest.

The Duchess. You hesitate, Miss Mary [*seizing her*]. Do not take your hand away. You are smiling. God bless you! I know you will take my boy. Speak to me, Miss Mary.

Miss Mary [*aloud*]. I will take your child. More than that, I will take him to his father.

The Duchess. No, no! for God's sake, no, Miss Mary! He has never seen him from his birth: he does not know him. He will disown him. He will curse him,—will curse me!

Miss Mary. Why should he? Surely his crime is worse than yours.

The Duchess. Hear me, Miss Mary. [*Aside.*] How can I tell her? [*Aloud.*] One moment, miss. I was once—ye may not believe it, miss—as good, as pure, as you. I had a husband, the father of this child. He was kind, good, easy, forgiving,—too good for me, miss, too simple and unsuspecting. He was what the world calls a fool, miss: he loved me too well,—the kind o' crime, miss,—beggin' your pardon, and all precepts to the contrairy,—the one thing that women like me never forgives. He had a pardner, miss, that governed him as *he* never governed me; that held him with the stronger will, and maybe *me* too. I was young, miss,—no older than yourself then; and I ran away with him,—left all, and ran away with my husband's pardner. My husband—nat'rally—took to drink. I axes your pardin', miss; but ye'll see now, allowin' your larnin', that Alexander Morton ain't the man as will take my child.

Miss Mary. Nonsense! you are wrong. He has reformed; he has been restored to his home,—your child's

home,—your home if you will but claim it. Do not fear:
I will make that right.

Enter SANDY, *slowly and sheepishly*, R.; *stops on observing the*
DUCHESS, *and stands amazed and motionless.*

Miss Mary [*observing* SANDY—*aside*]. He *has* returned.
Poor fellow! How shall I get rid of this woman? [*Aloud.*]
Enough! If you are sincere, I will take your child, and,
God help me! bring him to his home and yours. Are you
satisfied?

The Duchess. Thank ye! Thank ye, miss; but—but
thar's a mistake somewhar. In course it's natural. Ye
don't know the father of that child, my boy Tommy, under
the name o' Alexander Morton. Yer thinkin', like as not, of
another man. The man I mean lives 'yer, in this camp:
they calls him Sandy, miss,—*Sandy!*

Miss Mary [*after a pause, coming forward passionately*].
Hush! I have given you my answer, be it Alexander
Morton or Sandy. Go now: bring me the child this evening
at my house. I will meet you there. [*Leads the* DUCHESS
to wing. The DUCHESS *endeavours to fall at her feet.*]

Duchess. God bless you, miss!

Miss Mary [*hurriedly embracing her.*] No more, no more
—but go!

Exit DUCHESS. MISS MARY *returns hurriedly
to centre, confronting* SANDY.

Miss Mary [*to* SANDY, *hurriedly and excitedly*]. You
have heard what that woman said. I do not ask you
under what *alias* you are known here: I only ask a single
question,—Is *she* your wife? are you the father of her child?

Sandy [*sinking upon his knees before her, and covering his
face with his hands*]. I am!

Miss Mary. Enough! [*Taking flower from her bosom.*]
Here, I give you back the flower you gave me this morning.

It has faded and died here upon my breast. But I shall replace it with your foundling,—the child of that woman, born like that flower in the snow! And I go now, Sandy, and leave behind me, as you said this morning, the snow and rocks in which it bloomed. Good-bye! Farewell, farewell—forever! [*Goes toward schoolhouse as—*

Enter COL. STARBOTTLE.

Miss Mary [*to* STARBOTTLE]. You are here in season, sir. You must have come for an answer to your question. You must first give me one to mine. Who is this man [*pointing to* SANDY], the man you met upon the rocks this morning?

Col. Starbottle. Ahem! I am—er—now fully prepared and responsible, I may say, miss—er—personally responsible, to answer that question. When you asked it this morning, the ordinary courtesy of the—er—code of honour threw a —er—cloak around the—er—antecedents of the—er—man whom I had—er—elected, by a demand for personal satisfaction, to the equality of myself, an—er—gentleman! That—er—cloak is now removed. I have waited six hours for an apology or a—er—reply to my demand. I am now free to confess that the—er—person you allude to was first known by me, three months ago, as an inebriated menial,— a groom in the household of my friend Don José Castro,— by the—er—simple name of "Diego."

Miss Mary [*slowly*]. I am satisfied. I accept my cousin's invitation. [*Exit slowly, supported by* COL. STARBOTTLE, R.]

> [*As* STARBOTTLE *and* MISS MARY *exeunt* R., CONCHO *and* HOP SING *enter cautiously* L. SANDY *slowly rises to his feet, passes his hand across his forehead, looks around toward exit of* STARBOTTLE *and* MISS MARY.

Sandy [*slowly, but with more calmness of demeanour*]. Gone, gone—forever! No: I am not mad, nor crazed with drink. My hands no longer tremble. There is no confusion here. [*Feeling his forehead.*] I heard them all. It was no dream. I heard her every word. Alexander Morton, yes, they spoke of Alexander Morton. She is going to him, to my father. She is going—she, Mary, my cousin—she is going to my father. He has been seeking me—has found—ah! [*Groans.*] No, no, Sandy! Be patient, be calm: you are not crazy—no, no, good Sandy, good old boy! Be patient, be patient: it is coming, it is coming. Yes, I see: some one has leaped into my place; some one has leaped into the old man's arms. Some one will creep into *her* heart! No! by God! No! I *am* Alexander Morton. Yes, yes! But how, how shall I prove it?—how? Who [CONCHO *steps cautiously forward towards* SANDY *unobserved*] will believe the vagabond, the outcast—my God!—the crazy drunkard?

Concho [*advancing, and laying his hand on* SANDY]. I will!

Sandy [*staggering back amazedly*]. You!

Concho. Yes—I—I—Concho! You know me, Diego, you know me,—Concho, the major-domo of the Blessed Innocents. Ha! you know me now. Yes, I have come to save you. I have come to make you strong. So! I have come to help you strip the Judas that has stepped into your place,—the sham prodigal that has had the fatted calf and the ring,—ah! ah!

Sandy. You? You do not know me!

Concho. Ah! you think, you think, eh? Listen! Since you left me I have tracked *him—the impostor*, this Judas, this coyote—step by step, until his tracks crossed yours; and then I sought you out. I know all. I found a letter you had dropped; that brought me to Poker Flat. Ah! you start! I have seen those who knew you as Alexander Morton. You see! Ah! I am wise.

Sandy [*aside*]. It is true. [*Aloud.*] But [*suspiciously*] why have you done this? You, Concho?—you were not my friend.

Concho. No, but *he* is my enemy. Ah! you start. Look at me, Alexander Morton, Sandy, Diego! You knew a man, strong, active, like yourself. Eh! look at me now! Look at me, a cripple! Eh! lame and crushed here [*pointing to his leg*], broken and crushed here [*pointing to his heart*], by him,—the impostor! Listen, Diego! The night I was sent to track you from the rancho, he—this man—struck me from the wall, dashed me to the earth, and made *my body*, broken and bruised, a stepping-stone to leap the wall into your place, Diego—into your father's heart —into my master's home. They found me dead, they thought,—no, not dead, Diego! It was sad, they said,— unfortunate. They nursed me; they talked of money—eh! Diego!—money! They would have pensioned me to hush scandal—eh! I was a dog, a foreigner, a Greaser! Eh! That is why I am here. No! I love you not, Diego; you are of his race; but I hate—Mother of God!—I *hate* him!

Sandy [*rising to his feet, aside*]. Good! I begin to feel my courage return; my nerves are stronger. Courage, Sandy! [*Aloud.*] Be it so, Concho: there is my hand! We will help each other,—you to my birthright, I to your revenge! Hark ye! [SANDY'S *manner becomes more calm and serious.*] This impostor is no craven, no coyote. Whoever he is, he must be strong. He has most plausible evidences. We must have rigid proofs. I will go with you to Poker Flat. There is one man, if he be living, knows me better than any man who lives. He has done me wrong,—a great wrong, Concho,—but I will forgive him. I will do more,—I will ask his forgiveness. He will be a witness no man dare gainsay—my partner—God help him and forgive him as I do!—John Oakhurst.

Concho. Oakhurst your partner!

Sandy [*angrily*]. Yes. Look ye, Concho, he has wronged me in a private way: that is *my* business, not *yours;* but he was *my* partner,—no one shall abuse him before me.

Concho. Be it so! Then sink here! Rot here! Go back to your husks, O prodigal! wallow in the ditches of this camp, and see your birthright sold for a dram of *aguardiente!* Lie here, dog and coyote that you are, with your mistress under the protection of your destroyer! For I tell you—I, Concho, the cripple—that the man who struck me down, the man who stepped into your birthright, the man who to-morrow welcomes your sweetheart in his arms, who holds the custody of your child, is your partner—John Oakhurst!

Sandy [*who has been sinking under* CONCHO'S *words, rising convulsively to his feet*]. God be merciful to me a sinner! [*Faints.*]

Concho [*standing over his prostrate body exultingly*]. I am right. You are wise, Concho! you are wise! You have found Alexander Morton!

Hop Sing [*advancing slowly to* SANDY'S *side, and extending open palm*]. Me washee shirt flo you, flowty dozen hab. You no payee me. Me wantee twenty dollar hep. Sabe.

[*Curtain.*]

END OF ACT II.

ACT III.

SCENE I.—*The bank parlour of Morton & Son, San Francisco. Room richly furnished; two square library desks left and right. At right, safe in wall; at left, same with practicable doors. Folding door in flat* C., *leading to counting-room. Door in left to private room of Alexander Morton, sen.; door in right to private room of Morton, jun.* ALEXANDER MORTON, sen., *discovered at desk* R., *opening and reading letter*

Morton, sen. [*laying down letter*]. Well, well! the usual story! Letters from all sorts of people who have done or intend to do all sorts of things for my reclaimed prodigal. [*Reads.*] "Dear Sir: five years ago I loaned some money to a stranger who answers the description of your recovered son. He will remember Jim Parker,—Limping Jim, of Poker Flat. Being at present short of funds, please send twenty dollars, amount loaned, by return mail. If not convenient, five dollars will do as instalment." Pshaw! [*Throws letter aside and takes up another.*] "Dear Sir: I invite your attention to enclosed circular for a proposed Home for Dissipated and Anonymous Gold-Miners. Your well-known reputation for liberality, and your late valuable experience in the reformation of your son, will naturally enlist your broadest sympathies. We enclose a draft for five thousand dollars for your signature." We shall see. Another: "Dear Sir: the Society for the Formation of Bible Classes in the

Upper Stanislaus acknowledge your recent munificent gift of five hundred dollars to the cause. Last Sabbath Brother Hawkins of Poker Flat related with touching effect the story of your prodigal to an assemblage of over two hundred miners. Owing to unusual expenses, we regret to be compelled to draw upon you for five hundred dollars more." So! [*Putting down letter.*] If we were given to pride and vainglory, we might well be puffed up with the fame of our works and the contagion of our example: yet I fear that, with the worldly-minded, this praise of charity to others is only the prayerful expectation of some personal application to the praiser. [*Rings hand-bell.*]

Enter JACKSON.

[*To* JACKSON.] File these letters [*handing letters*] with the others. There is no answer. Has young Mr. Alexander come in yet?

Jackson. He only left here an hour ago. It was steamer day yesterday: he was up all night, sir.

Old Morton [*aside*]. True. And the night before he travelled all night, riding two hours ahead of one of our defaulting agents, and saved the bank a hundred thousand dollars. Certainly his devotion to business is unremitting. [*Aloud.*] Any news from Col. Starbottle?

Jackson. He left this note, sir, early this morning.

Old Morton [*takes it and reads*]. "I think I may say, on my own personal responsibility, that the mission is successful. Miss Morris will arrive to-night with a female attendant and child." [*To* JACKSON.] That is all, sir. Stop! Has any one been smoking here?

Jackson. Not to my knowledge, sir.

Old Morton. There was a flavour of stale tobacco-smoke in the room this morning when I entered, and ashes on the carpet. I *know* that young Mr. Alexander has abandoned the pernicious habit. See that it does not occur again.

Jackson. Yes, sir. [*Aside.*] I must warn Mr. Alexander that his friends must be more careful; and yet those ashes were good for a deposit of fifty thousand.

Old Morton. Is any one waiting?

Jackson. Yes, sir,—Don José Castro and Mr. Capper.

Old Morton. Show in the Don: the policeman can wait.

Jackson. Yes, sir. [*Exit.*

Old Morton [*taking up* STARBOTTLE'S *note*]. "Miss Morris will arrive to-night." And yet he saw her only yesterday. This is not like her mother: no. She would never have forgiven and forgotten so quickly. Perhaps she knew not my sin and her mother's wrongs; perhaps she has—has—*Christian* forgiveness [*sarcastically*]; perhaps, like my prodigal, she will be immaculately perfect. Well, well! at least her presence will make my home less lonely. "An attendant and child." A child! Ah! if *he*, my boy, my Alexander, were still a child, I might warm this cold, cold heart in his sunshine! Strange that I cannot reconstruct from this dutiful, submissive, obedient, industrious Alexander,—this redeemed outcast, this son who shares my life, my fortunes, my heart, —the foolish, wilful, thoughtless, idle boy that once defied me. I remember [*musing with a smile*] how the little rascal, ha! ha! once struck me,—*struck me!*—when I corrected him: ha! ha! [*Rubbing his hands with amusement, and then suddenly becoming grave and lugubrious.*] No, no! These are the whisperings of the flesh. Why should I find fault with him for being all that a righteous conversion demands, —all that I asked and prayed for? No, Alexander Morton, it is you, *you* who are not yet regenerate. It is *you* who are ungrateful to Him who blessed you, to Him whose guiding hand led you to—

Enter JACKSON.

Jackson. Don José Castro.

Enter DON JOSÉ.

Don José. A thousand pardons, señor, for interrupting you in the hours of business; but it is—it is of business I would speak. [*Looking around.*]

Old Morton [*to* JACKSON]. You can retire. [*Exit* JACKSON.] Be seated, Mr. Castro: I am at your service.

Don José. It is of your—your—son—

Old Morton. Our firm is Morton & Son: in business we are one, Mr. Castro.

Don José. Bueno! Then to you as to him I will speak. Here is a letter I received yesterday. It has significance, importance perhaps. But, whatever it is, it is something for you, not me, to know. If I am wronged much, Don Alexandro, *you*, you are wronged still more. Shall I read it? Good! [*Reads.*] "The man to whom you have affianced your daughter is not the son of Alexander Morton. Have a care. If I do not prove him an impostor at the end of six days, believe me one, and not your true friend and servant, CONCHO." In six days, Don Alexandro, the year of probation is over, and I have promised my daughter's hand to your son. [*Hands letter to* MORTON.]

Old Morton [*ringing bell*]. Is that all, Mr. Castro?

Don José. All! Mr. Castro? *Carramba!* is it not enough?

Enter JACKSON.

Old Morton [*to* JACKSON]. You have kept a record of this business during the last eighteen months. Look at this letter. [*Handing letter.*] Is the handwriting familiar?

Jackson [*taking letter*]. Can't say, sir. The form is the old one.

Old Morton. How many such letters have you received?

Jackson. Four hundred and forty-one, sir. This is the four hundred and forty-second application for your son's position, sir.

Don José. Pardon! This is not an application: it is only information or caution.

Old Morton [*to* JACKSON]. How many letters of information or caution have we received?

Jackson. This makes seven hundred and eighty-one, sir.

Old Morton. How, sir! [*Quickly.*] There were but seven hundred and seventy-nine last night.

Jackson. Beg pardon, sir! The gentleman who carried Mr. Alexander's valise from the boat was the seven hundred and eightieth.

Old Morton. Explain yourself, sir.

Jackson. He imparted to me, while receiving his stipend, the fact that he did not believe young Mr. Alexander was your son. An hour later, sir, he also imparted to me confidentially that he believed you were his father, and requested the loan of five dollars, to be repaid by you, to enable him to purchase a clean shirt, and appear before you in respectable condition. He waited for you an hour, and expressed some indignation that he had not an equal show with others, to throw himself into your arms.

Don José [*rising, aside, and uplifting his hands*]. Carramba! These Americaños are of the devil! [*Aloud.*] Enough, Don Alexandro! Then you think this letter is only worth—

Old Morton. One moment. I can perhaps tell you exactly its market value. [*To* JACKSON.] Go on, sir.

Jackson. At half-past ten, sir, then being slightly under

the influence of liquor, he accepted the price of a deck passage to Stockton.

Old Morton. How much was that, sir?

Jackson. Fifty cents.

Old Morton. Exactly so! There you have, sir [*to* Don José], the market value of the information you have received. I would advise you, as a business matter, not to pay more. As a business matter, you can at any time draw upon us for the amount. [*To* Jackson.] Admit Mr. Capper. [*Exit* Jackson.]

Don José [*rising with dignity*]. This is an insult, Don Alexandro.

Old Morton. You are wrong, Mr. Castro: it is *business*, sought, I believe, by yourself. Now that it is transacted, I beg you to dine with me to-morrow to meet my niece. No offence, sir, no offence! Come, come! Business, you know, business!

Don José [*relaxing*]. Be it so! I will come. [*Aside.*] These Americaños, these Americaños are of the devil! [*Aloud.*] Adios. [*Going.*] I hear, by report, that you have met with the misfortune of a serious loss by robbery.

Old Morton [*aside*]. So our mishap is known everywhere! [*Aloud.*] No serious misfortune, Mr. Castro, even if we do not recover the money. Adios. [*Exit* Don José.]

Old Morton. The stiff-necked Papist! That he should dare, for the sake of his black-browed, froward daughter, to question the faith on which I have pinned my future! Well, with God's blessing, I gave him some wholesome discipline. If it were not for my covenant with Alexander, —and nobly he has fulfilled his part,—I should forbid his alliance with the blood of this spying Jesuit.

Enter Mr. Jackson, *leading in* Capper.

Jackson. Policeman, sir. [*Exit.*
Capper [*turning sharply*]. Who's that man?
Old Morton. Jackson, clerk.
Capper. Umph! Been here long?
Old Morton. A year. He was appointed by my son.
Capper. Know anything of his previous life?
Old Morton [*stiffly*]. I have already told you he is an appointee of my son's.
Capper. Yes! [*Aside.*] "Like master, like man." [*Aloud.*] Well, to business. We have worked up the robbery. We have reached two conclusions,—one, that the work was not done by professionals; the other, consequent upon this, that you can't recover the money.
Old Morton. Excuse me, sir, but I do not see the last conclusion.
Capper. Then listen. The professional thief has only one or two ways of disposing of his plunder, and these ways are always well known to us. Good! Your stolen coin has not been disposed of in the regular way, through the usual hands which we could at any time seize. Of this we are satisfied.
Old Morton. How do you know it?
Capper. In this way. The only clue we have to the identification of the missing money were two boxes of Mexican doubloons.
Old Morton [*aside*]. Mr. Castro's special deposit! He may have reason for his interest. [*Aloud.*] Go on.
Capper. It is a coin rare in circulation in the interior. The night after the robbery, the dealer of a monte-table in Sacramento paid out five thousand dollars in doubloons. He declared it was taken in at the table, and could not

identify the players. Of course, *of course!* So far, you
see, you are helpless. We have only established one fact,—
that the robber is—is [*significantly*] a gambler.

Old Morton [*quietly*]. The regular trade of the thief
seems to me to be of little importance if you cannot identify
him or recover my money. But go on, sir, go on: or is
this all?

Capper [*aside*]. The old fool is blind. That is natural.
[*Aloud.*] It is not all. The crime will doubtless be repeated. The man who has access to your vaults, who has
taken only thirty thousand dollars when he could have
secured half a million,—this man, who has already gambled
that thirty thousand away,—will not stop there. He will
in a day or two, perhaps to-day, try to retrieve his losses
out of *your* capital. *I* am here to prevent it.

Old Morton [*becoming interested*]. How?

Capper. Give me, for forty-eight hours, free access to
this building. Let me conceal myself somewhere, anywhere
within these walls. Let it be without the knowledge of
your clerks, even of *your son!*

Old Morton [*proudly*]. Mr. Alexander Morton is absent
to-day. There is no other reason why he should not be
here to consent to the acts of his partner and father.

Capper [*quickly*]. Very good. It is only to ensure absolute secrecy.

Old Morton [*aside*]. Another robbery might excite a
suspicion worse for our credit than our actual loss. There
is a significant earnestness about this man that awakens
my fears. If Alexander were only here! [*Aloud.*] I accept.

[CAPPER *has been trying doors* R. *and* L.

Capper. What room is this? [*At* R.]

Old Morton. My son's. I would prefer—

Capper. And this? [*At* L.]

Old Morton. Mine, sir; if you choose—

Capper [*locking door and putting key in his pocket*]. This will do. Oblige me by making the necessary arrangements in your counting-room.

Old Morton [*hesitating and aside*]. He is right: perhaps it is only prudence, and I am saving Alexander additional care and annoyance. [*Exit.*

Enter Mr. Shadow *cautiously,* c.

Shadow [*in a lisping whisper to* Capper.] I've got the litht of the clerkth complete.

Capper [*triumphantly*]. Put it in your pocket, Shadow. We don't care for the lackeys now: we are after the master.

Shadow. Eh! the mathter?

Capper. Yes, the master,—the young master, the reclaimed son, the reformed prodigal! ha, ha!—the young man who compensates himself for all his austere devotion to business and principle by dipping into the old man's vaults when he wants a *pasear*—eh, Shadow? That's the man we're after. Look here! *I* never took any stock in that young man's reformation. Ye don't teach old sports like him new tricks. They're a bad lot, father and son,—eh, Shadow?—and he's a chip of the old block, I spotted him before this robbery, before we were ever called in here professionally. I've had my eye on Alexander Morton, *alias* John Oakhurst; and, when I found the old man's doubloons raked over a monte-table at Sacramento, I knew where to look for the thief. Eh, Shadow?

Shadow [*aside*]. He ith enormouth, thith Mithter Capper.

Enter Old Morton.

Old Morton. I have arranged everything. You will

not be disturbed or suspected here in my private office. Eh! [*Looking at* SHADOW.] Who has slipped in here?

Capper. Only my shadow, Mr. Morton; but I can rid myself even of that. [*Crosses to* SHADOW.] Take this card to the office, and wait for further orders. Vanish, Shadow!
[*Exit* SHADOW.

Enter JACKSON.

Jackson. Mr. Alexander has come in, sir. [OLD MORTON *and* CAPPER *start.*]

Old Morton. Where is he?

Jackson. In his private room, sir.

Old Morton. Enough; you can go. [*Exit* JACKSON.

Capper [*crossing to* MORTON]. Remember, you have given your pledge of secrecy. Beware! Your honour, your property, the credit and reputation of your bank, are at stake.

Old Morton [*after a pause of hesitation, with dignity*]. I gave you my word, sir, while my son was not present. I shall save myself from breaking my word with you or concealing anything from him, by withdrawing myself. For the next twenty-four hours, this room [*pointing to private room* R.] is yours.

[*Each regards the other. Exit* OLD MORTON C., *as* CAPPER *exit in private room* R. *After a pause, door of room opens, and* HARRY YORK *appears, slightly intoxicated, followed by* JOHN OAKHURST.

Harry York [*looking around*]. By Jove! Morton, but you've got things in style here. And this 'yer's the gov'nor's desk; and here old Praise-God Barebones sits opposite ye. Look 'yer, old boy [*throwing himself in chair*], I kin allow how it comes easy for ye to run this bank, for it's about as exciting, these times, as faro was to ye in '49, when I first knew ye as Jack Oakhurst; but how the devil you can sit opposite that stiff embodiment of all the Ten Commandments day by day, damn it! that's wot *gets* me! Why, the first day I came here on business, the old man froze me so that I couldn't thaw a deposit out of my pocket. It chills me to think of it.

Oakhurst [*hastily*]. I suppose I am accustomed to him. But come, Harry, let me warm you. [*Opens door of safe* L. *and discovers cupboard, decanter, and glasses.*]

York [*laughing*]. By Jove! under the old man's very nose. Jack, this is like you. [*Takes a drink.*] Well, old boy, this is like old times. But you don't drink.

Oakhurst. No, nor smoke. The fact is, Harry, I've taken a year's pledge. I've six days still to run; after that [*gloomily*], why [*with a reckless laugh*], I shall be Jack Oakhurst again.

York. Lord! to think of your turning out to be anybody's son, Jack!—least of all, *his!* [*Pointing to chair.*]

Oakhurst [*laughing recklessly*]. Not more strange than that I should find Harry York, the spendthrift of Poker Flat, the rich and respected Mr. York, produce merchant of San Francisco.

York. Yes; but, my boy, you see I didn't strike it—in a rich father. I gave up gambling, married, and settled down, saved my money, invested a little here and there, and worked for it, Jack, damn me,—worked for it like a damned horse!

Oakhurst [*aside*]. True, this is not work.

York. But that ain't my business with ye now, old boy; it's this. You've had some trials and troubles in the bank lately,—a defalcation of agents one day, a robbery next. It's luck, my boy, luck! but ye know people will talk. You don't mind my sayin' that there's rumours 'round. The old man's mighty unpopular because he's a saint; and folks don't entirely fancy you because you used to be the reverse. Well, Jack, it amounts to 'bout this: I've withdrawn my account from Parkinson's in Sacramento, and I've got a pretty heavy balance on hand—nigh on two hundred thousand—in bonds and certificates here; and if it will help you over the rough places, old boy, as a deposit, 'yer it is [*drawing pocket-book*].

Oakhurst [*greatly affected, but endeavouring to conceal it*]. Thank you, Harry, old fellow, but—

York [*quickly*]. I know; I'll take the risk, a business risk. You'll stand by me all you can, old boy; you'll make it pay all you can; and if you lose it—why—all right!

Oakhurst [*embarrassed*]. As a deposit with Morton & Son, drawing two per cent. monthly interest—

York. Damn Morton & Son! I'll back it with Jack Oakhurst, the man I know.

Oakhurst [*advancing slowly*]. I'll take it, Harry.

York [*extending his hand*]. It's a square game, Jack!

Oakhurst [*seizing his hand with repressed emotion*]. It's a square game, Harry York, if I live.

York. Then I'll travel. Good-night, old boy. I'll send my clerk around in the morning to put things right. Good-night [*going*].

Oakhurst [*grasping* YORK'S *hand*]. One moment—no—nothing! Good-night. [*Exit* YORK.

> [OAKHURST *follows him to door, and then returns to desk, throwing himself in chair, and burying his face in his hands.*

Oakhurst [*with deep feeling*]. It needed but this to fill the measure of my degradation. I have borne the suspicions of the old man's enemies, the half-pitying, half-contemptuous sympathy of his friends, even his own cold, heartless, fanatical fulfilment of his sense of duty; but *this* —this confidence from one who had most reason to scorn me, this trust from one who knew me as I *was*,—this is the hardest burden. And he too in time will know me to be an impostor. He too—a reformed man; but he has honourably retraced his steps, and won the position I hold by a trick, an imposture. And what is all my labour beside his honest sincerity? I have fought against the chances that might discover my deception, against the enemies who would overthrow me, against the fate that put me here; and I have been successful—yes, a successful impostor! I have even fought against the human instinct that told this fierce, foolish old man that *I* was an alien to his house, to his blood; I have even felt him scan my face eagerly for some reflection of his long-lost boy, for some realisation for his dream; and I have seen him turn away, cold, heartsick, and despairing. What matters that I have been to him devoted, untiring, submissive, ay! a better son to him than his own weak flesh and blood would have been? He would to-morrow cast me forth to welcome the outcast, Sandy Morton. Well, what matters? [*Recklessly.*] Nothing. In six days it will be over; in six days the year of my probation will have passed; in six days I will disclose to him the deceit I have practised, and will face the world again as John Oakhurst the gambler, who staked and lost *all* on a single cast. And Jovita! Well, well!—the game is made; it is too late to draw out now. [*Rings bell. Enter* JACKSON.] Who has been here?

Jackson. Only Don José and Mr. Capper the detective.

Oakhurst. The detective? What for?

Jackson. To work up the robbery, sir.

Oakhurst. True! Capper, Capper, yes! A man of

wild and ridiculous theories, but well-meaning, brave, and honest. [*Aside.*] This is the old man's idea. He does not know that I was on the trail of the thieves an hour before the police were notified. [*Aloud.*] Well, sir?

Jackson. He told your father he thought the recovery of the money hopeless, but he came to caution us against a second attempt.

Oakhurst [*aside, starting*]. True! I had not thought of that. [*Excitedly.*] The success of their first attempt will incite them to another; the money they have stolen is gone by this time. [*Aloud.*] Jackson, I will stay here to-night and to-morrow night, and relieve your regular watchman. You will, of course, say nothing of my intention.

Jackson. Yes, sir. [*Lingering.*]

Oakhurst [*after a pause*]. That is all, Mr. Jackson.

Jackson. Beg your pardon, Mr. Morton; but Col. Starbottle, with two ladies, was here half an hour ago, and said they would come again when you were alone.

Oakhurst. Very well: admit them.

Jackson. Beg pardon, sir; but they seemed to avoid seeing your father until they had seen you. It looked mysterious, and I thought I would tell you first.

Oakhurst [*laughing*]. Admit them, Mr. Jackson. [*Exit* JACKSON.] This poor fellow's devotion is increasing. He too believes that his old associate in dissipation, John Oakhurst, *is* the son of Alexander Morton. He too will have to share in the disgrace of the impostor. Ladies! umph! [*Looking down at his clothes.*] I'm afraid the reform of Alexander Morton hasn't improved the usual neatness of John Oakhurst. I haven't slept nor changed my clothes for three days. [*Goes to door of* MORTON, sen.'s, *room.*] Locked, and the key on the inside! That's strange. Nonsense! the old man has locked his door, and gone out through the private entrance. Well, I'll find means of making my toilet here. [*Exit into private room* L.

Enter JACKSON, *leading in* COL. STARBOTTLE, MISS MARY, *the* DUCHESS, *and child of three years.*

Jackson. Mr. Alexander Morton, jun., is in his private oom. He will be here in a moment. [*Exit* JACKSON.
Starbottle. One moment, a single moment, Miss Mary. Permit me to—er—if I may so express myself, to—er—group the party, to—er—place the—er—present company into position. I have—er—observed, as part of my—er—legal experience, that in cases of moral illustration a great, I may say—er—tremendous, effect on the—er—jury, I mean the—er—guilty party, has been produced by the attitude of the—er—victim and martyr. You, madam, as the—er—injured wife [*placing her*], shall stand here, firm yet expectant, protecting your child, yet looking hopefully for assistance toward its natural protector. You, Miss Mary, shall stand here [*placing her*], as Moral Retribution, leaning toward and appealing to me, the image of—er—er—Inflexible Justice! [*Inflates his chest, puts his hand in his bosom, and strikes an attitude.*]

> [*Door of young* MORTON'S *room opens, and discloses* MR. OAKHURST *gazing at the group. He starts slightly on observing the* DUCHESS, *but instantly recovers himself, and faces the company coldly. The* DUCHESS *starts on observing* OAKHURST, *and struggles in confusion towards the door, dragging with her the child and* MISS MARY, *who endeavours to reassure her.* COL. STARBOTTLE *looks in astonishment from one to the other, and advances to front.*

Col. Starbottle [*aside*]. The — er — tableau, although

striking in moral force, is apparently—er—deficient in moral stamina.

Miss Mary [*angrily to the* DUCHESS]. I'm ashamed of you! [*To* OAKHURST, *advancing.*] I don't ask pardon for my intrusion. If you are Alexander Morton, you are my kinsman, and you will know that I cannot introduce myself better than as the protector of an injured woman. Come here! [*To the* DUCHESS, *dragging her towards* OAKHURST. *To* OAKHURST.] Look upon this woman : she claims to be—

Starbottle [*stepping between* MISS MARY *and the* DUCHESS]. A moment, Miss Mary, a single moment! Permit me to—er—explain. The whole thing, the—er—situation reminds me, demn me, of most amusing incident at Sacramento in '52. Large party at Hank Suedecois: know Hank? Confirmed old bach of sixty. Dinner for forty. Everything in style, first families, Ged,—Judge Beeswinger, Mat Boompointer, and Maje Blodgett of Ahlabam: know old Maje Blodgett? Well, Maje was there. Ged, sir, delay,—everybody waiting. I went to Hank. "Hank," I says, "what's matter? why delay?" "Star," he says,—always called me Star,—"Star,—it's cook!" "Demn cook," I says: "discharge cook,—only a black mulatto any way!" "Can't, Star," he says: "impossible!" "Can't?" says I. "No," says he. "Listen, Star," he says, "family secret! Honour! Can't discharge cook, because cook—demn it—'s *my wife!*" Fact, sir, fact—showed marriage certificate—married privately seven years! Fact, sir—

The Duchess [*to* MISS MARY]. Some other time, miss. Let us go now. There's a mistake, miss, I can't explain. Some other time, miss! See, miss, how cold and stern he looks! another time, miss! [*Struggling.*] For God's sake, miss, let me go!

Miss Mary. No! This mystery must be cleared up now, before I enter *his* house,—before I accept the charge of this—

Starbottle [*interrupting, and crossing before* MISS MARY]. A moment—a single moment, miss. [*To* OAKHURST.] Mr. Morton, you will pardon the exuberance, and perhaps, under the circumstances, somewhat natural impulsiveness, of the—er—sex, for which I am perhaps responsible; I may say—er—personally, sir,—personally responsible—

Oakhurst [*coldly*]. Go on, sir.

Starbottle. The lady on my right is—er—the niece of your father,—your cousin. The lady on my left, engaged in soothing the—er—bashful timidity of infancy, is—er—that is—er—claims to be, the mother of the child of Alexander Morton.

Oakhurst [*calmly*]. She is right.

Miss Mary [*rushing forward*]. Then you are—

Oakhurst [*gently restraining her*]. You have another question to ask: you hesitate: let me ask it. [*Crossing to the* DUCHESS.] You have heard my answer. Madam, are you the legal wife of Alexander Morton?

The Duchess [*sinking upon her knees and dropping her face in her hands*]. No!

Oakhurst. Enough! I will take the child. Pardon me, Miss Morris, but you have heard enough to know that your mission is accomplished, but that what else passes between this woman and myself becomes no stranger to hear. [*Motions toward room* L.]

Miss Mary [*aside*]. It is *his* son. I am satisfied [*going*]. Come, Colonel. [*Exeunt into room* L., STARBOTTLE *and* MISS MARY.]

The Duchess [*crossing to* OAKHURST *and falling at his feet*]. Forgive me, Jack, forgive me! It was no fault of mine. I did not know that you were here. I did not know that you had taken his name!

Oakhurst. Hush—on your life!

The Duchess. Hear me, Jack! I was anxious only for a home for my child. I came to *her*—the schoolmistress of Red Gulch—for aid. I told her the name of my boy's father. She—she brought me here. Oh, forgive me, Jack! I have offended you!

Oakhurst. How can I believe you? You have deceived *him.* You have deceived me. Listen! When I said, a moment ago, you were not the wife of Alexander Morton, it was because I knew that your first husband—the Australian convict Pritchard—was still living; that you had deceived Sandy Morton as you had deceived me. That was why I left you. Tell me, have you deceived me also about him, as you did about the other? Is *he* living, and with you; or dead, as you declared?

The Duchess [*aside*]. He will kill me if I tell him. [*Aloud.*] No, no! He is gone—is dead these three years.

Oakhurst. You swear?

The Duchess [*hesitates, gasps, and looks around for her child; then seizing it, and drawing it towards her*]. I swear!

Oakhurst. Enough! Seek not to know why *I* am here, and under his name. Enough for you that it has saved your child's future, and secured him his heritage past all revocation. Yet remember! a word from you within the next few days destroys it all. After that, I care not what you say.

The Duchess. Jack! One word, Jack, before I go. I never thought to bring my shame to you!—to *him!*

Oakhurst. It was no trick, then, no contrivance, that brought her here. No: it was fate. And at least I shall save his child.

Re-enter STARBOTTLE, MISS MARY, *and* DUCHESS.

Col. Starbottle [*impressively*]. Permit me, Mr. Alexander Morton, as the friend of my—er—principal, to declare that we have received—honourable—honourable—satisfaction. Allow me, sir, to grasp the hand, the—er—cherished hand of a gentleman, who, demn me! has fulfilled all his duties to—er—society and gentlemen. And allow me to add, sir, should any invidious criticism of the present—er—settlement be uttered in my presence, I shall hold that critic responsible, sir—er—personally responsible!

Miss Mary [*sweeping truculently and aggressively up to* JOHN OAKHURST]. And permit *me* to add, sir, that, if you can see your way clearly out of this wretched muddle, it's more than I can. This arrangement may be according to the Californian code of morality, but it doesn't accord with my Eastern ideas of right and wrong. If this foolish, wretched creature chooses to abandon all claim upon you, chooses to run away from you,—why, I suppose, as a *gentleman*, according to your laws of honour, you are absolved. Good-night, Mr. Alexander Morton.

> [*Goes to door* C., *and exit, pushing out* STARBOTTLE, *the* DUCHESS, *and child.* MR. OAKHURST *sinks into chair at desk, burying his face in his hands. Re-enter, slowly and embarrassedly,* MISS MARY: *looks toward* OAKHURST, *and comes slowly down stage.*

ɉ *Miss Mary* [*aside*]. I was too hard on him. I was not so hard on Sandy when I thought that he—he—was the father of her child. And he's my own flesh and blood, too; and—he's crying. [*Aloud.*] Mr. Morton.

Oakhurst [*slowly lifting his head*]. Yes, Miss Mary.

Miss Mary. I spoke hastily just then. I—I—thought —you see—I—[*angrily and passionately*]—I mean this. I'm a stranger. I don't understand your Californian ways, and I don't want to. But I believe you've done what you thought was right, according to a *man's* idea of right; and —there's my hand. Take it, take it; for it's a novelty, Mr. Morton: it's the hand of an honest girl!

Oakhurst [*hesitates, then rises, sinks on one knee, and raises* MISS MARY'S *fingers to his lips*]. God bless you, miss! God bless you!

Miss Mary [*retreating to centre door*]. Good-night, good-night [*slowly*],—cousin—Alexander.

[*Exit. Dark stage.*

Oakhurst [*rising swiftly*]. No, no: it is false! Ah! She's gone. Another moment, and I would have told her all. Pshaw! courage, man! It is only six days more, and you are free, and this year's shame and agony forever ended.

Enter JACKSON.

Jackson. As you ordered, sir, the night watchman has been relieved, and has just gone.

Oakhurst. Very good, sir; and you?

Jackson. I relieved the porter, sir; and I shall bunk on two chairs in the counting-room. You'll find me handy, if you want me, sir. Good-night, sir. [*Exit* C.

Oakhurst. I fear these rascals will not dare to make their second attempt to night. A quiet scrimmage with them, enough to keep me awake or from thinking, would be a good fortune. No, no! no such luck for you to-night, John Oakhurst! You are playing a losing game. . . . Yet the robbery was a bold one. At eleven o'clock, while the bank was yet lighted, and Mr. Jackson and another clerk were at work here, three well-dressed men pick the lock of the counting-house door, enter, and turn the key on the clerks in this parlour, and carry away a box of doubloons not yet placed in the vaults by the porter; and all this done so cautiously that the clerks within knew nothing of it until notified of the open street-door by the private watchman, and so boldly that the watchman, seeing them here, believed them clerks of the bank, and let them go unmolested. No: this was the coincidence of good luck, not of bold premeditation. There will be no second attempt. [*Yawns.*] If they don't come soon I shall fall asleep. Four nights without rest will tell on a man, unless he has some excitement to back him. [*Nods.*] Hallo! What was that? Oh! Jackson in the counting-room getting to bed. I'll look at that front door myself.

> [*Takes revolver from desk and goes to door* C., *tries lock, comes down stage with revolver, examines it, and lays it down.*

Oakhurst [*slowly and quietly*]. The door is locked on the outside: that may have been an accident. The caps are taken from my pistol: *that* was not! Well, here is the vault, and here is John Oakhurst: to reach the one they must pass the other. [*Takes off his coat, seizes poker from grate, and approaches safe.*] Ha! some one is moving in the old man's room. [*Approaches door of room* R. *as*—

Enter noiselessly and cautiously from room L., PRITCHARD, SILKY, *and* SOAPY. PRITCHARD *and his confederates approach* OAKHURST *from behind, carrying lariat, or slip-noose.*

Oakhurst [*listening at door* R.]. Good! At least I know from what quarter to expect the attack. Ah!

> [PRITCHARD *throws slip-noose over* OAKHURST *from behind;* OAKHURST *puts his hand in his breast as the slip-noose is drawn across his bosom, pinioning one arm over his breast, and the other*

at his side. SILKY *and* SOAPY, *directed by* PRITCHARD, *drag* OAKHURST *to chair front, and pinion his legs.* PRITCHARD C., *regarding him.*

Oakhurst [*very coolly*]. You have left me my voice, I suppose, because it is useless.

Pritchard. That's so, pard. 'Twon't be no help to ye.

Oakhurst. Then you have killed Jackson.

Pritchard. Lord love ye, no! That ain't like us, pard! Jackson's tendin' door for us, and kinder lookin' out gin'rally for the boys. Thar's nothin' mean about Jackson.

Soapy. No! Jackson's a square man. Eh, Silky?

Silky. Ez white a man ez ther is, pard!

Oakhurst [*aside*]. The traitor! [*Aloud.*] Well!

Pritchard. Well, you want ter know our business. Call upon a business man in business hours. Our little game is this, Mr. Jack Morton Alexander Oakhurst. When we was here the other night, we was wantin' a key to that theer lock [*pointing to vault*], and we sorter dropped in passin' to get it.

Oakhurst. And suppose I refuse to give it up?

Pritchard. We were kalkilatin' on yer being even that impolite: wasn't we, boys?

Silky and Soapy. We was that.

Pritchard. And so we got Mr. Jackson to take an impression of it in wax. Oh, he's a square man, is Mr. Jackson!

Silky. Jackson is a white man, Soapy.

Soapy. They don't make no better men nor Jackson, Silky.

Pritchard. And we've got a duplicate key here. But we don't want any differences, pard: we only want a square game. It seemed to us—some of yer old pards as knew ye, Jack—that ye had a rather soft thing here reformin'; and we thought ye was kinder throwin' off on the boys, not givin' 'em any hand in the game. But thar ain't anythin' mean about us. Eh, boys?

Soapy. We is allers ready to chip in ekal in the game. Eh, Silky?

Silky. That's me, Soapy.

Pritchard. Ye see, the boys is free and open-handed, Jack. And so the proposition we wanter make to ye, Jack, is this. It's reg'lar on the square. We reckon, takin' Mr. Jackson's word,—and thar ain't no man's word ez is better nor Jackson's—that there's nigh onto two millions in that vault, not to speak of a little speshil de-posit o' York's, ez we learn from that accomodatin' friend Mr. Jackson. We propose to share it with ye, on ekal terms—us five—countin' Jackson, a square man. In course, we takes the risk o' packin' it away to-night comfortable. Ez your friends, Jack, we allow this 'yer little arrangement to be a deuced sight easier for you than playin' Sandy Morton on a riglar salary, with the chance o' the real Sandy poppin' in upon ye any night.

Oakhurst. It's a lie. Sandy is dead.

Pritchard. In course, in course! that is your little game! But we kalkilated, Jack, even on that, on yer bein' rambunktious and contrary; and so we went ter Red Gulch, and found Sandy. Ye know I take a kind o' interest in Sandy: he's the second husband of my wife, the woman you run away with, pard. But thar's nothin' mean about me! eh, boys?

Silky. No! he's the forgivingest kind of a man, is Pritchard.

Soapy. That's so, Silky.

Pritchard. And, thinkin' ye might be dubious, we filled Sandy about full o' rye-whisky, and brought him along; and one of our pards is preambulatin' the streets with him, ready to bring him on call.

Oakhurst. It's a lie, Pritchard,—a cowardly lie!
Pritchard. Is it? Hush!
Sandy [*without, singing*].

> Oh, 'yer's yer Sandy Morton,
> > Drink him down!
> Oh, 'yer's yer Sandy Morton,
> > Drink him down!
> Oh, 'yer's yer Sandy Morton,
> > All alive and just a-snortin!
> Oh, 'yer's yer Sandy Morton,
> > Drink him down!

Pritchard. We don't propose to run him in 'yer, 'cept we're took, or yer unaccomodatin' to the boys.

Oakhurst. And if I refuse?

Pritchard. Why, we'll take what we can get; and we'll leave Sandy Morton with you 'yer, to sorter alleviate the old man's feelin's over the loss of his money. There's nothin' mean about us; no! eh, boys? [*Going towards safe.*]

Oakhurst. Hear me a moment, Henry Pritchard. [PRITCHARD *stops abreast of* OAKHURST.] Four years ago you were assaulted in the Arcade Saloon in Sacramento. You would have been killed, but your assailant suddenly fell dead by a pistol-shot fired from some unknown hand. I stood twenty feet from you with folded arms; but that shot was fired by me,—me, Henry Pritchard,—through my clothes, from a derringer hidden in my waistcoat! Understand me, I do not ask your gratitude now. But that pistol is in my right hand, and now covers you. Make a single motion,—of a muscle,—and it is your last.

Pritchard [*motionless, but excitedly*]. You dare not fire! No, dare not! A shot here will bring my pal and Sandy Morton to confront you. You will have killed me to save exposure, have added murder to imposture! You have no witness to this attempt!

Capper [*opening door of room* L., *at the same moment that two policemen appear at door* C., *and two at room* R.] You are wrong; he has five [*crossing to* SILKY *and* SOAPY, *and laying his hands on their shoulders*]; and, if I mistake not, he has two more in these gentlemen, whom I know, and who will be quite as willing to furnish the necessary State's evidence of the robbery, as of the fact that they never knew any other Alexander Morton than the gentleman who sits in that chair.

Soapy. That's so, Silky.

Silky. That's so, Soapy.

Capper [*to policeman*]. Take them away.

[*Exit policeman with* PRITCHARD, SOAPY, *and* SILKY.

CAPPER *unbinds* OAKHURST.

Oakhurst. Then I have to thank you, Mr. C.

Capper. Yes! "A man of ridiculous theories, but well-meaning, brave, and honest." No, sir; don't apologise: you were right, Mr. Oakhurst. It is I who owe you an apology. I came here believing *you* were the robber, having no faith in you or your reformation, expecting,—yes, sir,—hoping, to detect you in the act. Hear me! From the hour you first entered the bank, I have shadowed your every movement, I have been the silent witness of all that has passed in this room. You have played a desperate game, Mr. Oakhurst; but I'll see you through it. If you are true to your resolve for the next six days, I will hold these wretches silent. I will protect your imposture with the strong arm of the law. I don't like *your* theories, sir; but I believe you to be well-meaning, and I know you to be brave and honest.

Oakhurst [*grasping his hand*]. I shall not forget this. But Sandy—

Capper. I will put my men on his track, and have him brought quietly here. I can give you no aid beyond that.

As an honourable man, I need not tell you your duty. Settle it with *him* as best you can.

Oakhurst. You are right; I *will* see him! [*Aside.*] Unless he has changed, he will listen to me, he will obey me.

Capper. Hush! [*Blows out candle.*] Stand here!

[CAPPER *and* OAKHURST *retreat to wing* L., *as enter* MORTON, sen., *from room* R.

Morton. The private door open, the room dark, and Capper gone. I don't like this. The more I think of the mystery of that man's manner this morning, the more it seems to hide some terrible secret I must fathom! There are matches here. [*Strikes a light, as* CAPPER *draws* OAKHURST, *struggling, back into shadow.*] What's this? [*Picking up key.*] The key of the vault. A chair overturned! [*Touches bell.*] No answer! Jackson gone! My God! A terrible suspicion haunts me! No! Hush! [*Retreats to private room* R., *as door of* L. *opens and*

Enter SANDY.

Sandy [*drunkenly*]. Shoo! Shoo! boys, whar are ye, boys, eh? Pritchard, Silky, Soapy! Whar are ye, boys?

Morton [*aside*]. A crime has been committed, and here is one of the gang. God has delivered him into my hands.

[*Draws revolver and fires, as* OAKHURST *breaks from* CAPPER, *and strikes up* MORTON'S *pistol.* CAPPER *at same moment seizes* SANDY, *and drags him in room* L. MORTON *and* OAKHURST *struggle to centre.*

Morton [*relaxing hold of* OAKHURST]. Alexander! Good God! Why are you here? Why have you stepped between me and retribution? You hesitate. God in heaven! Speak, Alexander, my son, speak, for God's sake! Tell me—tell me that this detective's suspicions are not true. Tell me that you are not—not—no, I cannot say it. Speak, Alexander Morton, I command you! Who is this man you have saved? Is it—is it—your accomplice?

Oakhurst [sinking at his feet]. Don't ask me! You know not what you ask! I implore you—

Capper [appearing quietly from room L., *and locking the door behind him].* Your son has acted under *my* orders. The man he has saved, as he has saved you, was a *decoy,*—one of my policemen.

TABLEAU.

CAPPER, MORTON, OAKHURST.

[*Curtain.*]

END OF ACT III.

ACT IV.

SCENE I.—MR. MORTON'S *villa, Russian Hill. Night.* OAKHURST'S *bedroom. Sofa in alcove* C., *door in flat left of* C. SANDY MORTON *discovered unconscious lying on sofa;* OAKHURST *standing at his head, two policemen at his feet. Candles on table* L.

Oakhurst. That will do. You are sure he was unconscious as you brought him in?

1st Policeman. Sure, sir! He hasn't known anything since we picked him up on the sidewalk outside the bank.

Oakhurst. Good! You have fulfilled your orders well, and your chief shall know it. Go now. Be as cautious in going out as you were on entering. Here is the private staircase. [*Opens door* L.] [*Exit Policemen.*

Oakhurst [*listening*]. Gone! and without disturbing any one. So far luck has befriended me. He will sleep tonight beneath his father's roof. His father! umph! would the old man recognise him here? Would he take to his heart this drunken outcast, picked from the gutters of the street, and brought here by the strong arm of the law? Hush! [*A knock without.*] Ah! it is the Colonel: he is prompt to the hour. [*Opens door cautiously, and admits* COL. STARBOTTLE.]

Starbottle [*looking around, and overlooking* SANDY]. I presume the other—er—principal is not yet on the ground?

Oakhurst [motioning to sofa]. He *is!*

Starbottle [starting as he looks towards sofa]. Ged! you don't mean to say it's all *over*, without witnesses, without my—er—presence?

Oakhurst. Pardon me, Col. Starbottle; but, if you look again, you will perceive that the gentleman is only drunk.

Starbottle. Eh? Ged! not uncommon, sir, not uncommon! I remember singular incident at—er—Louisville in '47. Old Judge Tollim—know old Judge Tolly?—Ged! he came to ground drunk, sir; couldn't stand! Demn me, sir, had to put him into position with kitchen poker down his back, and two sections of lightning-rod in his—er—trousers, demn me! Firm, sir, firm, you understand, here [*striking his breast*], but—here [*striking his legs*]—er—er—wobbly! No, sir! Intoxication of principal not a bar, sir, to personal satisfaction! [*Goes towards sofa with eyeglass.*] Good Ged! why, it's Diego! [*Returning stiffly to* OAKHURST.] Excuse me, sir, but this is a case in which I cannot act. Cannot, sir,—impossible! absurd! pre—post—er—ous. I recognise in the—er—inebriated menial on yonder sofa a person, sir, who having already declined my personal challenge, is—er—excluded from the consideration of gentlemen. The person who lies there, sir, is Diego,—a menial of Don José Castro,—*alias* "Sandy," the vagabond of Red Gulch.

Oakhurst. You have omitted one title, his true one. He is Alexander Morton, the son of the master of this house.

Starbottle [starting in bewilderment]. Alexander Morton! [*Aside.*] Ged! my first suspicions were correct. Star, you have lost the opportunity of making your fortune as a scoundrel; but you have, at a pecuniary sacrifice, preserved your honour.

Oakhurst. Yes. Hear me, Col. Starbottle. I have summoned you here to-night, as I have already intimated, on an ffair of honour. I have sought you as my father's legal counsel, as a disir'erested witness, as a gentleman of honour. The man who lies before you was once my friend and partner. I have wronged him doubly. As his partner, I ran away with the woman he believed, and still believes, to be his wife; as his friend, I have for a twelvemonth kept him from the enjoyment of his home, his patrimony, by a shameful deception. I have summoned you to-night to witness my confession; as a lawyer, to arrange those details necessary to restore to him his property; as a man of honour, to receive from me whatever retribution he demands. You will be a witness to our interview. Whatever befalls me here, you will explain to Mr. Morton—to Jovita—that I accepted it as a man, and did not avoid, here or elsewhere, the penalty of my crime. [*Folding his arms.*]

Starbottle. Umph! the case is, as you say, a delicate one, but not—not—peculiar. No, sir!. Ged, sir, I remember Tom Marshall—know Tom Marshall of Kentucky?—said to me, "Star!"—always called me Star,—"how in blank, sir, can you remember the *real* names of your clients?" "Why," says I, "Tom,"—always called him Tom,—"yesterday I was called to make will—most distinguished family of Virginia—as lawyer and gentleman, you understand, can't mention name. Waited for signature—most distinguished name. Ged, sir, man signed Bloggins—Peter Bloggins. Fact, demme! 'Mistake,' I said,—'excitement; exaltation of fever. *Non compos.* Compose yourself, Bob.' —'Star,' he said,—always called me Star,—'for forty-seven years I have been an impostor!'—his very words, sir. 'I am not'—you understand: 'I *am* Peter Bloggins!'"

Oakhurst. But, my dear Colonel, I—

Starbottle [*loftily*]. Say no more, sir! I accept the—

er—position. Let us see! The gentleman will, on recognition, probably make a personal attack. You are armed. Ah! no? Umph! On reflection, I would not permit him to strike a single blow—I would anticipate it. It will provoke the challenge from him, leaving *you*, sir, the—er—choice of weapons.

Oakhurst. Hush! he is moving! Take your stand here, in this alcove. Remember, as a gentleman and a man of honour, Col. Starbottle, I trust you not to interfere between the injured man and—justice! [*Pushes* COL. STARBOTTLE *into alcove behind couch and approaches* SANDY.]

Sandy [*waking slowly and incoherently*]. Hush! Silky! Hush! Eh? Oh, hush yourself. [*Sings.*]

<blockquote>Oh, 'yer's yer Sandy Morton,
Drink him down!</blockquote>

Eh! Oh! [*Half sits up on couch.*] Eh! [*Looking around him.*] Where the devil am I?

Oakhurst [*advancing and leaning over* SANDY'S *couch*]. In the house of your father, Alexander Morton.

Sandy [*recoiling in astonishment*]. His voice—John Oakhurst! What—ah! [*Rises, and rushes towards* OAKHURST *with uplifted hand.*]

Starbottle [*gesticulating in whisper*]. A blow! a single blow would be sufficient.

Sandy [*looking at* OAKHURST, *who regards him calmly*]. I—eh! I—eh! Ha, ha! I'm glad to see—old pard! I'm glad to see ye! [COL. STARBOTTLE *lifts his hand in amazement.*]

Oakhurst [*declining his hand*]. Do you understand me, Sandy Morton? Listen! I am John Oakhurst,—the man who has deceived your father, who has deceived you.

Sandy [*without heeding his words, but regarding him affectionately*] To think of it—Jack Oakhurst! It's like him,

like Jack. He was allers onsartain, the darned little cuss!
Jack! Look at him, will ye, boys? look at him! Growed too,
and dressed to kill, and sittin' in this 'yer house as natril as
a jaybird! [*Looking around.*] Natty, ain't it, Jack? and
this 'yer's your house—the old man's house—eh? Why, this
is—this is where she came. Jack, Jack! [*Eagerly.*] Tell
me, pard,—where is she?

Starbottle [*aside, rubbing his hands*]. We shall have it
now!

Oakhurst. She has gone,—gone! But hear me! She
had deceived you, as she has me. She has gone,—gone
with her first husband, Henry Pritchard.

Sandy [*stupefied.*] Gone! Her first husband! Pritchard!

Oakhurst. Ay! your wife!

Sandy. Oh, damn my wife! I'm talking of Mary,—Miss
Mary,—the little schoolma'am, Jack; the little rose of
Poker Flat. Oh! I see—ye didn't know her, Jack,—the
pertiest, sweetest little—

Oakhurst [*turning away coldly.*] Ay, ay! She is here!

Sandy [*looking after him affectionately*]. Look at him,
boys! Allers the same,—high-toned, cold, even to his
pardner! That's him,—Jack Oakhurst! But Jack, Jack,
you're goin' to shake hands, ain't ye? [*Extends his hand
after a pause.* OAKHURST *takes it gloomily.*]

Col. Starbottle [*who has been regarding interview with
visible scorn and disgust, advancing to* OAKHURST.] You will
—er—pardon me if, under the—er—circumstances, I withdraw from this—er—disgraceful proceeding. The condon-
ation, by that man, of two of the most tremendous offences
to society and to the code, without apology or satisfaction,
Ged, sir, is—er—er—of itself an insult to the spectator. I
go, sir—

Oakhurst. But, Col. Starbottle—

Starbottle. Permit me to say, sir, that I hold myself for this, sir, responsible, sir,—personally responsible.

[*Exit* STARBOTTLE, *glancing furiously at* SANDY, *who sinks on sofa laughing.*]

Oakhurst [*aside*]. He will change his mind in half an hour. But, in the meantime, time is precious. [*Aloud.*] Sandy, come!

Sandy. [*rising with alacrity*]. Yes, Jack, I'm ready.

Oakhurst. We are going [*slowly and solemnly*]—we are going to see your father.

Sandy [*dropping back with bashful embarrassment, and struggling to release his arm from* OAKHURST]. No, Jack! Not just yet, Jack; in a little while, ole boy! in about six months, or mebbe a year, Jack, not now, not now! I ain't feelin' exactly well, Jack,—I ain't.

Oakhurst. Nonsense, Sandy! Consider your duty and my honour.

Sandy [*regaining his seat*]. That's all very well, Jack; but ye see, pard, you've known the old man for nigh on a year, and it's twenty-five since I met him. No, Jack; you don't play any ole man on to me to-night, Jack. No, you and me'll just drop out for a *pasear.* Jack, eh? [*Taking* OAKHURST'S *arm.*] Come!

Oakhurst. Impossible! Hush! [*Listening.*] It is *he* passing through the corridor. [*Goes to wing* R. *and listens.*]

Sandy [*crowding hastily behind* OAKHURST *in alarm*]. But, I say, Jack! he won't come in here? He's goin' to bed, you know. Eh? It ain't right for a man o' his years —and he must be goin' on ninety, Jack—to be up like this. It ain't healthy.

Oakhurst. You know him not. He seems to need no rest [*sadly*]. Night after night, long after the servants are abed and the house is still, I hear that step slowly pacing the corridor. It is the last sound as I close my eyes, the first challenge of the morning.

Sandy. The ole scound—[*checking himself*]—I mean, Jack, the ole man has suthin' on his mind. But, Jack [*in great alarm*], he don't waltz in upon ye, Jack? He don't p'int them feet in 'yer, Jack? Ye ain't got to put up with that, Jack, along o' yer other trials?

Oakhurst. He often seeks me here. Ah! yes—he is coming this way now.

Sandy [*in ludicrous terror*]. Jack, pard, quick! hide me somewhere, Jack!

Oakhurst [*opening door* R.]. In there, quick! Not a sound, as you value your future!

[*Exit* SANDY *hurriedly* R.

SCENE 2.—*The same. Enter door* R. OLD MORTON, *in dressing-gown, with candle.*

Old Morton. Not abed yet, Alexander? Well, well! I don't blame you, my son: it has been for you a trying, trying night. Yes, I see: like me, you are a little nervous and wakeful. [*Slowly takes chair, and comfortably composes himself.*]

Oakhurst [*aside*]. He is in for a midnight gossip. How shall I dispose of Sandy?

Old Morton. Yes [*meditatively*],—yes, you have overworked lately. Never mind. In a day or two more you shall have a vacation, sir,—a vacation!

Oakhurst [*aside*]. He knows not how truly he speaks. [*Aloud.*] Yes, sir, I was still up. I have only just now dismissed the policemen.

Old Morton. Ay! I heard voices, and saw a light in your window. I came to tell you, Alexander, Capper has explained all about—about the decoy! More; he has told me of your courage and your invaluable assistance. For a moment, sir,—I don't mind telling you now in confidence, —I doubted *you*—

Oakhurst [*in feigned deprecation*]. Oh, sir!

Old Morton. Only for a moment. You will find, Alexander, that even that doubt shall have full apology when the year of your probation has expired. Besides, sir, I know all.

Oakhurst [*starting*]. All!

Old Morton. Yes, the story about the Duchess and your child. You are surprised. Col. Starbottle told me all. I forgive you, Alexander, for the sake of your boy.

Oakhurst. My boy, sir!

Old Morton. Yes, your boy. And let me tell you, sir, he's a fine young fellow. Looks like you,—looks as you did when *you* were a boy. He's a Morton, too, every inch of him, there's no denying that. No, sir. *You* may have changed; but he—he is the living image of my little Alexander. He took to me, too,—lifted his little arms,—and —and—[*Becomes affected, and leans his head in his hands.*]

Oakhurst [*rising*]. You are not well, sir. Let me lead you to your room.

Old Morton. No! It is nothing: a glass of water, Alexander!

Oakhurst [*aside*]. He is very pale. The agitation of the night has overcome him. [*Goes to table* R.] A little spirits will revive him. [*Pours from decanter in glass, and returns to* MORTON.]

Old Morton [*after drinking*]. There was spirits in that water, Alexander. Five years ago, I vowed at your mother's grave to abandon the use of intoxicating liquors.

Oakhurst. Believe me, sir, my mother will forgive you.

Old Morton. Doubtless. It has revived me. I am

getting to be an old man, Aleck. [*Holds out his glass half unconsciously, and* OAKHURST *replenishes it from decanter.*] Yes, an old man, Aleck; but the boy,—ah! I live again in him. The little rascal! He asked me, Aleck, for a "chaw tobacker!" and wanted to know if I was the "ole duffer." Ha, ha! He did. Ha, ha! Come, come! don't be despondent. I was like you once, damn it,—ahem—it's all for the best, my boy, all for the best. I'll take the young rascal [*aside*]—damn it, he's already taken me—[*aloud*] on equal terms. There, Aleck, what do you say?

Oakhurst. Really, sir, this forbearance,—this kindness —[*aside*] I see a ray of light.

Old Morton. Nonsense! I'll take the boy, I tell you, and do well for him—the little rascal!—as if he were the legal heir. But I say, Aleck [*laughing*], ha, ha!—what about—ha, ha!—what about Doña Jovita, eh? and what about Don José Castro, eh? How will the lady like a ready-made family, eh? [*Poking* OAKHURST *in the ribs.*] What will the Don say to the family succession? Ha, ha!

Oakhurst [*proudly*]. Really, sir, I care but little.

Old Morton [*aside*]. Oh, ho! I'll sound him. [*Aloud.*] Look ye, Alexander, I have given my word to you and Don José Castro, and I'll keep it. But if you can do any better, eh?—if—eh?—the schoolma'am's a mighty pretty girl, and a bright one, eh, Aleck? And it's all in the family—eh? And she thinks well of you; and I will say, for a girl brought up as she's been, and knowin' your relations with the Duchess and the boy, to say a kind word for ye, Aleck, is a good sign,—you follow me, Aleck?—if you think—why, old Don José might whistle for a son-in-law, eh?

Oakhurst [*interrupting indignantly*]. Sir! [*Aside.*] Stop! [*Aloud.*] Do you mean to say, sir, that if I should consent to this—suggestion—that, if the lady were willing, *you* **would** offer no impediment?

Old Morton. Impediment! my dear boy, you should have my blessing.

Oakhurst. Pardon me a moment. You have in the last year, sir, taught me the importance of business formality in all the relations of life. Following that idea, the conditions of my engagement with Jovita Castro were drawn up with your hand. Are you willing to make this recantation as formal, this new contract as business-like and valid?

Old Morton [eagerly]. I am.

Oakhurst. Then sit here, and write at my dictation. [*Pointing to table* L. OLD MORTON *takes seat at table.*] "In view of the evident preference of my son Alexander Morton and of certain family interests, I hereby revoke my consent to his marriage with the Doña Jovita Castro, and accord him full permission to woo and win his cousin, Miss Mary Morris; promising him the same aid and assistance previously offered in his suit with Miss Castro."

Old Morton [signing]. Alexander Morton, sen. There, Aleck! You have forgotten one legal formality. We have no witness. Ha, ha!

Oakhurst [significantly]. *I* will be a sufficient witness.

Old Morton. Ha, ha! [*Fills glass from decanter, after which* OAKHURST *quietly removes decanter beyond his reach.*] Very good! Aleck, I've been thinking of a plan,—I've been thinking of retiring from the bank. I'm getting old, and my ways are not the popular ways of business here. I've been thinking of you, you dog,—of leaving the bank to you, —to you, sir,—eh—the day—the day you marry the schoolma'am—eh! I'll stay at home, and take care of the boy— eh!—hic! The little rascal!—lifted his arms to me—did, Aleck! by God! [*incoherently.*] Eh!

Oakhurst. Hush! [*Aside.*] Sandy will overhear him, and appear.

Old Morton [greatly affected by liquor]. Hush! eh!—of

course—shoo! shoo! [*The actor will here endeavour to reproduce in* OLD MORTON'S *drunken behaviour, without exactly imitating him, the general characteristics of his son's intoxication.*] Eh! I say, Aleck, old boy! what will the Don say? eh? Ha, ha, ha! And Jovita, that firebrand, how will she—hic—like it, eh? [*Laughs immoderately.*]

Oakhurst. Hush! We will be overheard! The servants, sir!

Old Morton. Damn the servants! Don't I—hic—pay them wages—eh?

Oakhurst. Let me lead you to your own room. You are nervously excited. A little rest, sir, will do you good. [*Taking his arm.*]

Old Morton. No shir, no shir, 'm nerrer goin' to bed any more. Bed's bad habit!—hic—drunken habit. Lesh stay up all ni, Aleck! You and me! Lesh nev'r—go—bed any more! Whar's whisky—eh? [*Staggers to the table for decanter as* OAKHURST *seizes him, struggles up stage, and then* OLD MORTON, *in struggle, falls helplessly on sofa, in same attitude as* SANDY *was discovered.*]

Enter SANDY *cautiously from door* L.

Sandy [*to* OAKHURST]. Jack! Eh, Jack—

Oakhurst. Hush! Go! I will follow you in a moment. [*Pushes him back to door* L.]

Sandy [*catching sight of* OLD MORTON]. Hallo! What's up?

Oakhurst. Nothing. He was overtaken with a sudden faintness. He will revive presently: go!

Sandy [*hesitating*]. I say, Jack, he wasn't taken sick along o' me, eh, Jack?

Oakhurst. No! no! But go! [*pushing him toward door*].

Sandy. Hold on! I am going. But, Jack, I've got a kind of faintness 'yer, too. [*Goes to side-table, and takes up decanter.*] And thar's nothin' reaches that faintness like whisky. [*Fills glass.*]

Old Morton [*drunkenly and half-consciously from couch*]. Whisky—who shed—whisky—eh? Eh!—O—gim'me some. Aleck—Aleck, my son,—my son!—my old prodigal—Old Proddy, my boy—gim me—whisky—[*sings*]—

> Oh, 'yer's yer good old whisky,
> Drink it down!

Eh? I com—mand you—pass the whisky!

[SANDY, *at first panicstricken, and then remorsefully conscious, throws glass down with gesture of fear and loathing.* OAKHURST *advances to his side hurriedly.*

Oakhurst [*in hurried whisper*]. Give him the whisky, quick! It will keep him quiet. [*Is about to take decanter when* SANDY *seizes it: struggle with* OAKHURST.]

Sandy [*with feeling*]. No, no, Jack, no! [*Suddenly with great strength and determination breaks from him, and throws decanter from window.*] No, never!

Old Morton [*struggling drunkenly to his feet*]. Eh—who sh'd never? [OAKHURST *shoves* SANDY *in room* L., *and follows him, closing door.*] Eh! Aleck? [*Groping.*] Eh! where'sh light? All gone! [*Lapses on sofa again, after an ineffectual struggle to get up, and then resumes his old attitude.*]

[*Change scene quickly.*]

SCENE 3.—*Ante-room in* MR. MORTON'S *villa.* *Front scene.*
Enter DON JOSÉ CASTRO *and* CONCHO, *preceded by*
SERVANT, L.

Servant. This way, gentlemen.

Don José. Carry this card to Alexander Morton, sen.

Servant. Beg pardon, sir, but there's only one name here, sir [*looking at* CONCHO].

Don José [*proudly*]. That is my servant, sir.

[*Exit* SERVANT.

Don José [*aside*]. I don't half like this business. But my money locked up in his bank, and my daughter's hand bound to his son, demand it. [*Aloud.*] This is no child's play, Concho, you understand.

Concho. Ah! I am wise! Believe me, if I have not proofs which shall blanch the cheek of this old man, I am a fool, Don José!

Re-enter SERVANT.

Servant. Mr. Morton, sen., passed a bad night, and has left word not to be disturbed this morning. But Mr. Morton, jun., will attend you, sir.

Concho [*aside*]. So the impostor will face it out. Well, let him come.

Don José [*to* SERVANT]. I wait his pleasure.

[*Exit* SERVANT.

Don José. You hear, Concho? You shall face this man. I shall repeat to him all you have told me. If you fail to make good your charge, on your head rests the consequences.

Concho. He will of course deny. He is a desperate man: he will perhaps attack me. Eh! Ah! [*Drawing revolver.*]

Don José. Put up your foolish weapon. The sight of

the father he has deceived will be more terrible to him than the pistol of the spy.

Enter COL. STARBOTTLE, C.

Starbottle. Mr. Alexander Morton, jun., will be with you in a moment. [*Takes attitude by door, puts his hand in his breast, and inflates himself.*]

Concho [*to* DON JOSÉ *aside*]. It is the bullying lawyer. They will try to outface us, my patron; but we shall triumph. [*Aloud.*] He comes, eh!—Mr. Alexander Morton, gentlemen! I will show you a cheat, an impostor!

Enter, in correct, precise morning dress, SANDY MORTON. *There is in his make-up and manner a suggestion of the father.*

Concho [*recoiling, aside*]. Diego! The real son! [*Aloud, furiously.*] It is a trick to defeat justice,—eh!—a miserable trick! But it shall fail, it shall fail!

Col. Starbottle. Permit me, a moment,—a single moment. [*To* CONCHO.] You have—er—er—characterised my introduction of this—er—gentleman as a "cheat" and an "imposture." Are you prepared to deny that this is Alexander Morton?

Don José [*astonished, aside*]. These Americaños are of the devil! [*Aloud and sternly.*] Answer him, Concho, I command you.

Concho [*in half-insane rage.*] It is Alexander Morton; but it is a trick,—a cowardly trick! Where is the other impostor, this Mr. John Oakhurst?

Sandy [*advancing with dignity and something of his father's cold manner*]. He will answer for himself when called for. [*To* DON JOSÉ.] You have asked for me, sir: may I inquire your business?

Concho. Eh! It is a trick,—a trick!

Don José [*to* CONCHO]. Silence, sir! [*To* SANDY, *with dignity.*] I know not the meaning of this masquerade. I only know that you are *not* the gentleman hitherto known to me as the son of Alexander Morton. I am here, sir, to demand my rights as a man of property and a father. I have received this morning a cheque from the house of Morton & Son for the amount of my deposit with them. So far—in view of this complication—it is well. Who knows? *Bueno!* But the signature of Morton & Son to the cheque is not in the handwriting I have known. Look at it, sir. [*To* SANDY, *handing cheque.*]

Sandy [*examining cheque*]. It is my handwriting, sir, and was signed this morning. Has it been refused?

Don José. Pardon me, sir. It has not been presented. With this doubt in my mind, I preferred to submit it first to you.

Starbottle. A moment, a single moment, sir. While as a—er—gentleman and a man of honour, I—er—appreciate your motives, permit me to say, sir, as a lawyer, that your visit is premature. On the testimony of your own witness, the identification of Mr. Alexander Morton, jun., is—er—complete; he has admitted the signature as his own; you have not yet presented the cheque to the bank.

Don José. Pardon me, Col. Starbottle. It is not all. [*To* SANDY.] By a written agreement with Alexander Morton, sen., the hand of my daughter is promised to his son, who now stands before me, as my former servant, dismissed from my service for drunkenness.

Sandy. That agreement is revoked.

Don José. Revoked!

Sandy [*handing paper*]. Cast your eyes over that paper. At least you will recognise *that* signature.

Don José [*reads*]. "In view of the evident preference of

my son Alexander Morton, and of certain family interests, I hereby revoke my consent to his marriage with the Doña Jovita Castro, and accord him full permission to woo and win his cousin, Miss Mary Morris; promising him the same aid and assistance previously offered in his suit with Miss Castro.—ALEXANDER MORTON, SEN."

Concho. Ah! *Carramba!* Do you not see the trick,— eh, the conspiracy? It was this man, as Diego, your daughter's groom, helped his friend Mr. Oakhurst to the heiress. Ah! you comprehend? It was an old trick! You shall see! you shall see! Ah! I am wise—I am wise!

Don José [*aside*]. Could I have been deceived? But no! This paper that releases *him* gives the impostor no claim.

Sandy [*resuming his old easy manner, dropping his formality, and placing his hand on* DON JOSÉ'S *shoulder*]. Look 'yar, ole man: I didn't allow to ever see ye agin, and this 'yer ain't none o' *my* seekin'. But, since yer here, I don't mind tellin' ye that but for me that gal of yours would have run away a year ago, and married an unknown lover. And I don't mind adding, that, hed I known that unknown lover was my friend John Oakhurst, I'd have helped her to do it. [*Going.*] Good-morning, Don José.

Don José. Insolent! I shall expect an account for this from your—father, sir.

Sandy. Adios, Don José. [*Exit* C.

Concho. It is a trick—I told you. Ah! I am wise! [*Going to* DON JOSÉ.]

Don José [*throwing him off*]. Fool! [*Exit* DON JOSÉ.]

Concho [*infuriated*]. Eh! Fool yourself—dotard! No matter! I will expose all—ah! I will see Jovita;—I will revenge myself on this impostor! [*Is about to follow, when* COL. STARBOTTLE *leaves his position by the door and touches* CONCHO *on the shoulder.*]

Starbottle. Excuse me.

Concho. Eh?

Starbottle. You have forgotten something.

Concho. Something?

Starbottle. An apology, sir. You were good enough to express—er—incredulity—when I presented Mr. Morton: you were kynd enough to characterise the conduct of my —er—principal by—an epithet. You have alluded to me, sir,—ME—

Concho [*wrathfully*]. Bully! [*Aside.*] I have heard that this *pomposo*, this braggart, is a Yankee trick too; that he has the front of a lion, the liver of the chicken. [*Aloud.*] Yes, I have said, you hear I have said, I, Concho [*striking his breast*], have said you are a—bully!

Starbottle [*coolly.*] Then you are prepared to give me satisfaction, sir,—personal satisfaction?

Concho [*raging*]. Yes, sir, now—you understand, now [*taking out pistol*], anywhere, here! Yes, here! Ah! you start,—yes, here and now! Face to face, you understand, without seconds,—face to face. So! [*Presenting pistol.*]

Starbottle [*quietly*]. Permit me to—er—apologise—

Concho. Ah! It is too late!

Starbottle [*interrupting*]. Excuse me, but I feared you would not honour me so completely and satisfactorily. Ged, sir, I begin to respect you! I accede to all your propositions of time and position. The pistol you hold in your hand is a derringer, I presume, loaded. Ah—er—I am right. The one I now produce [*showing pistol*] is—er —as you will perceive, the same size and pattern, and—er —unloaded. We will place them both, so, under the cloth of this table. You shall draw one pistol, I will take the other. I will put that clock at ten minutes to nine, when we will take our positions across this table; as you—er—happily express it, "face to face." As the clock strikes the hour, we will fire on the second stroke.

Concho [*aside*]. It is a trick—a Yankee trick! [*Aloud.*] I am ready. Now—at once!

Starbottle [*gravely*]. Permit me, sir, to thank you. Your conduct, sir, reminds me of singular incident—

Concho [*angrily interrupting*]. Come, come! It is no child's-play. We have too much of this talk, eh! It is action, eh, you comprehend,—action.

> [STARBOTTLE *places pistols under the cloth, and sets clock.* CONCHO *draws pistol from cloth;* STARBOTTLE *takes remaining pistol. Both men assume position, presenting their weapons,* STARBOTTLE *pompously but seriously,* CONCHO *angrily and nervously.*

Starbottle [*after a pause*]. One moment, a single moment—

Concho. Ah, a trick! Coward! you cannot destroy my aim.

Starbottle. I overlook the—er—epithet. I wished only to ask, if you should be—er—unfortunate, if there was anything I could say to your—er—friends.

Concho. You cannot make the fool of me, coward. No!

Starbottle. My object was only precautionary. Owing to the position in which you—er—persist in holding your weapon, in a line with my right eye, I perceive that a ray of light enters the nipple, and—er—illuminates the barrel. I judge from this, that you have been unfortunate enough to draw the—er—er—unloaded pistol.

Concho [*tremulously lowering weapon*]. Eh! Ah! This is murder! [*Drops pistol.*] Murder!—eh—help! [*retreating*], help! [*Exit hurriedly door* C., *as clock strikes.* COL. STAR-BOTTLE *lowers his pistol, and moves with great pomposity to the other side of the table, taking up pistol.*]

Starbottle [*examining pistol*]. Ah! [*Lifts it, and discharges it.*] It seems that I am mistaken. [*Going.*] The pistol was—er—loaded! [*Exit.*

SCENE 4.—*Front scene. Room in villa. Enter* MISS MARY *and* JOVITA.

Miss Mary. I tell you, you are wrong. You are not only misunderstanding your lover, which is a woman's privilege; but you are abusing my cousin, which, as his relative, I won't put up with.

Jovita [*passionately*]. But hear me, Miss Mary. It is a year since we were betrothed; and such a betrothal! Why, I was signed, sealed, and delivered to him, on conditions, as if I were a part of the rancho; and the very night, too, I had engaged to run away with him! And during that year I have seen the gentleman twice,—yes, twice!

Miss Mary. But he has written?

Jovita. Mother of God! Yes,—letters delivered by my father, sent to *his care*, read by him first, of course; letters hoping that I was well, and obeying my father's commands; letters assuring me of his unaltered devotion; letters that, compared with the ones he used to hide in the confessional of the ruined mission church, were as ice to fire, were as that snowflower you value so much, Mary, to this mariposa blossom I wear in my hair. And then to think that this man —this John Oakhurst, as I knew him; this man who used to ride twenty miles for a smile from me on the church porch; this Don Juan who leaped that garden wall (fifteen feet, Mary, if it is an inch), and made old Concho his stepping stone; this man, who daily perilled death for my sake—is changed into this formal, methodical man of business—is—is—I tell you there's a *woman* at the bottom of it! I know it sure!

Miss Mary [*aside*]. How can I tell her about the Duchess? I won't! [*Aloud.*] But listen, my dear Jovita. You know he is under probation for you, Jovita. All this is for you. His father is cold, methodical, unsympathetic. *He* looks only to his bond with this son,—this son that he treats, even in matters of the heart, as a *business* partner. Remember, on his complete reformation and subjection to his father's will depends your hand. Remember the agreement!

Jovita. The agreement; yes! It is the agreement, always the agreement. May the devil fly away with the agreement! Look you, Miss Mary, I, Doña Jovita, didn't fall in love with an agreement: it was with a man! Why, I might have married a dozen agreements—yes, of a shorter limitation than this! [*Crossing.*]

Miss Mary. Yes. But what if your lover had failed to keep those promises by which he was to gain your hand? what if he were a man incapable of self-control? what if he were—a—a—drunkard!

Jovita [*musing*]. A drunkard! [*Aside.*] There was Diego, he was a drunkard; but he was faithless. [*Aloud.*] You mean, a weak, faithless drunkard?

Miss Mary. No! [*Sadly.*] Faithless only to himself, but devoted—yes, devoted to *you.*

Jovita. Miss Mary, I have found that one big vice in a man is apt to keep out a great many smaller ones.

Miss Mary. Yes; but if he were a slave to liquor?

Jovita. My dear, I should try to change his mistress. Oh, give me a man that is capable of a devotion to anything, rather than a cold, calculating average of all the virtues!

Miss Mary [*aside*]. I, who aspire to be her teacher, am only her pupil. [*Aloud.*] But what if, in this very drunkenness, this recklessness, he had once loved and worshipped another woman? What if you discovered all this after—after—he had won your heart?

Jovita. I should adore him! Ah, Miss Mary! love differs from all the other contagious diseases; the last time a man is exposed to it, he takes it most readily, and has it the worst! But you, *you*, you cannot sympathise with me. You have some lover, the ideal of the virtues; some man as correct, as well regulated, as calm as—yourself; some one who addresses you in the fixed morality and severe penmanship of the copy-books. He will never precipitate himself over a garden wall or through a window. Your Jacob will wait for you through seven years, and receive you from the hands of your cousin and guardian—as a reward of merit! No, you could not love a vagabond.

Miss Mary [*very slowly and quietly*]. No?

Jovita. No! [*Passionately.*] You are good: No, it is impossible! Forgive me, Miss Mary: a better girl than I am. But think of me! A year ago my lover leaped a wall at midnight to fly with me: to-day, the day that gives me to him, he writes a few cold lines saying that he has business, *business*—you understand—business, and that he shall not see me until we meet in the presence of—of—of—our fathers.

Miss Mary. Yes; but you will see him at least, perhaps alone. Listen! it is no formal meeting, but one of festivity. My guardian has told me, in his quaint scriptural way, it is the killing of the fatted calf over his long-lost prodigal. Have patience, little one. Ah! Jovita, we are of a different race, but we are of one sex; and as a woman I know how to accept another woman's abuse of her lover. Come, come. [*Exeunt* MISS MARY *and* JOVITA.

SCENE 5.—*The drawing-room of* MR. MORTON'S *villa. Large open arch in centre, leading to veranda, looking on distant view of San Francisco; richly furnished,—sofas, arm-chairs, and tête-à-tête. Enter* COL. STARBOTTLE C., *carrying bouquet, preceded by* SERVANT *bowing.*

Starbottle. Take my kyard to Miss Morris. [*Exit* SERVANT.]

Starbottle. Star! this is the momentous epoch of your life! It is a moment for which you—are—I may say alone responsible,—personally responsible! She will be naturally gratified by the—er—flowers. She will at once recognise this bouquet as a delicate souvenir of Red Gulch, and will appreciate your recollection. And the fact, the crushing fact, that you have overlooked the—er—ungentlemanly conduct of her *own* cousin Sandy, the real Alexander Morton, that you have—er—assisted to restore the *ex-vaquero* to his rights, will—er—er—at once open the door to—er—mutual confidence and—er—a continuance of that—er—prepossession I have already noticed. Ahem! here she is.

Enter MISS MARY *in full dress.*

Miss Mary. You are early, Col. Starbottle. This promptitude does honour to our poor occasion.

Col. Starbottle. Ged, Miss Mary, promptness with a lady and an adversary is the first duty of—er—gentleman. I wished that—er—the morning dew might still be—er—fresh in these flowers. I gathered them myself [*presenting bouquet*] at—er—flower-stand in the—er—California market.

Miss Mary [*aside*]. Flowers! I needed no such reminder of poor Sandy. [*Aloud.*] I thank you, Colonel.

Starbottle. Ged, ma'am, I am repaid doubly. Your conduct, Miss Mary, reminds me of little incident that occurred at Richmond in '53. Dinner party—came early—but obliged to go—as now—on important business, before dessert—before dessert. Lady sat next to me—beautiful woman—excuse me if I don't mention names—said to me, "Star,"—always called me Star,—"Star, you remind me of the month of May." "Ged, madam," I said, "delighted, proud; but why?" "Because," she said, "you come in with the—er—oysters." No! Ged, pardon me—ridiculous mistake! I mean—er—" you come in with the—er—flowers, and go before the—er—fruits."

Miss Mary. Ah, Colonel! I appreciate her disappointment. Let us hope, however, that some day you may find that happy woman who will be able to keep you through the whole dinner and the whole season, until December and the ices!

Starbottle. Ged! excellent! capital! [*seriously.*] Miss Mary [*suddenly inflating his chest, striking attitude, and gazing on* MISS MARY *with languishing eyes*]. There is—er—such a woman!

Miss Mary [*aside*]. What can he mean?

Starbottle [*taking seat beside her*]. Allow me, Miss Mary, a few moments of confidential—er—confidential disclosure. To-day is, as you are aware, the day on which, according to—er—agreement between parties, my friend and client Mr. Morton, sen., formally accepts his prodigal son. It is my—er—duty to state that—er—the gentleman who has for the past year occupied that position has behaved with great discretion, and—er—fulfilled his part of the—er—agreement. But it would—er—appear that there has been a—er—slight delusion regarding the identity of that prodigal,—a delusion shared by all the parties except, perhaps, myself. I have to prepare you for a shock. The gentleman whom you have recently known as Alexander Morton, jun., is not the prodigal son; is not your—er—cousin; is, in fact, no relation to you. Prepare yourself, Miss Mary, for a little disappointment,—for—er—degradation. The genuine son has been—er—discovered in the person of—er—low menial —er—vagabond,—"Sandy," the—er—outcast of Red Gulch!

Miss Mary [*rising in astonishment*]. Sandy! Then he was right. [*Aside.*] The child is his! and that woman—

Starbottle. Compose yourself, Miss Mary. I know the —er—effect of—er—revelation like this upon—er—proud and aristocratic nature. Ged! my own, I assure you, beats in—er—responsive indignation. You can never consent to remain beneath this roof, and—er—receive a—er vagabond and—er—menial on equal terms. The—er—necessities of my—er—profession may—er—compel me; but you -er— never! Holding myself—er—er—responsible for having introduced you here, it is my—er—duty to provide you with—another home! It is my—er—duty to protect—

Miss Mary [*aside*]. Sandy here, and beneath this roof! Why has he not sought me? Ah! I know too well: he dare not face me with his child!

Starbottle [*aside*]. She turns away! it is maiden coyness. [*Aloud.*] If, Miss Mary, the—er—devotion of a lifetime; if the—er—chivalrous and respectful adoration of a man—er —whose record is—er—not unknown in the Court of Honour [*dropping on one knee with excessive gallantry*]; if the—er—measure—

Miss Mary [*oblivious of* COL. STARBOTTLE]. I *will*—I *must* see him! Ah! [*looking* L.] he is coming!

Enter SANDY.

Starbottle [*rising with great readiness and tact*]. I have found it [*presenting flower*]. It had fallen beneath the sofa.

Sandy [*to* MISS MARY, *stopping short in embarrassment*]. I did not know you—I—I—thought there was no one here.

Miss Mary [*to* STARBOTTLE]. May I ask you to excuse me for a moment? I have a few words to say to—to my cousin!

[STARBOTTLE *bows gallantly to* MISS MARY, *and stiffly to* SANDY, *and exit* R. *A long pause.* MISS MARY *remains seated pulling flowers,* SANDY *remains standing by wing foolish and embarrassed. Business.*

Miss Mary [*impatiently*]. Well?

Sandy [*slowly*]. I axes your pardon, miss; but you told *that* gentleman you had a few words—to say to me.

Miss Mary [*passionately, aside*]. Fool! [*Aloud.*] I had; but I am waiting to first answer your inquiries about your—your—child. I have fulfilled my trust, sir.

Sandy. You have, Miss Mary, and I thank you.

Miss Mary. I might perhaps have expected that this revelation of our kinship would have come from other lips than a stranger's; but—no matter! I wish you joy, sir, of your heritage. [*Going.*] You have found a home, sir, at last, for yourself and—and—your child. Good day, sir.

Sandy. Miss Mary!

Miss Mary. I must make ready to receive your father's guests. It is his orders: I am only his poor relation. Good-bye, sir. [*Exit* L.

Sandy [*watching her*]. She is gone!—gone! No! She has dropped on the sofa in the ante-room, and is crying. Crying! I promised Jack I wouldn't speak until the time came. I'll go back. [*Hesitating and looking towards* L.] Poor girl! how she must hate me! I might just say a word, one word to thank her for her kindness to Johnny,—only one word, and then go away. I—I—can keep from liquor.

I swore I would to Jack, that night I saw the old man—drunk,—and I have. But—I can't keep—from—her! No—damn it! [*Going toward* L.] No!—I'll go! [*Exit* L.

Enter hurriedly and excitedly JOVITA R., *followed by* MANUELA.

Jovita. Where is she? Where is *he?*—the traitor!

Manuela [*entreatingly*]. Compose yourself, Doña Jovita, for the love of God! This is madness: believe me, there is some mistake. It is some trick of an enemy,—of that ingrate, that coyote, Concho, who hates the Don Alexandro.

Jovita. A trick! Call you this a trick? Look at this paper, put into my hands by my father a moment ago. Read it. Ah! listen. [*Reads.*] "In view of the *evident preference* of my son, Alexander Morton, I hereby revoke my consent to his marriage with the Doña Jovita Castro, and accord him full permission to woo and win his cousin, Miss Mary Morris!" Call you this a trick, eh? No, it is their perfidy! ·This is why *she* was brought here on the eve of my betrothal. This accounts for his silence, his absence. Oh, I shall go mad!

Manuela. Compose yourself, miss. If I am not deceived, there is one here who will aid us,—who will expose this deceit. Listen! an hour ago; as I passed through the hall, I saw Diego, our old Diego,—your friend and confidant, Diego.

Jovita. The drunkard—the faithless Diego!

Manuela. Never, Miss Jovita; not drunken! For, as he passed before me, he was as straight, as upright, as fine as your lover. Come, miss, we will seek him.

Jovita. Never! He too is a traitor.

Manuela. Believe me, no! Come, Miss Jovita. [*Looking toward* L.] See, he is there. Some one is with him.

Jovita [*looking*]. You are right; and it is *she—she*, Miss Mary! What? he is kissing her hand! and she—*she*, the double traitress—drops her head upon his shoulder! Oh, this is infamy!

Manuela. Hush! Some one is coming. The guests are arriving. They must not see you thus. This way, Miss Jovita,—this way. After a little, a little, the mystery will be explained. [*Taking* JOVITA'S *hand, and leading her* R.]

Jovita [*going*]. And this was the correct schoolmistress, the preceptress, and example of all the virtues! ha! [*laughing hysterically*] ha!

[*Exeunt* JOVITA *and* MANUELA.

SCENE 6.—*The same. Enter* SERVANT; *opens folding-doors* C., *revealing veranda, and view of distant city beyond. Stage, fog effect from without. Enter* STARBOTTLE *and* OAKHURST R., *in full evening dress.*

Starbottle [*walking towards veranda*]. A foggy evening for our anniversary.

Oakhurst. Yes. [*Aside.*] It was such a night as this I first stepped into Sandy's place, I first met the old man. Well, it will be soon over. [*Aloud.*] You have the papers and transfers all ready?

Starbottle. In my—er—pocket. Mr. Morton, sen., should be here to receive his guests.

Oakhurst. He will be here presently; until then the duty devolves on me. He has secluded himself even from me! [*Aside.*] Perhaps it is in very shame for his recent weakness.

Enter SERVANT.

Servant. Don José Castro, Miss Castro, and Miss Morris.

Enter DON JOSÉ *with* JOVITA *and* MISS MARY *on either arm. All formally salute* MR. OAKHURST, *except* MISS JOVITA, *who turns coldly away, taking seat remotely on sofa.* COL. STARBOTTLE *gallantly approaches* MISS MARY, *and takes seat beside her.*

Oakhurst [*aside*]. They are here to see my punishment. There is no sympathy even in her eyes.

Enter SERVANT.

Servant. Mr. Concepcion Garcia and Mr. Capper.

Concho [*approaching* OAKHURST, *rubbing his hands*]. I wish you joy, Mr. Alexander Morton!

Oakhurst [*excitedly, aside*]. Shall I throw him from the window? The dog!—even he!

Capper [*approaching* MR. OAKHURST]. You have done well. Be bold. *I* will see you through. As for *that* man [*pointing to* CONCHO], leave him to *me!*

   [*Lays his hand on* CONCHO'S *shoulder, and leads him to sofa* R. OAKHURST *takes seat in chair* L. *as* SANDY *enters quietly from door* L., *and stands leaning upon his chair.*

Starbottle [*rising*]. Ladies and gentlemen, we are waiting only for the presence of Mr. Alexander Morton, sen. I regret to say that for the last twenty-four hours he has been—er—exceedingly preoccupied with the momentous cares of the—er—occasion. You who know the austere habits of my friend and—er—client will probably understand that he may be at this very moment engaged in prayerful and Christian meditation, invoking the Throne of Grace, previous to the solemn duties of—er—er—to-night.

Enter SERVANT.

Servant. Mr. Alexander Morton, sen.

Enter OLD MORTON, *drunk, in evening costume, cravat awry, coat half buttoned up, and half surly, half idiotic manner. All rise in astonishment.* SANDY *starts forward.* OAKHURST *pulls him back.*

Morton [*thickly*]. Don't rish! Don't rish! We'll all sit down! How do you do, sir? I wish ye well, miss. [*Goes around and laboriously shakes hands with everybody.*] Now lesh all take a drink! lesh you take a drink, and you take a drink, and you take a drink!

Starbottle. Permit me, ladies and gentlemen, to—er—explain: our friend is—er—evidently labouring under—er—er—accident of hospitality! In a moment he will be himself.

Old Morton. Hush up! Dry up—yourself—old turkey-cock! Eh!

Sandy [*despairingly*]. He will not understand us! [*To* STARBOTTLE.] He will not know me! What is to be done?

Old Morton. Give me some whishky. Lesh all take a drink! [*Enter* SERVANT *with decanter and glasses.*]

Old Morton [*starting forward*]. Lesh all take a drink!

Sandy. Stop!

Old Morton [*recovering himself slightly*]. Who says stop? Who dares countermand my orderish?

Concho [*coming forward*]. Who? I will tell you: eh! eh! Diego—dismissed from the rancho of Don José for drunkenness! Sandy—the vagabond of Red Gulch!

Sandy [*passionately seizing* OLD MORTON'S *arm*]. Yes, Diego—Sandy—the outcast—but, God help me! no longer the drunkard! I forbid you to touch that glass!—I, your son, Alexander Morton! Yes, look at me, father: I, with drunkenness in my blood, planted by you, fostered by you —I whom you sought to save—I—I, stand here to save you! Go! [*To* SERVANT.] Go! While he is thus, I—*I*, am master here!

Old Morton [*cowed and frightened*]. That voice! [*Passing his hand over his forehead.*] Am I dreaming? Aleck, where are you? Alexander, speak, I command you: is this the truth?

Oakhurst [*slowly*]. It is!

Starbottle. One moment—a single moment: permit me to—er—er—explain. The gentleman who has just—er— dismissed the refreshment is, to the best of my legal knowledge, your son. The gentleman who for the past year has so admirably filled the functions of that office is—er—prepared to admit this. The proofs are—er—conclusive. It is with the—er—intention of offering them, and—er— returning your lawful heir, that we—er—are here to-night.

Old Morton [*rising to his feet*]. And I renounce you both! Out of my house, out of my sight, out of my heart, for ever! Go! liars, swindlers, confederates! Drunk—

Oakhurst [*retiring slowly with* SANDY]. We are going, sir!

Old Morton. Go! open the doors there *wide*, wide enough for such a breadth of infamy! Do you hear me? *I* am master here!

[*Stands erect, as* OAKHURST *and* SANDY, *hand in hand, slowly retreat backward to centre,—then suddenly utters a cry and falls heavily on sofa. Both pause.* OAKHURST *remains quiet and motionless;* SANDY, *after a moment's hesitation, rushes forward, and falls at his feet.*

Sandy. Father, forgive me!

Old Morton [*putting his hand round* SANDY'S *neck, and motioning him to door*]. Go! both of you, both of you! [*Resisting* SANDY'S *attempt to rise.*] Did you hear me? Go!

Starbottle. Permit me to explain. Your conduct, Mr. Morton, reminds me of sing'lar incident in '47—

Old Morton. Silence!

Oakhurst. One word, Mr. Morton! Shamed and disgraced as I am, I leave this roof more gladly than I entered it. How I came here, you best know. How I yielded madly to the temptation, the promise of a better life; how I fell, through the hope of reformation,—no one should know better than you, sir, the reformer. I do not ask your pardon. You know that I did my duty to you as your presumed son. Your real son will bear witness that, from the hour I knew of his existence, I did my duty equally to him. Col. Starbottle has all the legal transfers and papers necessary to make the restoration of your son—the integrity of your business name—complete. I take nothing out of this life that I did not bring in it,—except my self-respect! I go—as I came—alone!

Jovita [*rushing towards him*]. No! no! You shall take *me!* I have wronged you, Jack, cruelly; I have doubted you; but you shall not go alone. I care not for this contract! You are more to me, by your own right, Jack, than by any kinship with such as these!

Oakhurst [*raising her gently*]. I thank you, darling. But it is too late now. To be more worthy of you, to win *you,* I waived the title I had to you in my own manhood, to borrow another's more legal claim. I, who would not win you as a gambler, cannot make you now the wife of a convicted impostor. No! Hear me, darling! do not make my disgrace greater than it is. In the years to come, Jovita, think of me as one who loved you well enough to go through shame to win you, but too well to ask you to share with him that shame. Farewell, darling, farewell! [*Releases himself from* JOVITA'S *arms, who falls beside him.*]

Concho [*rubbing his hands, and standing before him*]. Oho! Mr. John Oakhurst—eh—was it for this, eh—you leaped the garden wall, eh? was it for this you struck me down, eh? You are not wise, eh? You should have run away with the Doña when you could—ah, ah, impostor!

Sandy [*leaping to his feet*]. Jack, you shall not go! I will go with you!

Oakhurst. No! Your place is there [*pointing to* OLD MORTON, *whose head has sunk drunkenly on his breast.*] Heed not this man; his tongue carries only the borrowed lash of his master.

Concho. Eh! you are bold now—bold; but I said I would have revenge—ah, revenge!

Sandy [*rushing towards him*]. Coward!

Don José. Hold your hand, sir! Hold! I allow no one to correct my menials but myself. Concho, order my carriage!

Concho. It is ready, sir.

Don José. Then lead the way to it, for my daughter and her husband, John Oakhurst. Good night, Mr. Morton. I can sympathise with you; for we have both found a son. I am willing to exchange my dismissed servant for your dismissed *partner*.

Starbottle [*advancing*]. Ged, sir, I respect you! Ged, sir, permit me, sir, to grasp that honourable hand!

Old Morton [*excitedly*]. He is right, my partner! What have I done! The house of Morton & Son dissolved. The man known as my partner—a fugitive! No, Alexander!

Starbottle. One moment—a single moment! As a

lawyer, permit me to say, sir, that the whole complication may be settled, sir, by the—er—addition of—er—single letter! The house of Morton & Son shall hereafter read Morton & Sons. The papers for the legal adoption of Mr. Oakhurst are—er—in my pocket.

Old Morton [*more soberly*]. Have it your own way, sir! Morton & Sons be it. Hark ye, Don José! We are equal at last. But—hark ye, Aleck! How about the boy, eh?—my grandson, eh? Is this one of the sons by adoption?

Sandy [*embarrassedly*]. It is my own, sir.

Capper [*advancing*]. He can with safety claim it; for the mother is on her way to Australia with her husband.

Old Morton. And the schoolma'am, eh?

Miss Mary. She will claim the usual year of probation for your prodigal, and then—

Sandy. God bless ye, Miss Mary!

Old Morton. I am in a dream! But the world—my friends—my patrons—how can I explain?

Starbottle. I will—er—explain. [*Advancing slowly to front—to audience.*] One moment—er—a single moment! If anything that has—er—transpired this evening—might seem to you, ladies and gentlemen—er—morally or—er—legally—or honourably to require—er—apology or—er—explanation!—permit me to say—that I, Col. Culpepper Starbottle, hold myself responsible — er — personally responsible.

Capper.   *Concho.*

Old Morton. Sandy. Miss Mary. Don José. Jovita. Oakhurst.

Col. Starbottle.

[*Curtain.*]

Cadet Grey.

CANTO I.

I.

ACT first, scene first. A study. Of a kind
   Half cell, half *salon*, opulent yet grave;
Rare books, low shelved, yet far above the mind
   Of common man to compass or to crave;
Some slight relief of pamphlets that inclined
   The soul at first to trifling, till dismayed
By text and title, it drew back resigned,
   Nor cared with levity to vex a shade.
   That to itself such perfect concord made.

II.

Some thoughts like these perplexed the patriot brain
   Of Jones—Lawgiver to the Commonwealth,
As on the threshold of this chaste domain
   He paused expectant, and looked up in stealth
To darkened canvases that frowned amain,
   With stern-eyed Puritans, who first began
To spread their roots in "*Georgius Primus'*" reign,
   Nor dropped till now, obedient to some plan,
   Their century fruit—the perfect Boston man.

III.

Somewhere within that Russia-scented gloom
   A voice catarrhal thrilled the Member's ear:

"Brief is our business, Jones. Look round this
    room!
  Regard yon portraits! Read their meaning clear!
These much proclaim '*my*' station. I presume
    You are our Congressman, before whose wit
And sober judgment shall the youth appear
    Who for West Point is deemed most just and fit
    To serve his country and to honour it."

IV.

"Such is my son! Elsewhere perhaps 'twere wise
    Trial competitive should guide your choice.
There are some people I can well surmise
    Themselves must show their merits. History's
        voice
Spares me that trouble, all desert that lies
    In yonder ancestor of Queen Anne's day,
Or yon grave Governor—is all my boy's,
    Reverts to him; entailed, as one might say;
    In brief, result in Winthrop Adams Grey!"

V.

He turned and laid his well-bred hand, and smiled,
    On the cropped head of one who stood beside.
Ah me! in sooth it was no ruddy child,
    Nor brawny youth that thrilled the father's pride—
'Twas but a *Mind* that somehow had beguiled
    From soulless *Matter* processes that served
For speech and motion and digestion mild,
    Content if all one moral purpose nerved,
    Nor recked thereby its spine were somewhat curved.

VI.

He was scarce eighteen. Yet ere he was eight
    He had despoiled the classics; much he knew

Of Sanscrit; not that he placed undue weight
    On this, but that it helped him with Hebrew,
His favourite tongue. He learned, alas! too late,
    One can't begin too early—would regret
That boyish whim to ascertain the state
    Of Venus' atmosphere made him forget
    That philologic goal on which his soul was set.

VII.

He too had travelled; at the age of ten
    Found Paris empty, dull except for art
And accent. "*Mabille*" with its glories then
    Less than Egyptian "*Almees*" touched a heart
Nothing if not pure classic. If some men
    Thought him a prig, it vexed not his conceit,
But moved his pity, and ofttimes his pen,
    The better to instruct them, through some sheet
    Published in Boston, and signed "Beacon Street."

VIII.

From premises so plain the blind could see
    But one deduction, and it came next day.
"In times like these, the very name of G.
    Speaks volumes," wrote the Honourable J.
"Enclosed please find appointment." Presently
    Came a reception to which Harvard lent
Fourteen professors, and, to give "*esprit*,"
    The Liberal Club some eighteen ladies sent,
    Five that spoke Greek, and thirteen sentiment.

IX.

Four poets came who loved each others' song,
    And two philosophers, who thought that they

Were in most things impractical and wrong;
   And two Reformers, each in his own way
Peculiar—one who had waxed strong
   On herbs and water, and such simple fare;
Two foreign lions, " Ram See " and " Chy Long,"
   And several artists claimed attention there,
     Based on the fact they had been snubbed elsewhere.

X.

With this endorsement nothing now remained
   But counsel, God speed, and some calm adieux;
No foolish tear the father's eyelash stained,
   And Winthrop's cheek as guiltless shone of dew.
A slight publicity, such as obtained
   In classic Rome, these few last hours attended.
The day arrived, the train and depot gained,
   The mayor's own presence this last act commended;
   The train moved off, and here the first act ended.

CANTO II

I.

Where West Point crouches, and with lifted shield
   Turns the whole river eastward through the pass;
Whose jutting crags, half silver, stand revealed
   Like bossy bucklers of Leonidas;
Where buttressed low against the storms that wield
   Their summer lightnings where her eaglets' swarm,
By Freedom's cradle Nature's self has steeled
   Her heart, like Winkelried, and to that storm
   Of levelled lances bares her bosom warm.

II.

But not to-night.   The air and woods are still,
    The faintest rustle in the trees below,
The lowest tremor from the mountain rill,
    Come to the ear as but the trailing flow
Of spirit robes that walk unseen the hill;
    The moon low sailing o'er the upland farm,
The moon low sailing where the waters fill
      The lozenge lake, beside the banks of balm,
      Gleams like a chevron on the river's arm.

III.

All space breathes languor; from the hill-top high,
    Where Putnam's bastion crumbles in the past,
To swooning depths where drowsy cannon lie
    And wide-mouthed mortars gape in slumbers vast;
Stroke upon stroke, the far oars glance and die
    On the hushed bosom of the sleeping stream;
Bright for one moment drifts a white sail by,
    Bright for one moment shows a bayonet gleam
    Far on the level plain, then passes as a dream.

IV.

Soft down the line of darkened battlements,
    Bright on each lattice of the barrack walls,
Where the low arching sallyport indents,
    Seen through its gloom beyond, the moonbeam falls.
All is repose save where the camping tents
    Mock the white gravestones farther on, where sound
No morning guns for "*reveille*," nor whence
    No drum-beat calls retreat, but still is ever found
    Waiting and present on each sentry's round.

V.

Within the camp they lie, the young, the brave,
    Half knight, half schoolboy, acolytes of fame,
Pledged to one altar, and perchance one grave;
    Bred to fear nothing but reproach and blame,
Ascetic dandies o'er whom vestals rave,
    Clean-limbed young Spartans, disciplined young elves,
Taught to destroy, that they may live to save,
    Students embattled, soldiers at their shelves,
    Heroes whose conquests are at first themselves.

VI.

Within the camp they lie, in dreams are freed
    From the grim discipline they learn to love;
In dreams no more the sentry's challenge heed,
    In dreams afar beyond their pickets rove;
One treads once more the piney paths that lead
    To his green mountain home, and pausing hears
The cattle call; one treads the tangled weed
    Of slippery rocks beside Atlantic piers;
    One smiles in sleep, one wakens wet with tears.

VII.

One scents the breath of jasmine flowers that twine
    The pillared porches of his Southern home;
One hears the coo of pigeons in the pine
    Of Western woods where he was wont to roam;
One sees the sunset fire the distant line
    Where the long prairie sweeps its levels down;
One treads the snowpeaks; one by lamps that shine
    Down the broad highways of the sea-girt town,
    And two are missing—Cadets Grey and Brown!

VIII.

Much as I grieve to chronicle the fact,
   That self-same truant known as "*Cadet Grey*"
Was the young hero of our moral tract,
   Shorn of his twofold names on entrance-day.
"Winthrop" and "Adams" dropped in that one act
   Of martial curtness, and the roll-call thinned
Of his ancestors, he with youthful tact
     Indulgence claimed, since Winthrop no more sinned,
     Nor sainted Adams winced when he, plain Grey was "skinned."

IX.

He had known trials since we saw him last,
   By sheer good luck had just escaped rejection,
Not for his learning, but that it was cast
   In a spare frame scarce fit for drill inspection;
But when he ope'd his lips a stream so vast
   Of information flooded each professor,
They quite forgot his eyeglass—something past
     All precedent—accepting the transgressor,
     Weak eyes and all of which he was possessor.

X.

E'en the first day he touched a blackboard's space—
   So the tradition of his glory lingers—
Two wise professors fainted, each with face
   White as the chalk within his rapid fingers:
All day he ciphered, at such frantic pace,
   His form was hid in chalk precipitation
Of every problem, till they said his case
     Could meet from them no fair examination
     Till Congress made a new appropriation.

XI.

Famous in molecules, he demonstrated
   From the mess hash to many a listening classful;
Great as a botanist, he separated
   Three kinds of "*Mentha*" in one julep's glassful;
High in astronomy, it has been stated
   He was the first at West Point to discover
Mars' missing satellites, and calculated
   Their true positions, not the heavens over,
   But 'neath the window of Miss Kitty Rover.

XII.

Indeed I fear this novelty celestial
   That very night was visible and clear;
At least two youths of aspect most terrestrial,
   And clad in uniform, were loitering near
A villa's casement, where a gentle vestal
   Took their impatience somewhat patiently,
Knowing the youths were somewhat green and
     "bestial"—
   (A certain slang of the Academy,
   I beg the reader won't refer to me).

XIII.

For when they ceased their ardent strain, Miss Kitty
   Glowed not with anger nor a kindred flame,
But rather flushed with an odd sort of pity,
   Half matron's kindness, and half coquette's shame;
Proud yet quite blameful, when she heard their ditty
   She gave her soul poetical expression,
And being clever too, as she was pretty,
   From her high casement warbled this confession—
   Half provocation and one half repression :—

NOT YET.

Not yet, O friend, not yet ! the patient stars
Lean from their lattices, content to wait.
All is illusion till the morning bars
Slip from the levels of the Eastern gate.
Night is too young, O friend ! day is too near;
Wait for the day that maketh all things clear.
    Not yet, O friend, not yet !

Not yet, O love, not yet ! all is not true,
All is not ever, as it seemeth now.
Soon shall the river take another blue,
Soon dies yon light upon the mountain brow.
What lieth dark, O love, bright day will fill.
Wait for thy morning, be it good or ill—
    Not yet, O love, not yet !

XIV.

The strain was finished; softly as the night
  Her voice died from the window, yet e'en then
Fluttered and fell likewise a kerchief white;
  But that no doubt was accident, for when
She sought her couch she deemed her conduct quite
  Beyond the reach of scandalous commentor—
Washing her hands of either gallant wight
  Knowing the moralist might compliment her—
Thus voicing Siren with the words of Mentor.

XV.

She little knew the youths below, who straight
  Dived for her kerchief, and quite overlooked
The pregnant moral she would inculcate;
  Nor dreamed the less how little Winthrop brooked
Her right to doubt his soul's maturer state.
  Brown—who was Western, amiable, and new—
Might take the moral and accept his fate;
  The which he did, but, being stronger too,
Took the white kerchief, also, as his due.

XVI.

They did not quarrel, which no doubt seemed queer
   To those who knew not how their friendship blended;
Each were opposed, and each the other's peer,
   Yet each other in some things transcended.
Where Brown lacked culture, brains—and oft, I fear,
   Cash in his pocket—Grey of course supplied him;
Where Grey lacked frankness, force, and faith sincere,
   Brown of his manhood suffered none to chide him,
But in his faults stood manfully beside him.

XVII.

In academic walks and studies grave,
   In the camp drill and martial occupation,
They helped each other; but just here I crave
   Space for the reader's full imagination—
The fact is patent, Grey became a slave!—
   A tool, a fag, a "pleb!" To state it plainer,
All that blue blood and ancestry e'er gave,
   Cleaned guns, brought water!—was, in fact, retainer
To Jones, whose uncle was a paper-stainer!

XVIII.

How they bore this at home I cannot say:
   I only know so runs the gossip's tale.
It chanced one day that the paternal Grey
   Came to West Point that he himself might hail
The future hero in some proper way
   Consistent with his lineage. With him came
A judge, a poet, and a brave array
   Of aunts and uncles, bearing each a name,
Eyeglass and respirator with the same.

XIX.

"Observe!" quoth Grey the elder to his friends,
  "Not in these giddy youths at base-ball playing
You'll notice Winthrop Adams! Greater ends
  Than these absorb *his* leisure. No doubt straying
With Cæsar's Commentaries, he attends
  Some Roman council. Let us ask, however,
Yon grimy urchin, who my soul offends
  By wheeling offal, if he will endeavour
    To find——What! heaven! Winthrop! Oh! no! never!"

XX.

Alas! too true! The last of all the Greys
  Was "doing police detail;" it had come
To this; in vain were the historic bays
  That crowned the pictured Puritans at home!
And yet 'twas certain that in grosser ways
  Of health and physique he was quite improving.
Straighter he stood, and had achieved some praise
  In other exercise, much more behooving
    A soldier's taste than merely dirt removing.

XXI.

But to resume: we left the youthful pair,
  Some stanzas back, before a lady's bower;
'Tis to be hoped they were no longer there,
  For stars were pointing to the morning hour.
Their escapade discovered, ill 'twould fare
  With our two heroes, derelict of orders;
But, like the ghost, they "scent the morning air,"
  And back again they steal across the borders,
    Unseen, unheeded, by their martial warders.

XXII.

They got to bed with speed : young Grey to dream
    Of some vague future with a general's star,
And Mistress Kitty basking in its gleam ;
    While Brown, content to worship her afar,
Dreamed himself dying by some lonely stream,
    Having snatched Kitty from eighteen Nez Perces,
Till a far bugle, with the morning beam,
    In his dull ear its fateful song rehearses,
    Which Winthrop Adams after put to verses.

XXIII.

So passed three years of their noviciate,
    The first real boyhood Grey had ever known.
His youth ran clear—not choked like his Cochituate,
    In civic pipes, but free and pure alone ;
Yet knew repression, could himself habituate
    To having mind and body well rubbed down,
Could read himself in others, and could situate
    Themselves in him—except, I grieve to own,
    He couldn't see what Kitty saw in Brown !

XXIV.

At last came graduation ; Brown received
    In the One Hundredth Cavalry commission ;
Then frolic, flirting, parting—when none grieved
    Save Brown, who loved our young Academician,
And Grey, who felt his friend was still deceived
    By Mistress Kitty, who with other beauties
Graced the occasion, and it was believed
    Had promised Brown that when he could recruit his
    Promised command, she'd share with him those duties.

XXV.

Howe'er this I know not ; all I know,
    The night was June's, the moon rode high and clear,

"'Twas such a night as this"—three years ago
  Miss Kitty sang the song that two might hear.
There is a walk where trees o'erarching grow,
  Too wide for one, not wide enough for three
(A fact precluding any plural beau),
  Which quite explained Miss Kitty's company,
But not why Grey that favoured one should be.

XXVI

There is a spring, whose limpid waters hide
  Somewhere within the shadows of that path
Called Kosciusko's. There two figures bide—
  Grey and Miss Kitty. Surely Nature hath
No fairer mirror for a might-be bride
  Than this same pool that caught our gentle belle
To its dark heart one moment. At her side
  Grey bent. A something trembled o'er the well,
Bright, spherical—a tear? Ah! no, a button fell!

XXVII.

"Material minds might think that gravitation,"
  Quoth Grey, "drew yon metallic spheroid down.
The soul poetic views the situation
  Fraught with more meaning. When thy girlish crown .
Was mirrored there, there was disintegration
  Of me, and all my spirit moved to you,
Taking the form of slow precipitation!"—
  But here came "Taps," a start, a smile, adieu!
  A blush, a sigh, and end of Canto II.

BUGLE SONG.

Fades the light,   Love, good night!
  And afar   Must thou go
Goeth day, cometh night   When the day
  And a star   And the light
    Leadeth all,   Need thee so—
    Speedeth all   Needeth all
      To their rest!   Heedeth all,
        That is best?

CANTO III.

I.

Where the sun sinks through leagues of arid sky,
    Where the sun dies o'er leagues of arid plain,
Where the dead bones of wasted rivers lie,
    Trailed from their channels in yon mountain chain;
Where day by day naught takes the wearied eye
    But the low-rimming mountains, sharply based
On the dead levels, moving far or nigh,
    As the sick vision wanders o'er the waste,
    But ever day by day against the sunset traced:

II.

There moving through a poisonous cloud that stings
    With dust of alkali the trampling band
Of Indian ponies, ride on dusky wings
    The red marauders of the Western land;
Heavy with spoil, they seek the trail that brings
    Their flaunting lances to that sheltered bank
Where lie their lodges; and the river sings
    Forgetful of the plain beyond, that drank
    Its life blood, where the wasted caravan sank.

III.

They brought with them the thief's ignoble spoil,
    The beggar's dole, the greed of *chiffonier*,
The scum of camps, the implements of toil
    Snatched from dead hands, to rust as useless here;
All they could rake or glean from hut or soil
    Piled their lean ponies, with the jackdaw's greed
For vacant glitter. It were scarce a foil
    To all this tinsel that one feathered reed
    Bore on its barb two scalps that freshly bleed!

IV.

They brought with them, alas! a wounded foe,
  Bound hand and foot, yet nursed with cruel care,
Lest that in death he might escape one throe
  They had decreed his living flesh should bear:
A youthful officer, by one foul blow
  Of treachery surprised, yet fighting still
Amid his ambushed train, calm as the snow
  Above him; hopeless, yet content to spill
  His blood with theirs, and fighting but to kill.

V.

He had fought nobly, and in that brief spell
  Had won the awe of those rude border men
Who gathered round him, and beside him fell
  In loyal faith and silence, save that when
By smoke embarrassed, and near sight as well,
  He paused to wipe his eyeglass, and decide
Its nearer focus, there arose a yell
  Of approbation, and Bob Barker cried
  "Wade in, Dundreary!" tossed his cap and—died.

VI.

Their sole survivor now! his captors bear
  Him all unconscious, and beside the stream
Leave him to rest; meantime the squaws prepare
  The stake for sacrifice: nor wakes a gleam
Of pity in those Furies' eyes that glare
  Expectant of the torture; yet alway
His steadfast spirit shines and mocks them there
  With peace they know not, till at close of day
  On his dull ear there thrills a whispered "Grey!"

VII.

He starts! Was it a trick? Had angels kind
   Touched with compassion some weak woman's
      breast?
Such things he'd read of! Faintly to his mind
   Came Pocohontas pleading for her guest.
But then this voice, though soft, was still inclined
   To baritone! A squaw in ragged gown
Stood near him frowning hatred. Was he blind?
   Whose eye was this beneath that beetling frown?
   The frown was painted, but that wink meant—
      Brown!

VIII.

"Hush! for your life and mine! the thongs are cut,"
   He whispers; "in yon thicket stands my horse,
One dash!—I follow close, as if to glut
   My own revenge, yet bar the other's course.
Now!" And 'tis done. Grey speeds, Brown follows;
      but
Ere yet they reach the shade, Grey, fainting, reels—
Yet not before Brown's circling arms close shut
   His in, uplifting him! Anon he feels
   A horse beneath him bound, and hears the rattling
      heels.

IX.

Then rose a yell of baffled hate, and sprang
   Headlong the savages in swift pursuit;
Though speed the fugitives, they hope to hang
   Hot on their heels, like wolves, with tireless foot.
Long is the chase; Brown hears with inward pang
   The short, hard panting of his gallant steed
Beneath its double burden; vainly rang

Both voice and spur. The heaving flanks may
    bleed,
Yet comes the sequel that they still must heed!

X.

Brown saw it—reined his steed; dismounting, stood
    Calm and inflexible. "Old chap! you see
There is but *one* escape. You know it? Good!
    There is *one* man to take it. You are he,
The horse won't carry double. If he could,
    'Twould but protract this bother. I shall stay:
I've business with these devils—they with me;
    I will occupy them till you get away.
    Hush! quick time, forward. There! God bless
        you, Grey!"

XI.

But as he finished, Grey slipped to his feet,
    Calm as his ancestors in voice and eye:
    You do forget yourself when you compete
With him whose *right* it is to stay here and to die:
That's not your duty. Please regain your seat:
    And take my *orders*—since I rank you here!—
Mount and rejoin your men, and my defeat
    Report at quarters. Take this letter; ne'er
    Give it to aught but *her*, though death should
        interfere."

XII.

And, shamed and blushing, Brown the letter took
    Obediently and placed it in his pocket,
Then drawing forth another, said, "I look
    For death as you do, wherefore take this locket
And letter." Here his comrade's hand he shook
    In silence. "Should we both together fall,
Some other man"—but here all speech forsook

His lips, as ringing cheerily o'er all
He heard afar his own dear bugle-call!

XIII.

'Twas his command and succour, but e'en then
    Grey fainted, with poor Brown, who had forgot
He likewise had been wounded, and both men
    Were picked up quite unconscious of their lot.
Long lay they in extremity, and when
    They both grew stronger, and once more exchanged
Old vows and memories, one common "*den*"
    In hospital was theirs, and free they ranged,
    Awaiting orders, but no more estranged.

XIV.

And yet 'twas strange—nor can I end my tale
    Without this moral, to be fair and just:
They never sought to know why each did fail
    The prompt fulfilment of the other's trust.
It was suggested they could not avail
    Themselves of either letter, since they were
Duly dispatched to their address by mail
    By Captain X., who knew Miss Rover fair
    Now meant stout Mistress Bloggs of Blank Blank Square.

END OF VOL. I.

STANDARD AND POPULAR

Library Books

SELECTED FROM THE CATALOGUE OF

HOUGHTON, MIFFLIN AND CO.

CONSIDER what you have in the smallest chosen library. A company of the wisest and wittiest men that could be picked out of all civil countries, in a thousand years, have set in best order the results of their learning and wisdom. The men themselves were hid and inaccessible, solitary, impatient of interruptions, fenced by etiquette; but the thought which they did not uncover to their bosom friend is here written out in transparent words to us, the strangers of another age. — Ralph Waldo Emerson.

Library Books

OHN ADAMS and Abigail Adams.
Familiar Letters of John Adams and his wife, Abigail Adams, during the Revolution. Crown 8vo, $2.00.

Louis Agassiz.
Methods of Study in Natural History. 16mo, $1.50.
Geological Sketches. 16mo, $1.50.
Geological Sketches. Second Series. 16mo, $1.50.
A Journey in Brazil. Illustrated. 8vo, $5.00.

Thomas Bailey Aldrich.
Story of a Bad Boy. Illustrated. 16mo, $1.50.
Marjorie Daw and Other People. 16mo, $1.50.
Prudence Palfrey. 16mo, $1.50.
The Queen of Sheba. 16mo, $1.50.
The Stillwater Tragedy. $1.50.
Cloth of Gold and Other Poems. 16mo, $1.50.
Flower and Thorn. Later poems. 16mo, $1.25.

American Men of Letters.
Edited by CHARLES DUDLEY WARNER.

Washington Irving. By Charles Dudley Warner. 16mo, $1.25.
Noah Webster. By Horace E. Scudder. 16mo, $1.25.

(*In Preparation.*)

Nathaniel Hawthorne. By James Russell Lowell.
N. P. Willis. By Thomas Bailey Aldrich.
Henry D. Thoreau. By Frank B. Sanborn.
J. Fenimore Cooper. By Prof. T. R. Lounsbury.
William Gilmore Simms. By George W. Cable.
Benjamin Franklin. By T. W. Higginson.

Others to be announced.

American Statesmen.

Edited by JOHN T. MORSE, Jr.
(*In Preparation.*)

John Quincy Adams. By John T. Morse, Jr.
Alexander Hamilton. By Henry Cabot Lodge.
Andrew Jackson. By Prof. W. G. Sumner.
John C. Calhoun. By Dr. H. Von Holst.
John Randolph. By Henry Adams.
James Madison. By Sidney Howard Gay.
James Monroe. By Pres. D. C. Gilman.
Albert Gallatin. By John Austin Stevens.
Patrick Henry. By Prof. Moses Coit Tyler.
Henry Clay. By Hon. Carl Schurz.

Lives of Jefferson and Webster are expected, and others, to be announced later.

Hans Christian Andersen.

Complete Works. 8vo.
1. The Improvisatore ; or, Life in Italy.
2. The Two Baronesses.
3. O. T. ; or, Life in Denmark.
4. Only a Fiddler.
5. In Spain and Portugal.
6. A Poet's Bazaar.
7. Pictures of Travel.
8. The Story of my Life. With Portrait.
9. Wonder Stories told for Children. Ninety-two illustrations.
10. Stories and Tales. Illustrated.

Cloth, per volume, $1.50 ; price of sets in cloth, $15.00.

Francis Bacon.

Works. Collected and edited by Spedding, Ellis, and Heath. With Portraits and Index. In fifteen volumes, crown 8vo, cloth, $33.75.

The same. *Popular Edition.* In two volumes, crown 8vo, with Portraits and Index. Cloth, $5.00.

Bacon's Life.

Life and Times of Bacon. Abridged. By James Spedding. 2 vols. crown 8vo, $5.00.

Björnstjerne Björnson.

Norwegian Novels. 16mo, each $1.00.
Synnöve Solbakken.   A Happy Boy.
Arne.   The Fisher Maiden.

British Poets.

Riverside Edition. In 68 volumes, crown 8vo, cloth, gilt top, per vol. $1.75; the set complete, 68 volumes, cloth, $100.00.

Akenside and Beattie, 1 vol.
Ballads, 4 vols.
Burns, 1 vol.
Butler, 1 vol.
Byron, 5 vols.
Campbell and Falconer, 1 vol.
Chatterton, 1 vol.
Chaucer, 3 vols.
Churchill, Parnell, and Tickell, 2 vols.
Coleridge and Keats, 2 vols.
Cowper, 2 vols.
Dryden, 2 vols.
Gay, 1 vol.
Goldsmith and Gray, 1 vol.
Herbert and Vaughan, 1 vol.
Herrick, 1 vol.
Hood, 2 vols.
Milton and Marvell, 2 vols.
Montgomery, 2 vols.
Moore, 3 vols.
Pope and Collins, 2 vols.
Prior, 1 vol.
Scott, 5 vols.
Shakespeare and Jonson, 1 vol.
Shelley, 2 vols.
Skelton and Donne, 2 vols.
Southey, 5 vols.
Spenser, 3 vols.
Swift, 2 vols.
Thomson, 1 vol.
Watts and White, 1 vol.
Wordsworth, 3 vols.
Wyatt and Surrey, 1 vol.
Young, 1 vol.

John Brown, M. D.

Spare Hours. 2 vols. 16mo, each $1.50.

Robert Browning.

Poems and Dramas, etc. 13 vols. $19.50.

Wm. C. Bryant.

Translation of Homer. The Iliad. 2 vols. royal 8vo, $9.00. Crown 8vo, $4.50. 1 vol. 12mo, $3.00.
The Odyssey. 2 vols. royal 8vo, $9.00. Crown 8vo, $4.50. 1 vol. 12mo, $3.00.

John Burroughs.
Wake-Robin. Illustrated. 16mo, $1.50.
Winter Sunshine. 16mo, $1.50.
Birds and Poets. 16mo, $1.50.
Locusts and Wild Honey. 16mo, $1.50.
Pepacton, and Other Sketches. 16mo, $1.50.

Thomas Carlyle.
Essays. With Portrait and Index. Four volumes, crown 8vo, $7.50. *Popular Edition.* Two volumes, $3.50.

Alice and Phœbe Cary.
Poetical Works, including Memorial by Mary Clemmer. 1 vol. 8vo, $3.50.
Ballads for Little Folk. Illustrated. $1.50.

L. Maria Child.
Looking toward Sunset. 4to, $2.50.

James Freeman Clarke.
Ten Great Religions. 8vo, $3.00.
Common Sense in Religion. 12mo, $2.00.
Memorial and Biographical Sketches. 12mo, $2.00.
Exotics. $1.00.

J. Fenimore Cooper.
Works. *Household Edition.* Illustrated. 32 vols. 16mo. Cloth, per volume, $1.00; the set, $32.00.
Globe Edition. Illust'd. 16 vols. $20.00. (*Sold only in sets.*)
Sea Tales. Illustrated. 10 vols. 16mo, $10.00.
Leather Stocking Tales. *Household Edition.* Illustrated. 5 vols. $5.00. *Riverside Edition.* 5 vols. $11.25.

C. P. Cranch.
Translation of the Æneid of Virgil. Royal 8vo, $4.50.

Richard H. Dana.
To Cuba and Back. 16mo, $1.25.
Two Years Before the Mast. 16mo, $1.50.

Thomas De Quincey.
Works. *Riverside Edition.* In 12 vols. crown 8vo. Per volume, cloth, $1.50; the set, $18.00.
Globe Edition. Six vols. 12mo, $10.00. (*Sold only in sets.*)

Madame De Stael.
Germany. 1 vol. crown 8vo, $2.50.

Charles Dickens.
Works. *Illustrated Library Edition.* In 29 volumes, crown 8vo. Cloth, each, $1.50; the set, $43.50.
Globe Edition. In 15 vols. 12mo. Cloth, per volume, $1.25; the set, $18.75.

J. Lewis Diman.
The Theistic Argument as Affected by Recent Theories. 8vo, $2.00.
Orations and Essays. 8vo, $2.50.

F. S. Drake.
Dictionary of American Biography. 1 vol. 8vo, cloth, $6.00.

Charles L. Eastlake.
Hints on Household Taste. Illustrated. 12mo, $3.00.

George Eliot.
The Spanish Gypsy. 16mo, $1.50.

Ralph Waldo Emerson.
Works. 10 vols. 16mo, $1.50 each; the set, $15.00.
Fireside Edition. 5 vols. 16mo, $10.00. (*Sold only in sets.*)
"Little Classic" Edition. 9 vols. Cloth, each, $1.50.
Prose Works. Complete. 3 vols. 12mo, $7.50.
Parnassus. *Household Ed.* 12mo, $2.00. *Library Ed.*, $4.00.

Fénelon.
Adventures of Telemachus. Crown 8vo, $2.25.

James T. Fields.
Yesterdays with Authors. 12mo, $2.00. 8vo, $3.00.
Underbrush. $1.25.
Ballads and other Verses. 16mo, $1.00.
The Family Library of British Poetry, from Chaucer to the Present Time (1350–1878). Edited by James T. Fields and Edwin P. Whipple. Royal 8vo. 1,028 pages, with 12 fine Steel Portraits, $5.00.
Biographical Notes and Personal Sketches. 1 vol. 8vo, gilt top, $2.00.

John Fiske.
Myths and Mythmakers. 12mo, $2.00.
Outlines of Cosmic Philosophy. 2 vols. 8vo, $6.00.
The Unseen World, and other Essays. 12mo, $2.00.

Goethe.
Faust. Metrical Translation. By Rev. C. T. Brooks. 16mo, $1.25.
Faust. Translated into English Verse. By Bayard Taylor. 2 vols. royal 8vo, $9.00; crown 8vo, $4.50; in 1 vol. 12mo, $3.00.
Correspondence with a Child. Portrait of Bettina Brentano. 12mo, $1.50.
Wilhelm Meister. Translated by Thomas Carlyle. Portrait of Goethe. 2 vols. 12mo, $3.00.

Bret Harte.
Works. New complete edition. 5 vols. 12mo, each $2.00.

Nathaniel Hawthorne.
Works. *"Little Classic" Edition.* Illustrated. 24 vols. 18mo, each $1.25; the set $30.00.
Illustrated Library Edition. 13 vols. 12mo, per vol. $2.00.
Fireside Edition. Illustrated. 13 vols. 16mo, the set, $21.00.
New Globe Edition. 6 vols. 16mo, illustrated, the set, $10.00.
(*The Fireside and Globe Editions are sold only in sets.*)

George S. Hillard.
Six Months in Italy. 12mo, $2.00.

Oliver Wendell Holmes.
Poems. *Household Edition.* 12mo, $2.00.
Illustrated Library Edition. Illustrated, full gilt, 8vo, $4.00.
Handy Volume Edition. 2 vols. 18mo, gilt top, $2.50.
The Autocrat of the Breakfast-Table. 18mo, $1.50. 12mo, $2.00.
The Professor at the Breakfast-Table. 12mo, $2.00.
The Poet at the Breakfast-Table. 12mo, $2.00.
Elsie Venner. 12mo, $2.00.
The Guardian Angel. 12mo, $2.00.
Soundings from the Atlantic. 16mo, $1.75.
John Lothrop Motley. A Memoir. 16mo, $1.50.

W. D. Howells.
Venetian Life. 12mo, $1.50.
Italian Journeys. 12mo, $1.50.
Their Wedding Journey. Illus. 12mo, $1.50; 18mo, $1.25.
Suburban Sketches. Illustrated. 12mo, $1.50.
A Chance Acquaintance. Illus. 12mo, $1.50; 18mo, $1.25.
A Foregone Conclusion. 12mo, $1.50.
The Lady of the Aroostook. 12mo, $1.50.
The Undiscovered Country. $1.50.
Poems. 18mo, $1.25.
Out of the Question. A Comedy. 18mo, $1.25.
A Counterfeit Presentment. 18mo, $1.25.
Choice Autobiography. Edited by W. D. Howells. 18mo, per vol., $1.25.
   I., II. Memoirs of Frederica Sophia Wilhelmina, Margravine of Baireuth.
   III. Lord Herbert of Cherbury, and Thomas Ellwood.
   IV. Vittorio Alfieri. V. Carlo Goldoni.
   VI. Edward Gibbon. VII., VIII. François Marmontel.

Thomas Hughes.
Tom Brown's School-Days at Rugby. $1.00.
Tom Brown at Oxford. 16mo, $1.25.
The Manliness of Christ. 16mo, gilt top, $1.00.

Henry James, Jr.
Passionate Pilgrim and other Tales. $2.00.
Transatlantic Sketches. 12mo, $2.00.
Roderick Hudson. 12mo, $2.00.
The American. 12mo, $2.00.
Watch and Ward. 18mo, $1.25.
The Europeans. 12mo, $1.50.
Confidence. 12mo, $1.50.
The Portrait of a Lady. $2.00.

Mrs. Anna Jameson.
Writings upon Art subjects. 10 vols. 18mo, each $1.50.

Sarah O. Jewett.
Deephaven. 18mo, $1.25.
Old Friends and New. 18mo, $1.25.
Country By-Ways. 18mo, $1.25.
Play-Days. Stories for Children. Sq. 16mo, $1.50.

Rossiter Johnson.
Little Classics. Eighteen handy volumes containing the choicest Stories, Sketches, and short Poems in English literature. Each in one vol. 18mo, $1.00; the set, $18.00. In 9 vols. square 16mo, $13.50. (*Sold in sets only.*)

Samuel Johnson.
Oriental Religions: India, 8vo, $5.00. China, 8vo, $5.00.

T. Starr King.
Christianity and Humanity. 12mo, $2.00.
Substance and Show. 12mo, $2.00.

Lucy Larcom.
Poems. 16mo, $1.25.
Wild Roses of Cape Ann and other Poems. 16mo, $1.25.
An Idyl of Work. 16mo, $1.25.
Childhood Songs. Illustrated. 12mo, $1.50; 16mo, $1.00.
Breathings of the Better Life. 18mo, $1.25.

G. P. Lathrop.
A Study of Hawthorne. 18mo, $1.25.

G. H. Lewes.
The Story of Goethe's Life. Portrait. 12mo, $1.50.
Problems of Life and Mind. 5 vols. $14.00.

J. G. Lockhart.
Life of Sir Walter Scott. 3 vols. cr. 8vo, $4.50.

H. W. Longfellow.
Poems. *Cambridge Edition complete*. Portrait. 4 vols. cr. 8vo, $9.00. 2 vols. $7.00.
Octavo Edition. Portrait and 300 illustrations. $8.00.
Household Edition. Portrait. 12mo, $2.00.
Red-Line Edition. 12 illustrations and Portrait. $2.50.
Diamond Edition. $1.00.
Library Edition. Portrait and 32 illustrations. 8vo, 14.00.
Prose Works. *Cambridge Edition.* 2 vols. cr. 8vo, $4.50.
Hyperion. A Romance. 16mo, $1.50.
Outre-Mer. 16mo, $1.50.
Kavanagh. 16mo, $1.50.
Christus. *Red-Line Edition.* 16 illustrations. $2.50.
Translation of the Divina Commedia of Dante. 3 vols. royal 8vo, $13.50; cr. 8vo, $6.00; 1 vol. cr. 8vo, $3.00.

James Russell Lowell.
Poems. *Red-Line Ed.* 16 illustrations and Portrait. $2.50.
Household Edition. Portrait. 12mo, $2.00.
Library Edition. Portrait and 32 illustrations. 8vo, $4.00.
Fireside Travels. 16mo, $1.50.
Among my Books. 12mo, $2.00.
Among my Books. Second Series. 12mo, $2.00.
My Study Windows. 12mo, $2.00.

T. B. Macaulay.
England. *New Riverside Edition.* 4 vols., cloth, $5.00.
Essays. Portrait. *New Riverside Edition.* 3 vols., $3.75.
Speeches and Poems. *New Riverside Ed.* 1 vol., $1.25.

Harriet Martineau.
Autobiography. Portraits and illustrations. 2 vols. 8vo, $6.00.
Household Education. 18mo, $1.25.

Edwin D. Mead.
Philosophy of Carlyle. 16mo, $1.00.

Owen Meredith.
Poems. *Household Edition.* Illustrated. 12mo, $2.00.
Library Edition. Portrait and 32 illustrations. 8vo, $4.00.
Shawmut Edition. $1.50.
Lucile. *Red-Line Edition.* 8 illustrations. $2.50.
Diamond Edition. 8 illustrations, $1.00.

Michael de Montaigne.
Complete Works. Portrait. 4 vols. crown 8vo, $7.50.

E. Mulford.
The Nation. 8vo, $2.50.
The Republic of God. 8vo, $2.00.

D. M. Mulock.
Thirty Years. Poems. 1 vol. 16mo, $1.50.

T. T. Munger.
On the Threshold. 16mo, gilt top, $1.00.

J. A. W. Neander.
History of the Christian Religion and Church, with Index volume, 6 vols. 8vo, $20.00; Index alone, $3.00.

C. E. Norton.
Notes of Travel and Study in Italy. 16mo, $1.25.
Translation of Dante's New Life. Royal 8vo, $3.00.

Francis W. Palfrey.
Memoir of William Francis Bartlett. Portrait. 16mo, $1.50.

James Parton.
Life of Benjamin Franklin. 2 vols. 8vo, $4.00.
Life of Thomas Jefferson. 8vo, $2.00.
Life of Aaron Burr. 2 vols. 8vo, $4.00.
Life of Andrew Jackson. 3 vols. 8vo, $6.00.
Life of Horace Greeley. 8vo, $2.00.
Humorous Poetry of the English Language. 8vo, $2.00.
Famous Americans of Recent Times. 8vo, $2.00.
Life of Voltaire. 2 vols. 8vo, $6.00.
The French Parnassus. *Household Edition.* 12mo, $2.00.
   Holiday Edition. Crown 8vo, $3.50.

Blaise Pascal.
Thoughts, Letters, and Opuscules. Crown 8vo, $2.25.
Provincial Letters. Crown 8vo, $2.25.

Charles C. Perkins.
Raphael and Michael Angelo. 8vo, $5.00.

E. S. Phelps.
The Gates Ajar. 16mo, $1.50.
Men, Women, and Ghosts. 16mo, $1.50.
Hedged In. 16mo, $1.50.
The Silent Partner. 16mo, $1.50.
The Story of Avis. 16mo, $1.50.
Sealed Orders, and other Stories. 16mo, $1.50.
Friends: A Duet. 16mo, $1.25.
Poetic Studies. Square 16mo, $1.50.

Adelaide A. Procter.
Poems. *Diamond Edition.* $1.00.
Red-Line Edition. Portrait and 16 illustrations. $2.50.
Favorite Edition. Illustrated. 16mo, $1.50.

Henry Crabb Robinson.
Diary. Crown 8vo, $2.50.

A. P. Russell.
Library Notes. 12mo, $2.00.

John G. Saxe.
Works. Portrait. 16mo, $2.25.
Highgate Edition. 16mo, $1.50.

Sir Walter Scott.
Waverley Novels. *Illustrated Library Edition.* In 25 vols. cr. 8vo, each $1.00; the set, $25.00.
Globe Edition. 13 vols. 100 illustrations, $16.25.
(*Sold only in sets.*)
Tales of a Grandfather. *Library Edition.* 3 vols. $4.50.

Horace E. Scudder.
The Bodley Books. 5 vols. Each, $1.50.
The Dwellers in Five-Sisters' Court. 16mo, $1.25.
Stories and Romances. $1.25.
Dream Children. Illustrated. 16mo, $1.00.
Seven Little People. Illustrated. 16mo, $1.00.
Stories from my Attic. Illustrated. 16mo, $1.00.
The Children's Book. 4to, 450 pages, $3.50.
Boston Town. Illustrated. 12mo, $1.50.

J. C. Shairp.
Culture and Religion. 16mo, $.125.
Poetic Interpretation of Nature. 16mo, $1.25.
Studies in Poetry and Philosophy. 16mo, $1.50.
Aspects of Poetry. 16mo, $1.50.

Dr. William Smith.
Bible Dictionary. *American Edition.* In four vols. 8vo, the set, $20.00.

E. C. Stedman.
Poems. *Farringford Edition.* Portrait. 16mo, $2.00.
Victorian Poets. 12mo, $2.00.
Hawthorne, and other Poems. 16mo, $1.25.
Edgar Allan Poe. An Essay. Vellum, 18mo, $1.00.

Harriet Beecher Stowe.
    Agnes of Sorrento. 12mo, $1.50.
    The Pearl of Orr's Island. 12mo, $1.50.
    Uncle Tom's Cabin. *Popular Edition.* 12mo, $2.00.
    The Minister's Wooing. 12mo, $1.50.
    The May-flower, and other Sketches. 12mo, $1.50.
    Nina Gordon. 12mo, $1.50.
    Oldtown Folks. 12mo, $1.50.
    Sam Lawson's Fireside Stories. Illustrated. $1.50.
    Uncle Tom's Cabin. 100 Illustrations. 12mo, full gilt, $3.50.

Bayard Taylor.
    Poetical Works. *Household Edition.* 12mo, $2.00.
    Dramatic Works. Crown 8vo, $2.25.
    The Echo Club, and other Literary Diversions. $1.25.

Alfred Tennyson.
    Poems. *Household Ed.* Portrait and 60 illustrations. $2.00.
    Illustrated Crown Edition. 48 illustrations. 2 vols. $5.00.
    Library Edition. Portrait and 60 illustrations. $4.00.
    Red-Line Edition. Portrait and 16 illustrations. $2.50.
    Diamond Edition. $1.00.
    Shawmut Edition. Illustrated. Crown 8vo, $1.50.
    Idylls of the King. Complete. Illustrated. $1.50.

Celia Thaxter.
    Among the Isles of Shoals. $1.25.
    Poems. $1.50.
    Drift-Weed. Poems. $1.50.

Henry D. Thoreau.
    Walden. 12mo, $1.50.
    A Week on the Concord and Merrimack Rivers. $1.50.
    Excursions in Field and Forest. 12mo, $1.50.
    The Maine Woods. 12mo, $1.50.
    Cape Cod. 12mo, $1.50.
    Letters to various Persons. 12mo, $1.50.
    A Yankee in Canada. 12mo, $1.50.
    Early Spring in Massachusetts. 12mo, $1.50.

George Ticknor.
    History of Spanish Literature. 3 vols. 8vo, $10.00.
    Life, Letters, and Journals. Portraits. 2 vols. 8vo, $6.00.
        Cheaper edition. 2 vols. 12mo, $4.00.

J. T. Trowbridge.
A Home Idyl. 16mo, $1.25.
The Vagabonds. 16mo, $1.25.
The Emigrant's Story. 16mo, $1.25.

Voltaire.
History of Charles XII. Crown 8vo, $2.25.

Lew Wallace.
The Fair God. 12mo, $1.50.

George E. Waring, Jr.
Whip and Spur. 18mo, $1.25.
A Farmer's Vacation. Square 8vo, $3.00.
Village Improvements. Illustrated. 75 cents.
The Bride of the Rhine. Illustrated. $1.50.

Charles Dudley Warner.
My Summer in a Garden. 16mo, $1.00. *Illustrated.* $1.50.
Saunterings. 18mo, $1.25.
Back-Log Studies. Illustrated. $1.50.
Baddeck, and that Sort of Thing. $1.00.
My Winter on the Nile. 12mo, $2.00.
In the Levant. 12mo, $2.00.
Being a Boy. Illustrated. $1.50.
In the Wilderness. 75 cents.

William A. Wheeler.
Dictionary of the Noted Names of Fiction. $2.00.

Edwin P. Whipple.
Works. Critical Essays. 6 vols., $9.00.

Richard Grant White.
Every-Day English. 12mo, $2.00.
Words and their Uses. 12mo, $2.00.
England Without and Within. 12mo, $2.00.

Mrs. A. D. T. Whitney.
Faith Gartney's Girlhood. 12mo, $1.50.
Hitherto. 12mo, $1.50.
Patience Strong's Outings. 12mo, $1.50.
The Gayworthys. 12mo, $1.50.

Leslie Goldthwaite. Illustrated. 12mo, $1.50.
We Girls. Illustrated. 12mo, $1.50.
Real Folks. Illustrated. 12mo, $1.50.
The Other Girls. Illustrated. 12mo, $1.50.
Sights and Insights. 2 vols. 12mo, $3.00.
Odd or Even. $1.50.
Boys at Chequasset. $1.50.
Pansies. Square 16mo, $1.50.
Just How. 16mo, $1.00.

John G. Whittier.

Poems. *Household Edition.* Portrait. $2.00.
Cambridge Edition. Portrait. 3 vols. crown 8vo, $6.75.
Red-Line Edition. Portrait. 12 illustrations. $2.50.
Diamond Edition. 18mo, $1.00.
Library Edition. Portrait. 32 illustrations. 8vo, $4.00.
Prose Works. *Cambridge Edition.* 2 vols. $4.50.
John Woolman's Journal. Introduction by Whittier. $1.50.
Child Life in Poetry. Selected by Whittier. Illustrated. $2.25. Child Life in Prose. $2.25.
Songs of Three Centuries. Selected by J. G. Whittier. *Household Edition.* 12mo, $2.00. *Illustrated Library Edition.* 32 illustrations. $4.00.

Justin Winsor.

Reader's Handbook of the American Revolution. 16mo, $1.25.

A catalogue containing portraits of many of the above authors, with a description of their works, will be sent free, on application, to any address.

www.ingramcontent.com/pod-product-compliance
Lightning Source LLC
Chambersburg PA
CBHW022104300426
44117CB00007B/586